KT-195-682

angles on
criminal psychology

Books are to be returned on or before
the last date below.

-2. DEC. 2002	30. JAN. 2006	2 3 SEP 2014
-9. SEP. 2003	1. DEC. 2008	
12. SEP. 2003		
15. SEP. 2003	6 JUL. 2009	
-5. DEC. 2003	15. SEP. 2009	
-8. DEC. 2003	2. OCT. 2009	
15. DEC. 2003	2 4 NOV 2011	
-6. JAN. 2004	1 8 OCT 2013	
-6. FEB. 2004	0 4 NOV 2013	
22. APR. 2004	0 2 APR 2014	
14. SEP. 2004	0 1 APR 2014	
28. NOV. 2005		
-1. DEC. 2005	2 3 APR 2014	

LIBREX —

103925

043851

THE HENLEY COLLEGE LIBRARY

dedication

Shivaun and Joe – this one's for you, with lots of love and great pride in you both.

angles on criminal psychology

Diana Dwyer

Series Editors: Matt Jarvis Julia Russell

T

Text © Diana Dwyer 2001
Original line illustrations © Nelson Thornes Ltd 2001, with the exception of cartoons,
© Roy Hunt (pp. 17, 87) and © Catherine Baynham (p. 97)

The right of Diana Dwyer to be identified as author of this work has been asserted by
her in accordance with the Copyright, Designs and Patents Act 1988.

All rights reserved. No part of this publication may be reproduced or transmitted in any
form or by any means, electronic or mechanical, including photocopy, recording or
any information storage and retrieval system, without permission in writing from the
publisher or under licence from the Copyright Licensing Agency Limited, of 90
Tottenham Court Road, London W1T 4LP.

Any person who commits any unauthorised act in relation to this publication may be
liable to criminal prosecution and civil claims for damages.

Published in 2001 by:
Nelson Thornes Ltd
Delta Place
27 Bath Road
CHELTENHAM
GL53 7TH
United Kingdom

01 02 03 04 05 / 10 9 8 7 6 5 4 3 2 1

A catalogue record for this book is available from the British Library

ISBN 0 7487 5977 8

Illustrations by Steve Ballinger, Roy Hunt and Catherine Baynham
Page make-up by Northern Phototypesetting Co. Ltd

Printed and bound in Great Britain by The Bath Press

contents

Contents

acknowledgements

A very special thank you to Alan Woodcock for practical help in painstakingly checking the whole script and for his support throughout the writing.

Grateful thanks also to Matt 'Sigmund' Jarvis for his many well-informed, positive comments.

Last but not least, thanks to Roy Hunt and Catherine Baynham for their cartoons (and general good humour).

The authors and publishers are grateful to the following for permission to reproduce material:

- American Psychological Association for material from the *Journal of Personality and Social Psychology* (diagrams on pp. 109 and 110 from Anderson & Dill, 2000; and extract on pp. 132–6 from Pennington & Hastie, 1986)

- British Crime Survey for graphs on p. 12

- Brooks/Cole for extract from *Psychology and the Legal System*, 3rd edition, by Wrightsman, L.S. *et al.* (1994) on p.119

- *The Independent* for extract on pp. 12–13

- *The Observer* for extract on p. 56

- Oxford University Press for graph from *The Oxford Handbook of Criminology*, 2nd edition, by Maquire, M., *et al.* (1997) on p. 8

- Pearson Education Inc. for the diagram reproduced from Bartol (1995) on p. 18

- *The Sunday Times* for extract from the News Review on p. 57

- Telegraph Group Limited for the extract on pp. 101–2

Every effort has been made to contact copyright holders and we apologise if anyone has been overlooked.

Photo credits

- Associated Press (p. 93)

- Impact Photos (p. 167)

- Photofusion (p. 106)

- Photofusion/AFP (p. 119)

- Photos reproduced from *Defensible Space*, courtesy Oscar Newman (pp. 172, 173, 174)

- Popperfoto/Greg Bos–Reuters (p. 6)

- Popperfoto/John Giles–Reuters (p. 154)

- Presss Association (p. 55)

- United Artists (courtesy Kobal) (p. 145)

Coverage of examination board specifications

Chapter no	Topics covered	Edexcel	AQA B	OCR	AQA A
1 Introduction	Definitions of crime Morality and crime Measuring crime		Definitions of crime Criminal statistics and the measurement of crime, including official statistics and crime surveys	Morality and crime Who are the victims? Fear of crime Crime reporting and intervention	
2 Explanations of criminal behaviour	Biological theories Psychoanalytic theories Learning and social learning theory Social and familial correlates of crime		Theories of crime: biological theories, psychoanalytic theories and learning theories, including social learning theory	Theories of criminal behaviour Individual and cultural differences in criminal behaviour	
3 Offender profiling	Top-down approaches Bottom-up approaches Applying profiling Evaluation of offender profiling	Offender profiling: what is involved; comparison of 'bottom-up' and 'top-down' methods	Offender profiling	Offender profiling: definitions, approaches and developing a profile Biases and pitfalls in profiling A case study of profiling	
4 Witness testimony	Variables affecting witness testimony Earwitness testimony Children as witnesses Methods of improving witness testimony	Eyewitness testimony Evaluation of the role of hypnosis in memory recall		Psychology of testimony: cognitive processes and testimony; variables influencing accurate identification of suspect/event Aids to recall: identikit and identity parades	AS module 1 (Cognitive and Developmental Psychology): eyewitness testimony, including reconstructive memory; Loftus' research in this area

Chapter no	Topics covered	Edexcel	AQA B	OCR	AQA A
5 Media influences on criminal behaviour	Studies of media violence Effects of violent video games Effects of pornography	Effects of the media on aggressive behaviour, including limitations on research methods used			A2 module 4: explanations and research studies relating to media influences on pro- and anti-social behaviour
6 Jury decision making	Characteristics of defendants Attribution effects on juries and witnesses	Effects of attribution on witnesses and juries Influences on jury decision making Effects of social pressure or conformity on jury decision making Effects of characteristics of the defendant on the jury Just world hypothesis		Trial procedures and persuasion techniques Jury selection and decision making Children as witnesses	AS module 3 (Social Psychology and Research Methods): conformity and minority influence A2 module 4 (Attribution of Causality)
7 The treatment of offenders and the prevention of crime	Custodial and non-custodial sentencing Behaviour modification Social skills training Anger management Zero tolerance Environmental crime prevention	Means of controlling aggression, such as behavioural treatment, modelling, role playing Zero tolerance and its effectiveness	Punishment: custodial and non-custodial sentencing Psychological effects of imprisonment Evaluation of custodial sentencing, including recidivism Therapies and strategies used in treatment of offenders, including behaviour modification, social skills training and anger management	Types and effectiveness of punishments Offender treatment programmes Environmental crime prevention	

1

Introduction

Crime fascinates people and arouses strong emotions. Both in fact and fantasy, it is a very important part of our everyday lives; you only have to think of the numerous television programmes and books that are based on crime. Consider also the news stories of the last few weeks – there's almost bound to be some story of crime that has provoked heated arguments and debate.

Crime is a major player in shaping our attitudes and affecting our behaviour. But what exactly do we mean by crime? What is the recorded incidence of various types of crime and how accurately does this reflect actual crime statistics? Is crime on the increase? Does the general public have an accurate or a distorted picture of who the criminals are, who the victims are, and does fear of crime have a significant effect on our everyday behaviour? In this introductory chapter we will consider all of these questions and although the answers are not always simple or straightforward in this complex area of behaviour, they should for the most part be informative and intriguing.

Definitions of crime – what is crime?

There is no single definition of crime that is acceptable to everyone. The most straightforward definition is that crime is anything that is forbidden or punishable by the criminal justice system. What we need to consider is why within any society certain acts or omissions should be classed as criminal, and why this classification differs somewhat between societies.

In some cases it is very easy to see why certain behaviours, such as killing another person, are criminal. In order to function effectively, all societies need to prohibit certain behaviours, especially those that harm other people or their property; for this reason murder is universally a criminal act. However, in other cases the distinction between what is and is not criminal is not so easy. Whereas there is likely to be a consensus that murder should be a crime, not everyone would agree that, say, blockading a road to prevent a building programme going ahead should constitute a criminal act.

Intention and age

In order to judge whether an action is criminal, we need to consider not only the act itself but the *intention* and the *age* of the perpetrator. It would be unjust to punish people who could not help doing what they did, so if the act was not *intentional*, but was accidental, done under duress, a mistake or intended for good then it is not a crime. Thus the same action, such as cutting someone with a knife, is a criminal act if it involves malicious wounding but not if it was entirely accidental or part of a surgical operation. Intention cannot be proved if an individual does not have sufficient understanding to know what they are doing, so we need to consider whether someone has learning difficulties or a psychiatric illness before deciding whether their behaviour is criminal. With respect to age, because very young children cannot be held responsible for their actions, the legal system has introduced an age below which people are not considered criminally responsible – this differs between countries (for example, the age of criminal responsibility is 10 in England and Wales, 8 in Scotland and 15 in Sweden) but the principle is the same.

Culture and history

The concept of what constitutes a crime is also influenced by culture and history. Some actions are criminal in one culture but not in others. In Egypt and Sudan, female circumcision is legal, in England and many other countries it is prohibited. Private consumption of the drug marijuana has been decriminalised in the Netherlands but not in Britain. Changes over time in our ideas of what does or does not denote a crime reflect humanitarian concerns, scientific and industrial advances, and increasing affluence. Suicide, homosexual behaviour between consenting adults, adultery and prostitution are just a few examples of behaviour that has been wholly or partially removed from criminal law. On the other hand, neglect and abuse of children, employees and animals have been added. With the advent of the car and other motor vehicles, such acts as dangerous driving, speeding and failure to wear a seat belt are actions that are now illegal.

In essence then, crime can be considered a *social construct*, a product of social and cultural influences rather than a universal truth. The set of behaviours it encompasses are so diverse that they only have one thing in common: they are proscribed by the criminal law.

Approaches to deciding what is a criminal act

How does any society decide which acts are criminal? Hollin (1989) outlines three main approaches to defining crime.

Consensus view

The *consensus view* states that a society's legal system is based on an agreement (consensus) amongst most of its members about what behaviours will not be tolerated and should therefore incur punishment. By defining crime in this way, actions are only criminal if they are forbidden by law, so anti-social behaviour is not considered a crime unless the particular act is illegal. Some illegal acts are uniformly deemed to be wrong and have always been forbidden – crimes such as malicious wounding. Other actions, as discussed above, pass in and out of criminal law depending on the changing values of a society. Printing a book was once forbidden in this country; incest was once a legal act. The consensus view sees the main aim of a legal system as a means of preserving a stable society and is more or less of equal benefit to all its citizens.

Conflict view

The *conflict view*, a sociological approach rooted in Marxism, is a very different approach which maintains that the law benefits some far more than others. According to this approach, there are many competing groups within society, groups such as unions, industrialists and professional bodies, and they are in conflict with each other because some are more wealthy and powerful than others. Criminal laws exist to protect the rich and powerful from the remainder of the population. In this way the ruling group secures its interests at the expense of the underprivileged. Even when actions are forbidden in the common interest, they are defined in an unequal way so that the powerful tend to go unpunished. An example is the English law against rape, which was only recently extended to include sexual coercion within marriage. Before that the wife, who is the partner who is usually the weaker in both physical and economic terms, was not given the option to refuse unwanted sexual intercourse even though its imposition involves physical force.

Some neo-Marxist sociologists feel that the conflict view is too extreme an approach and have offered various modifications of it, but they all agree on one point: that crime is the product of inadequate social conditions. Objectors to this approach point out that crime is a harsh reality for many working-class people who suffer considerably from its effects and is not something to be glorified in a 'Robin Hood' way.

Interactionist view

The *interactionist view* takes a middle line between these two opposing approaches. It emphasises the fact that there are no absolute values of right and wrong because these depend on the *meaning* placed upon them by the individual. Each of us has a different view: taking a life is sometimes seen as criminal but not always. When killing occurs in wartime, when capital punishment is used or when someone is acting in self-defence then the act is not called 'murder' and it is not criminal. On the other hand, taking a life in the act of euthanasia is a criminal act in most societies but one that some people would like to see decriminalised. According to the interactionist view, the decision about when an act becomes a crime is not drawn from a consensus of the whole population but by those in power. In one way, this agrees with the conflict approach; however, it differs in that it does not see those in power as motivated by maintaining their economic supremacy but more by a belief in their own moral superiority. The interactionist view is concerned with the way in which legal standards are related to changing moral values.

This leads neatly on to our next consideration, the relationship between crime and morality.

Morality and crime

Morals are beliefs and values that are shared by a society or a section of society and are the means by which we judge what is right and what is wrong. Activities such as cheating, lying and stealing are deemed by most people to be morally wrong and we instil these values into our children, so that eventually they develop a conscience and uphold the social order (including obeying laws) through inner conviction, rather than simply through fear of punishment. The morals held by a society have a considerable influence on what is classed as criminal, but immorality and criminality are not the same thing. This means that not everything considered morally wrong is illegal (we do not have a law against telling lies) nor is everything illegal necessarily immoral (it's not immoral to park on a double yellow line but it is illegal).

The sociologist Durkheim highlighted the fact that within a complex society there is no set of moral values that are shared by everyone. Since individuals in such a society differ markedly in their social status, occupation, religion, ethnicity and so on, they are unlikely to share all their moral values. Given that these moral values, however strongly held, differ between groups, which group's moral opinions, if any, should be adopted by the law? Whereas it is easy to appreciate why the law should be used to protect persons and property, the question of whether it should reflect morality in cases where no harm is done to others is far more debatable. The controversial question is: should the law be used to direct the behaviour of private individuals simply because this behaviour violates a moral code, even though it is hurting no one (except maybe the perpetrator)? The kinds of behaviour this includes are those concerned with alcohol, sex, drugs and gambling.

There are two problems with using the legal system to punish so-called immoral behaviour. The first is that there is no general consensus as to what constitutes an immoral act; any decisions concerning what is and is not moral would be value judgements and who is to decide which set of values should predominate? The second problem is that even if there were agreement over what is moral or immoral, as long as no harm is done to others, why should such behaviour be criminal?

Many arguments have been offered as to what should constitute an appropriate relationship between morality and the law. We will consider two opposing ones.

Natural law approach

The natural law approach argues that law should strongly reflect morality. There is a variety of such theories so it is not possible to summarise a single approach but the one theme they have in common is the proposal that there is a higher law, known as the natural law, which should be the basis of the laws that societies make for themselves. The natural law approach argues that laws that do not reflect this code should never have been made and need not be obeyed.

However, there is no universal agreement amongst natural law theorists as to what should be the exact content of the laws and this is a weakness of their position. Usually it would encompass basic human rights; the Bill of Rights, like that in the US constitution, could be seen as being based on natural law principles.

The approach of John Stuart Mill

An opposing position was offered by the philosopher John Stuart Mill who argued that the criminal law should function primarily to prevent individuals harming others and should not concern itself with private morality. Modern theorists of this school focus on what is known as *victimless crimes*, crimes such as homosexuality and drug use which do no harm to anyone other than, on occasions, the participant. Since they do not do harm to others, supporters of this view argue that such acts should not be illegal. Indeed, it is on that basis that homosexual acts between consenting adults were decriminalised in Britain, but other forms of consensual sex between adults, such as some sado-masochistic behaviour, remain illegal (see Interactive Angles, below).

This view was reflected in a 1950s government report on homosexuality and pornography, known as the Wolfenden Report, which argued that the purpose of criminal law should not be to interfere in the lives of citizens or seek to enforce any particular behaviour other than that which was necessary 'to preserve public order and decency, to protect the citizen from what is offensive and injurious and to provide sufficient safeguards against exploitation and corruption of others especially the vulnerable, that is the young, weak in body or mind, inexperienced or those in a state of physical, official or economic dependence'. In other words, the argument was similar to that of John Stuart Mill: people should be free to make their own choices as long as they do not harm others.

Professor Hart, a supporter of the Wolfenden Report, argued that the law should not be used to enforce moral values and to do so was in itself morally unacceptable since it infringes the liberty of the individual. Hart (1963) further suggested that often it was not morality that prompted people to object to unusual behaviour; instead it was that such objections were often the result of prejudice, bigotry, ignorance or misunderstanding. (This is related to theories of prejudice, especially that of the Authoritarian Personality.) An opposing argument was put forward by Lord Devlin who proposed that a society could only be stable if it had a set of shared moral principles and that it was only in a stable society that individual freedom was possible.

The relationship between law and morality

The relationship between law and morality is a complex one, which is constantly being reviewed as new issues arise. For example, in vitro fertilisation has led to arguments on the extent to which 'test tube' embryos should be selected. The two views expressed above are not always entirely incompatible and both are still influential in the judgements that are made.

Civil rights campaigners protest against the 1994 Criminal Justice and Public Order Act

interactive
angles

In 1992 an interesting case led to a heated debate about the extent to which people should be punished for acts that harm no one except themselves: the case involved a group of homosexual men who were convicted of a variety of assaults against the person. These men had willingly participated in a number of sado-masochistic acts involving, amongst other things, safety-pins, nails, stinging nettles, heated wires and sandpaper. Although the acts had been videotaped, this was for personal use only. Any injuries sustained were not permanent nor serious enough to warrant medical attention. The acts had taken place in private and all the participants had freely consented and expressed no regrets whatsoever. The men lodged an unsuccessful appeal to the House of Lords and then took their case to the European Court of Human Rights. See if you can find out the decision made by this court.

The initial judgement made in this case was heavily criticised, since, it was argued, these individuals had done no harm to anyone except themselves and had not been involved in any corruption. Should these men have been convicted? What is your view?

Measuring crime

Methods of estimating crime rates

There are several sources of information about the prevalence of crime but none of them is wholly accurate. The data used by criminologists derives from three main sources:

- statistical records compiled by the police and criminal justice agencies

- large-scale surveys commissioned by the government

- small-scale surveys conducted by academic and other researchers.

We will concentrate on the first two of these.

Police recording of crime

The Home Office publication *Criminal Statistics* presents a record of the number and types of crime recorded by the police in England and Wales. Offences included in the recorded crime statistics cover a wide range of crimes, from homicides to minor theft and criminal damage.

These statistics show a marked change in the crime rate over time. From the first records in 1876 to the 1930s, the crime rate was relatively unchanged but then the picture altered dramatically. There was a significant rise from the 1930s up to the 1950s and an even more rapid rise thereafter. The annual figure for recorded crime was around 500,000 in the 1950s, which doubled in the next ten years to 1 million by the mid-1960s, doubled yet again to 2 million by the mid-1970s, and had reached more than 5.5 million by 1998. There has therefore been an eleven-fold increase in crime rates in England and Wales between 1950 and 1998.

Over the last eight years for which records are available (1992–2000) there has actually been a steady but relatively small fall in each year, the longest sustained fall since records began in 1876. Despite this, the underlying trend has been predominantly upwards; this underlying trend is reflected in the fact that the number of notifiable offences per 100,000 of the population has risen from 5,200 in 1978 to 9,800 in 1998/99, a rise of 65 per cent.

Crime statistics do not simply provide information on the variety and number of crimes that are committed, they also consider who the criminals and victims are. This data can be quite provocative for, as Maguire (1994) reports, many of our stereotypes of who constitutes a criminal are inaccurate. He points out that:

> *'criminal behaviour is not the near-monopoly of poor and deprived young males. For example, the sexual abuse of children (Baker & Duncan 1985), domestic violence (Dobash & Dobash 1992), football hooliganism (Murphy et al. 1990), workplace theft (Ditton 1977; Mars 1982) and drug offences (Pearson 1987) have all been shown to*

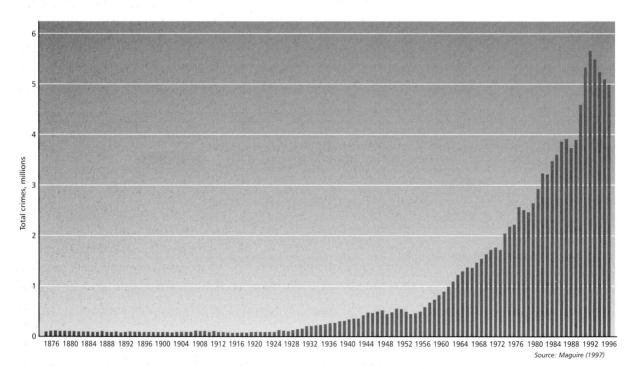

Source: Maguire (1997)

Crimes recorded by the police, 1876–1996

be committed by people from a wide range of age groups and social classes … while a series of major frauds … have demonstrated for all to see that criminals are to be found in suites as well as on the streets (Levi & Pithouse 1992).' (page 235)

Official crime statistics provide one important source of information on recorded crime but these greatly underestimate the amount of crime because many crimes go unreported. There are several reasons for this. People may consider the offence too trivial; they may doubt that the police can do anything about it; they may prefer to deal with the matter personally or not recognise the act as criminal. Some crimes such as vandalism and tax fraud have no responsive victim to report them. Yet other crimes such as drug dealing and soliciting have willing victims who indeed may be in trouble if they did report the crime. Even when crimes are reported they need not necessarily be recorded by the police, who may consider them too trivial to warrant intervention, for example, some minor domestic disputes.

In addition to this, some crimes are more likely to be reported than others; in general it is the more serious crimes that are reported but there are other considerations. For example, car theft is more often reported than theft of other property, because of insurance implications. Trends in the particular crimes reported may change over time. Rape, for example, is more likely to be reported now than it once was because of changing attitudes of both the police and the general public to victims of such an offence. Hence figures for rape have shown a relatively large increase, not all of which necessarily reflects an increase in actual rape.

It is worth noting that despite the fact that these crime figures should be treated with caution, they act as the main picture of crime used by politicians and highlighted in the media. They are also used in strategic planning by the Home Office and police forces.

Survey information

The amount of unknown crime has traditionally been referred to as the 'Dark Figure', and in order to reach an estimate of the extent of this, other sources of information are used. One of the most important of these is the British Crime Survey (BCS), a survey conducted every two years of adults (people over the age of 16) in private households about their experiences of victimisation in the previous year. The main purpose of the survey is to give estimates of the extent of household and personal crime in England and Wales and to compare these with official statistics in order to gauge the extent of unreported and unrecorded crimes. In addition, it also provides important information about attitudes to crime and punishment. As with all surveys, this is likely not to be wholly accurate. Variables that can result in bias are:

- the characteristics of the interviewer and how he or she is perceived by the interviewee

- the way in which the interview is conducted and the level of educational attainment of the respondent.

In addition, just as with official statistics, there are victimless crimes, which will not therefore be reported. Despite these limitations, surveys are still important sources of information about crime rates and attitudes to crime.

The BCS provides information on the amount of crime and concern about crime. When conducting the BCS, respondents are first asked whether they or anyone else in their household has been the victim of any of a series of crimes, each described in everyday language, since the beginning of the previous year. If the answer is 'yes' then a detailed interview is conducted.

research
now

what is the incidence of crime?

The 2000 British Crime Survey

Aim: The main aim is to measure crimes against people living in private households in England and Wales. The main purposes of the British Crime Survey are listed in the report (page 1) as to:

- provide an alternative measure of crime to offences recorded by the police

- provide information on crime risks

- provide a picture of the nature of crime

- take up other crime-related issues.

Method: This uses the survey method with a questionnaire. Respondents are questioned at home by interviewers using Computer Assisted Personal Interviewing. The questionnaire is a computer program which specifies the questions and the range and structure of permissible answers.

The 2000 survey, which measured crime in 1999, used a representative core sample of nearly 19,500 people, all interviewed face to face between January and April 2000, and an additional ethnic minority booster sample of over 3,800 (Kershaw *et al.*, 2000).

Results:

Incidence of crime: According to the BCS there are about four and a half times more crimes committed than are recorded by the police. As discussed earlier, this is mainly because many crimes are not reported to the police. Also, the police do not record all crimes that are reported to them. Some crimes, such as vehicle theft, were nearly all recorded, doubtless because people want police help in recovering their cars and need to report the theft for insurance purposes. On the other hand, attempted vehicle theft, common assault and vandalism are amongst the crimes least recorded.

There was a fall in most crime since the last survey, with the exception of robbery and theft from the person. The long-term trend from 1981–1999 shows a gradual rise during the 1980s and a decline in the 1990s. Overall the 1999 rate is a third higher than in 1981.

Public concern over crime: In order to monitor this the BCS looks at beliefs concerning crime trends, the perceived risk of being a victim of crime and emotional responses to specific offences.

People are in general very pessimistic about crime. One finding of the 2000 British Crime Survey, reflecting results from earlier such surveys, was that people tend to exaggerate the crime problem. One third believed that the national crime rate had increased 'a lot' between 1997 and 1999 when both the BCS and police figures show a decrease. Not surprisingly, worry about crime is higher among those living in high crime areas, those who are recent victims and those who are socially vulnerable.

Variables affecting fear of crime: As in previous surveys, the 2000 survey showed that age and sex are strongly related to fear of crime. Women were more worried than men about every type of crime except theft from a car and they were far more concerned about violent crime. Older people were more anxious than the young were about walking alone at night.

There were also ethnic differences in fear of crime. Black and Asian respondents were far more worried about all types of crime than white respondents. This is in part because ethnic minorities are more likely to live in inner-city areas.

Effect of crime on behaviour: The survey also looked at the effect of crime on people's behaviour. One in twelve people said that they rarely or never walk in their local areas after dark partly because of the fear of crime. This rises to almost one in five women over 60 years of age. About one in seventeen considered that crime greatly affected their quality of life.

Conclusion: Crime rates have dropped by 10 per cent over the past two years but it is very difficult to change people's perception of crime. Despite the drop in offences, public fear of crime remains high. Two out of three people believed crime was rising, and one in three believed it had risen 'a lot'.

Reasons for the drop in crime are difficult to identify but the Home Office expressed the view that the booming economy and more focused policing strategies have been important factors.

media watch

Criminal activity 'less fashionable' for young

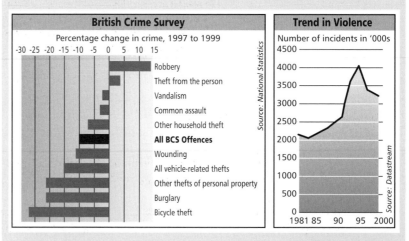

British Crime Survey

Percentage change in crime, 1997 to 1999

-30 -25 -20 -15 -10 -5 0 5 10 15

Robbery
Theft from the person
Vandalism
Common assault
Other household theft
All BCS Offences
Wounding
All vehicle-related thefts
Other thefts of personal property
Burglary
Bicycle theft

Source: National Statistics

Trend in Violence

Number of incidents in '000s

4500
4000
3500
3000
2500
2000
1500
1000
500
0
1981 85   90   95 2000

Source: Datastream

Crime in Britain has fallen by 10 per cent over the past two years, the Home Office said yesterday as it claimed that a "cultural change" may have made criminal activity "less fashionable" for young people.

Jack Straw, the Home Secretary, said he believed there had been a public backlash against law breakers and that "people have become less and less tolerant of crime".

Mr Straw spoke at the publication of the British Crime Survey 2000, which showed that between 1997 and 1999 burglary had fallen by 21 per cent, vehicle-related theft by 15 per cent and crimes of violence by four per cent.

The survey confounded the idea that rural crime was on the rise. It found that the risk of crime was less in rural areas and that declines in burglary, vehicle-related thefts and violent crime between 1997 and 1999 had been particularly marked in country districts.

The survey claimed that one of the factors for the falling crime levels, which mirror patterns in America, Canada and other European countries, was a broad change in attitude to crime among young people.

It stated: "There could be intricate cultural change, which is leading to crime simply becoming a less fashionable pursuit for high-risk age groups."

The British Crime Survey is based on people's actual experiences of crime rather than offences reported to the police and is believed to give a truer picture of crime than the recorded statistics.

Paul Wiles, director of research at the Home Office, said the 10 per cent fall was compatible with the five per cent fall in police recorded offences over the same two-year period. He said police figures had not fallen so sharply because officers now recorded a greater proportion of offences reported to them by the public.

The survey estimated that 14.7 million crimes had taken place in Britain last year, more than four and a half times the police recorded figure.

The Independent, 17 October 2000

Discussion points

1 What does the 'Trend in Violence' chart show us about the trend in the incidence of violent crimes since 1981?

2 What reasons are given in the report for the differences between police-recorded offences and those shown in the British Crime Survey?

3 Why is it important to have results from the British Crime Survey as well as statistics on the amount of police recorded crime?

where to now?

The following are good sources of further information on definitions and measurement of crime:

▶ **www.homeoffice.gov.uk/rds/bcs1.html** – this Home Office website provides a list of useful publications including the British Crime Survey and summary papers on its main findings. These can be downloaded at no charge.

▶ **Coolican, H. (1996) *Applied Psychology*. London: Hodder & Stoughton** – this contains a useful chapter on criminological psychology (by Julia Harrower) which covers what criminological psychologists do and the development of criminological psychology.

▶ **Maguire, M. *et al.* (1997) *The Oxford Handbook of Criminology*. Oxford: Clarendon Press** – this is a weighty tome but is divided up into many separate papers and is well worth a look. The particular chapter pertinent to patterns and trends in perception of crime is Chapter 6 by Mike Maguire.

▶ **Hollin, C.R. (1989) *Psychology and Crime: An Introduction to Criminological Psychology*. London: Routledge** – this book was written to support an undergraduate course in forensic psychology (run by Leicester University) and covers a range of material on psychology and crime. The first chapter provides useful ways of defining crime.

what do you know?

1   Describe and evaluate three approaches to defining crime.

2   Discuss the relationship between crime and morality.

3   How has the crime rate changed in England and Wales since the first records in 1876 up to the present time?

4   List some of the reasons why official crime statistics tend to underestimate the amount of crime.

5   Describe and discuss the findings from the 2000 British Crime Survey.

2

Explanations of Criminal Behaviour

what's
ahead?

Can there possibly be such a thing as a 'born criminal' or is this simply an outmoded Victorian view? If our biology is not responsible for criminal tendencies then what other factors may be important? In this chapter we look at various theories on the causes of crime, including some theories, such as psychoanalytic theory (based on the work of Freud) and Learning Theory, with which you may be familiar. You may even like to anticipate the reasons these theories put forward to account for antisocial behaviour.

Crime and its causes are by no means the exclusive province of psychology and we will briefly consider some sociological approaches. Finally, we will look at research that has investigated the type of family and social environment most likely to predict the onset of delinquency.

Biological theories

The born criminal: Lombroso's theory

The Victorians believed that it was possible to spot a criminal by his features. This idea was part of a tradition known as physiognomy, the idea that a person's character and intellect could be read in their head and face. A pioneer of this view as far as criminals were concerned was an Italian Army doctor, Cesare Lombroso (1836–1909) who, in 1876, published a book (*L'Uomo Delinquente* or *Criminal Man*) in which he proposed that some people are born with a strong, innate predisposition to behave antisocially.

Influenced by Darwin's theory of evolution, Lombroso suggested that criminals form a separate species which is a more primitive form of human being that has not evolved as fully as homo sapiens and is genetically somewhere between modern humans and their primitive ancestors. This retarded species, which he called homo delinquens, displayed certain physical characteristics which showed how primitive they were:

- a narrow sloping brow (low in intellect)

- prominent jaw (strong in passion)

- high cheekbones, large ears

- extra nipples, toes and fingers.

These subhuman creatures displayed characteristics useful for survival in the wild in primitive times, but could not adjust socially and morally to a modern civilised society. The biologically predisposed criminals were incapable of distinguishing right from wrong, showed no guilt or remorse and, because they had no feelings for others, were unable to form deep, meaningful, loving relationships.

Following his original book, Lombroso published several further volumes in which his view became rather less dogmatic. He and his followers retreated from the assertion that *all* criminals were evolutionary throw-backs to the view that this theory accounted for about a third of the criminal population (Lombroso-Ferrero, 1972: this reference, particularly the date, may seem strange – this book was written by Lombroso's son-in-law, who worked closely with him, especially on the revisions to the theory). He acknowledged the fact that environmental factors made a significant contribution to the causes of some types of criminal behaviour. Interestingly, he labelled prisons 'criminal universities' since he believed that they reinforced criminal tendencies. Nevertheless, essentially the message was the same: certain people were 'born criminals'.

Lombroso originally thought that female criminals, mostly represented by prostitutes, had the same biological features as their male counterparts. He later modified this view, stating that criminal women did not show these physical anomalies but were psychologically even worse than male criminals: jealous, vengeful and capable of monstrous cruelty. We will return to Lombroso's views on female criminals later in the chapter when we consider gender and crime.

Physiognomy as a whole, but especially when applied to criminals, encourages the worst prejudices of stereotyping and has caused much embarrassment to criminologists. There is no serious evidence in its support; Lombroso's own research was methodologically flawed. He did not use proper control groups and the criminal samples he used were often mentally disturbed or suffering from chromosomal abnormalities. Goring (1913, 1972) reported a study comparing the physical features of

3,000 convicts with 3,000 non-criminals and found no significant differences in any features. Although Goring's methodology was also open to criticism, it was less dubious than Lombroso's and his report did a great deal to close the door on such a concept.

Nevertheless, this theory, especially in its later formulation, had certain positive features. It was one of the first not to attribute criminal behaviour entirely to wickedness caused by a lack of will power and therefore it acknowledged that the causes of criminal behaviour cannot entirely be laid at the feet of the perpetrator. His later theories, in which he acknowledged the role of the environment as a contributor to shaping criminal behaviour, were certainly more enlightened than the original thesis, but have received relatively little attention. Hollin (1989) argues that Lombroso can 'with some justification be hailed as the "father of modern criminology" (Schaffer, 1976) as his later theories encompass the three major strands – biology, environment, and psychology – evident in much contemporary research.' (pages 23–24)

Body build

Shakespeare wrote:

> *Let me have men about me that are fat;*
> *Sleek-headed men and such as sleep o'nights;*
> *Yond Cassius has a mean and hungry look;*
> *He thinks too much; such men are dangerous.*
>
> *Julius Caesar* (1599) Act 1, Scene 2

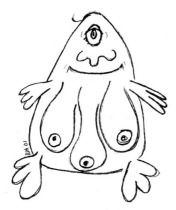

It was Edna's three nipples that made the police suspicious

The idea that personality is linked to body type dates right back to the time of Hippocrates, who drew up a list of typologies of physiques and tried to link them to character traits. As the Shakespearean quotation indicates, people of certain body build are not to be trusted.

In an attempt to develop a scientific theory, William Sheldon drew up his own classification system in which he related physique to characteristics that included delinquency (Sheldon & Stevens, 1942; Sheldon *et al.*, 1949). According to Sheldon's system, there are three basic body types:

- endomorphs, who are fat and soft

- ectomorphs, who are thin and fragile

- mesomorphs, who are muscular and hard.

The temperaments to which these correspond are that endomorphs are relaxed and pleasure loving, and enjoy food and the company of others. Ectomorphs are solitary, restrained and self-conscious. Mesomorphs are the ones associated with criminality since they are aggressive, have a high pain tolerance, are callous and are careless of others' feelings. Sheldon did not simply group people into these three types but rated individuals on a scale of

1 to 7 according to the amount of each of the three components they showed. The average body build would therefore be 4-4-4 in somatotype; a person with such a body build would be denoted as 'balanced'.

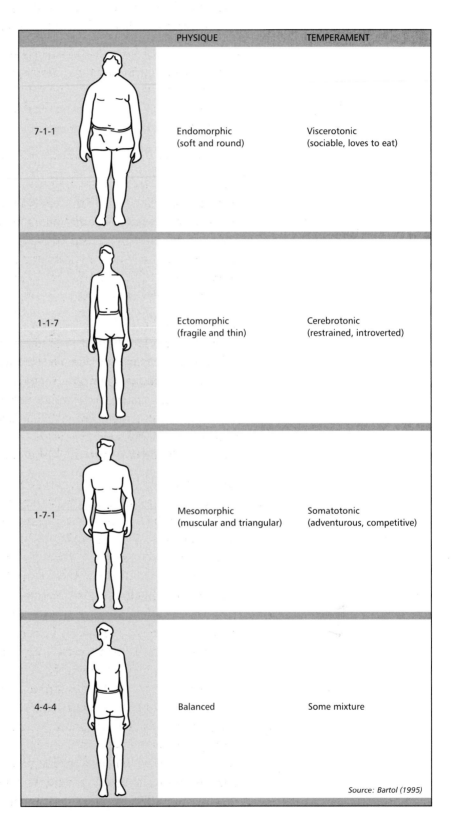

	PHYSIQUE	TEMPERAMENT
7-1-1	Endomorphic (soft and round)	Viscerotonic (sociable, loves to eat)
1-1-7	Ectomorphic (fragile and thin)	Cerebrotonic (restrained, introverted)
1-7-1	Mesomorphic (muscular and triangular)	Somatotonic (adventurous, competitive)
4-4-4	Balanced	Some mixture

Source: Bartol (1995)

Sheldon's somatotypes in relation to physique and temperament

Using full-length photographs Sheldon rated 200 college students and 200 male delinquents on each of the body types. He then divided the delinquents up into various groups according to type of degree of delinquency and compared the criminal group with other types of delinquents, such as the mentally ill. The results are shown in the following table.

Body build	Students	Delinquents	Criminal delinquents
endomorph	3.2	3.5	3.4
ectomorph	3.4	2.7	1.8
mesomorph	3.8	4.6	5.4

These results demonstrate that the student group had roughly the average somatotype, with approximately equal distribution of endomorphy, ectomorphy and mesomorphy. The delinquent group, on the other hand, were significantly more mesomorphic and less ectomorphic than a balanced somatotype. The criminal group were even more extreme in their imbalance: as the figures in the table show, they are very predominantly mesomorphic.

Cortes & Gatti (1972) point out several flaws in both the theory and the research. The classification into the somatotypes was unreliable, the delinquent group chosen was selective and the subdivision of the delinquents into criminal types was not based on legal definitions of a delinquent but on subjective criteria. Sutherland (1951) reclassified the delinquents using legal criteria and found far less difference in the somatotypes of delinquents and non-delinquents, although the delinquent youths did still show the highest ratings for mesomorphy.

Other studies have demonstrated conflicting results; some support the idea of the predominantly mesomorphic criminal while others have found no relationship between mesomorphy and delinquency. In support, Cortes & Gatti (1972) conducted a study of 100 institutionalised delinquents and found that 57 per cent were mesomorphic and 16 per cent ectomorphic compared with 19 per cent and 33 per cent respectively for controls. However, this study has been criticised on the grounds that the control group were from a private school whilst the delinquent group came mainly from the lower classes. The differences in physique could therefore have been due to social class differences, which may also have been at the root of the differences in antisocial behaviour. Certainly Cortes did not rule out the significance of environmental factors in the causation of antisocial behaviour, emphasising that both genetics *and* environment were influential. Contradicting the theory is a large-scale study using data from the British National Survey which reported that delinquents guilty of serious offences, rather than being strong and muscular, were actually smaller than average. Although they were not classified by somatotype, this certainly does not correspond to Sheldon's theory. The problem is that in all these studies there is little reliability in the assessment of the somatotypes and we must conclude that the evidence is unclear.

Even if there is a link between mesomorphy and aggressive behaviour, one fundamental problem still remains with this type of theory. Rather than the mesomorphic body build resulting in a temperament that leads to antisocial behaviour, there are several alternative (and probably more commonsense) explanations. Firstly, it may be that people of a muscular build learn from an early age that they can get their own way by being aggressive and dominant and so they continue to be so and eventually end up in trouble with the law. It's interesting to note that no research has been done to see whether those convicted of non-aggressive criminal acts such as fraud have a mesomorphic body build. Secondly, criminal justice agents may respond negatively to those who look 'tough' and be more inclined, therefore, to impose custodial sentences on them than on their more puny counterparts. Thirdly, mesomorphs accused of crime are often poor and may be so built because of the lifestyle they have been forced to adopt, a combination of poor diet and continued manual labour. It could then be poverty rather than body build that is the direct link with criminal behaviour.

It is clear that more reliable and well-executed research needs to be done before we can ascertain whether there is a relationship between body build and antisocial or aggressive acts and what exactly this link is.

Eysenck's theory of personality and crime

Eysenck's (1977) theory of criminal behaviour is not as biologically deterministic as the previous two: it postulates that it is the interaction of personality (which is biologically based) and the environment that produces antisocial behaviour. This theory is not intended as a theory of criminal behaviour in general but is one that seeks to explain why certain individuals fail to comply with rules. Indeed, Eysenck himself suggests that his theory applies only to certain crimes, namely 'victimful' crimes and that sociological theories are particularly relevant in relation to victimless crime.

Eysenck argues that personality is determined by an individual's biological constitution which is, in turn, determined by their genes. Certain personality traits are more likely to lend themselves to antisocial behaviour and if someone inherits these traits *and* is brought up in an environment that nurtures crime, then they are liable to engage in criminal acts. As Eysenck & Gudjonsson (1989) comment: 'What is inherited are certain peculiarities of the brain and nervous system that interact with certain environmental factors and thereby increase the likelihood that a given person will act in a particular antisocial manner in a given situation.' (page 247)

According to Eysenck's basic theory of personality, an individual's temperament can be measured on three dimensions:

- extraversion–introversion (E)
- neuroticism–stability (N)
- psychoticism–normality (P).

Most of the research on crime and personality has focused on extraversion and neuroticism – stability, so it is on these dimensions that we will concentrate.

Extraversion–introversion

Extraverts have a high need for excitement and for a varied, changing environment. They enjoy company, lively parties and are impulsive and optimistic. They are inclined easily to lose their temper and to be aggressive and unreliable. Introverts, on the other hand, are reserved, cautious and dislike change and noisy gatherings. They tend to keep themselves to themselves, are reliable, unaggressive and place great value on ethical standards.

Biologically, Eysenck contends, the dimension of extraversion–introversion is based on the nature of the reticular activating system (RAS), a part of the brain responsible for arousal levels. Everyone has an optimum level of arousal which they strive to achieve. In extraverts, the RAS strongly inhibits incoming sensations, resulting in the need to seek stimulation. By contrast, in introverts the RAS amplifies sensory input, hence they seek far less stimulation. Another important difference between introverts and extraverts is that the latter are much harder to condition, and therefore far more likely not to do as they are told when young or care about societal disapproval when older.

In contrast to an introvert, an extravert's need for constant stimulation and new and dangerous experiences is liable to bring them into conflict with the law, and they are more likely to engage in criminal activities, especially those such as joy riding, which bring excitement. In short, according to this theory, most criminals are extraverts.

Neuroticism–stability

The dimension of neuroticism–stability is controlled by the level of reactivity of the autonomic nervous system (ANS), that part of the nervous system which, by releasing the hormone adrenalin into your bloodstream, makes you 'jump' when something frightening happens. People who score highly on neuroticism have a more reactive ANS than those who score at the stable end of the continuum: they tend to be nervous, jumpy and anxious, and find it difficult to cope with stress. They are moody, easily upset by others and prone to physical ailments such as headaches and stomach upsets. Those at the stable end of the continuum are emotionally stable, calm, even-tempered and not easily upset by other people. They are unlikely to panic when confronted by extreme stress but keep their wits about them and respond to emergencies in a productive manner.

Eysenck assumed that people who score highly on the neuroticism scale, those whom he labelled as high on emotionality, are more likely to behave in a criminal manner than those low on neuroticism or emotionality. This is because emotionality acts as a drive and those high in emotionality are liable to repeat behaviours until they become habitual. If these habits are antisocial ones, then this may lead to criminality.

Since the two dimensions of extraversion–introversion and stability–neuroticism are independent, it is possible for individuals to be neurotic introverts, stable introverts, stable extraverts or neurotic extraverts. It follows from the theory of personality that it is the latter group, the neurotic extraverts, who are most likely to engage in criminal behaviour.

Psychoticism

Only a limited amount of research has been conducted on the dimension of psychoticism in relation to crime but Eysenck has suggested that this is likely to be a characteristic shown by a large proportion of the criminal population, especially hardcore, habitual, violent offenders. Psychoticism within this theory means a hostile and uncaring attitude to others, cold cruelty and a lack of empathy. (It is important to note however, that this use is not the same as the clinical term 'psychotic' as used to describe someone who is out of touch with reality.)

Evaluating Eysenck's theory

In evaluating Eysenck's theory, it is useful to look separately at the theory itself, and then at the research done on it.

Evaluation of the theory

There are numerous problems with the theory. Firstly, there is no evidence that there are consistent differences in EEG measures (which are used to ascertain cortical arousal) between introverts and extraverts (Gale & Edwards, 1983). Secondly, some studies indicate that sensation seeking is not necessarily related to extraversion (Zuckerman *et al.*, 1988). Indeed some theorists argue that boredom arises from *increased* rather than decreased arousal (e.g. Zuckerman, 1969). Smith *et al.* (1989) have carried out research which indicates that sensation seekers have an excitable central nervous system, being more aroused and arousable. This seriously compromises Eysenck's proposal that criminal behaviour is the result of stimulus seeking by extraverts attempting to achieve an optimum level of stimulation. Thirdly, several researchers have discovered personality traits other than ones identified by Eysenck which are related to criminal behaviour (McGurk *et al.*, 1981).

Evaluation of the research

Having considered problems with the theory, let us turn our attention to the research on which it is based. In support, some studies that have compared prisoners with non-criminals have found that the criminals score more highly on the scales of extraversion, neuroticism and psychoticism as measured by the Eysenck Personality Questionnaire (EPQ) (Eysenck, 1977). However, Passingham (1972) drew attention to some methodological flaws in these studies, namely that the control group of non-criminals was not matched with the criminals on relevant variables such as socioeconomic class, cultural background and intelligence.

Many other studies have not been supportive. Bartol *et al.* (1979) compared EPQ scores of 398 inmates of a maximum security jail in New York with a control group of 187 male job seekers in the same city who were, like the prisoners, mainly African-American and Hispanic and were matched in terms of age, race, socioeconomic class and employment record. The criminals were categorised into six groups according to their criminal history. Although, as predicted by the theory, sex offenders were the least extravert and robbers the most extravert of the criminals, *all* six groups of offenders were *less* extravert than the control group. Bartol *et al.* suggest that the main reason for this may be because their study was conducted on a completely different cultural group than that studied by Eysenck, whose sample was predominantly European White criminals guilty of property crimes. A theory that claims to be universal but cannot be generalised to other populations is not valid. Many other research studies have been, in various ways, equally unsupportive. Farrington *et al.* (1982), in a review of such research, concluded that neither the theory nor the personality scales were useful in explaining the origins of delinquency.

Nevertheless, on the positive side, this theory does recognise that both biology and the environment may be important determinants of criminality and, even if the specific mechanisms suggested are inaccurate, it draws attention to the possible importance of genetics in influencing behaviour. As Bartol (1995) comments, 'Criminology cannot afford to discount the existence of biological factors in antisocial behaviour, even if these factors account for the behaviour of only a small percentage of the population' (page 55).

Evaluating biological theories

In considering biological theories as a whole, it is unlikely that they alone can offer a convincing explanation for criminal behaviour. Even if some individuals' physiology predisposes them to be impulsive, aggressive and erratic, these characteristics can be channelled into legal activities. Any link between physiology and criminal behaviour is inevitably indirect and mediated by social factors, which will be considered later in this chapter. In humans, biology never imprisons us entirely.

for and against

biological theories of crime

+ They draw attention to the importance of biology, particularly genetics, in influencing behaviour.

+ They take account of personality differences that might exist from birth, such as impulsiveness and a desire for excitement.

+ They help us understand how genetic potential can lead to such problems as poor achievement in school and inadequate socialisation, which in turn may result in criminality.

– They are simplistic theories, taking account of only one factor (biology). It is very unlikely that criminal behaviour can be reduced to a biological explanation alone.

– They ignore or underestimate the social causes of crime such as antisocial role models and an emotionally deprived childhood.

where to now?

The following are good sources of further information on biological theories of crime:

▶ **Moir, A. & Jessel, D. (1997)** *A Mind to Crime: The Controversial Link Between Mind and Criminal Behaviour.* **London: Signet.**

▶ **Jones, S. (1998)** *Criminology.* **London: Butterworth.**

The three theories discussed above are by no means the only theories that highlight the importance of physiology in the development of criminal behaviour. Moir & Jessel examine a wide range of biological theories and Jones offers a critique of them (as well as many other up-to-date theories and discussions).

Psychoanalytic theory

Freud's theory

In order to understand Freud's psychoanalytic theory as it has been applied to crime, it would be useful to revise Freud's basic theory as discussed in detail in Jarvis *et al.* (2000), *Angles on Psychology*. Freud himself made little direct reference to criminal behaviour but his theory has been used to explain the origins of criminal behaviour by several psychoanalysts (e.g. Feldman, 1964; Kline, 1987). Since there are several such models, it is not possible to outline a single psychoanalytic theory, but certain themes can be described.

Freud's best known contribution to psychology is his emphasis on the unconscious and its influence on behaviour. The unconscious part of the mind contains repressed memories and instinctive drives, drives that cannot be ignored but must find expression in some form. According to Freud, the personality consists of three parts: the id, the ego and the superego.

Id, ego and superego

The id is the instinctual part of the personality, comprising biological urges such as the need for food, warmth and sex, which it seeks to satisfy urgently. When thwarted, as inevitably happens, aggressive urges emerge. It was because of the existence of the id that Freud formulated his belief that humans are inherently antisocial, driven by egocentric urges which are in conflict with harmonious living in a social group. The ego is the conscious part of the personality which seeks to channel the urges of the id within the constraints provided by parents and by society. The superego, which does not emerge fully until around four to five years of age, comprises the conscience and the ego-ideal. The conscience is concerned with moral rules and the ego-ideal represents standards to which the self aspires, thus providing the ego with a set of values and goals.

Until the superego is fully formed children have no internalised moral standards. When young children do as they are told, it is from fear of punishment rather than avoidance of guilt. This changes at around the age of four when both girls and boys experience the Oedipus complex (sometimes referred to as the Electra complex in girls, but not by Freud). At this stage, children develop a strong and powerful urge for sexual possession of the opposite sex parent. This unacceptable urge gives rise to serious problems. The young boy becomes extremely fearful that his vengeful father will castrate him for having such desires and he resolves this conflict by identifying with his father, and in so doing, internalises the father's moral standards. In this way the superego is formed and the boy

25

takes on the moral values of the father. If, because of a weak or absent father, the Oedipus complex is not fully resolved, the superego will be weak. If the father is over-strict then the superego may be so strong that the urges of the id are tightly controlled and thwarted in which case serious problems can arise.

The problems girls experience are rather different from those of boys. They fear losing the love of their mother and, believing that they have already been punished by castration, they also repress their urges and identify with the same-sex parent. Since girls do not have a penis they are unable to develop a conscience through fear of castration in the same way as boys do. The superegos of females are, therefore, weaker than those of males and they are morally inferior.

The id and superego are in constant conflict and it is the ego's unenviable task to strike a balance between them. In order to do this, it employs what Freud called ego defence mechanisms which prevent the system becoming so dangerously unbalanced that the individual's mental health is at risk. When the id, ego and superego are reasonably well balanced, then these defence mechanisms can usually channel the urges in a socially acceptable way; for example, aggression may be expressed in sport. However, if the urges are overwhelming or the systems not in balance, then problems arise. For example, a boy who feels very aggressive towards his violent father but cannot express this directly may use the defence mechanism of displacement and take out his violent urges on weaker children, thus becoming a bully.

Freudian psychoanalysts argue that an individual can only lead a stable life if the id, ego and superego are sufficiently balanced. If the id is strong and the superego is weak, the individual will seek pleasure and immediate gratification regardless of the needs of others and, although aware of the possibility of punishment, will not be deterred by it. Kline (1987) argued that many rational law-abiding citizens who have control over their id believe that harsh punishments will effectively act as a deterrent to crime. However, this is not the case, because an individual with a dominant id is ruled by the pleasure principle, not the reality principle.

Psychodynamic explanations of crime

Psychodynamic theorists have explained crime in several ways, focusing particularly on a harsh, weak or deviant superego which inevitably leads to an imbalance between the id, ego and superego. A harsh superego, resulting from identification with a strict parent, can lead to strong feelings of guilt and obsession whenever the id attempts to get any satisfaction at all. People with strong superegos will usually be law abiding, but a few such people will engage in antisocial acts and such strangely deviant behaviour as stealing women's underwear from a washing line. The unconscious desire for sex has led to such feelings of guilt that the individual unconsciously desires to be punished, and so commits a crime, and the crime is related to their problematic urges. As Jones (1998) states, 'Here, there is a reversal of the usual situation: guilt precedes crime.'

More commonly, crime arises from a weak, underdeveloped superego. In this case the individual is selfish and uncaring, full of uncontrolled aggression. The failure to develop a well functioning superego is believed by psychoanalysts to be the result of unloving or absent parenting. This is the basis of Bowlby's theory, as considered below.

A deviant superego may emerge in a boy if his father is deviant. In this case there may be a good relationship between father and son with the Oedipus complex fully resolved and a superego which has developed normally. However, the son's superego standards are those of the father, that is, antisocial, deviant ones. Freud called this phenomenon pseudo-heredity.

Evaluating the psychodynamic approach to crime

When applied to crime, there are several problems with the Freudian approach. As mentioned earlier, according to this approach, females have weaker superegos than males have. This would lead us to expect more female than male criminals. However, females constitute a very small percentage of the criminal population; furthermore, some research indicates that females show a stronger moral orientation than males at all ages (Hoffman, 1977).

The theory is rather limited in the types of crimes for which it can account; indeed, it does not claim to offer an explanation for *all* crime. Kline (1987) suggests that many white-collar crimes and even some aggressive crimes are carefully and deliberately planned and executed, and are motivated by a rational decision to profit from the proceeds of crime rather than by irrational thought processes.

Some criminals do show neurotic conflicts but even this does not necessarily support the psychoanalytic approach. The validity of the techniques used to assess these conflicts has been questioned (e.g. Balay & Shevrin, 1988) and these conflicts may result from, rather than cause, the criminal behaviour.

Nevertheless, the psychodynamic hypothesis cannot be summarily dismissed. It is the only theory that addresses the importance of emotional factors in criminal behaviour. It also offers a more plausible account than most theories for crimes that have no obvious gain and are incomprehensible to the logically minded, such as stealing women's underwear from washing lines or compulsive shoplifting by the rich of items for which they have no use. The notion that unconscious processes are an important determinant of behaviour is one that is still strongly held by a significant body of psychologists.

A theory based on the psychodynamic approach: Bowlby's theory of delinquency

John Bowlby, a psychoanalyst who worked with disturbed adolescents at a clinic in London, drew on Freud's theory to explain why children who are unloved are liable themselves to become uncaring, delinquent individuals (Bowlby, 1979). His study of juvenile thieves is considered below in Classic Research. You can see from this that Bowlby believed that separation from the main attachment figure in early life can result in delinquent behaviour because individuals who have suffered such deprivation do not consider other people's feelings, so they do as they wish without consideration for the hurt they may cause. In psychoanalytic terms, the young child has been unable to form a strong attachment and consequently has an inadequately formed superego. Bowlby has been criticised for concentrating on separation as a precursor to delinquency. The important factor that determines whether an antisocial personality may be formed is the failure to form a bond with someone, whether or not this is caused by separation (Rutter, 1971). It is quite possible to remain in contact with the mother (or main carer) but, if she (or he) is unloving and distant, then no proper bond will form. Some theorists (e.g. Marshall, 1983) argue that the hostility and apparent lack of anxiety shown by adolescents and adults who were neglected and unloved as children is an ego defence mechanism against the painful feelings of dependency and powerlessness they feel as a result of their harsh experiences.

classic
research

Can disruption to attachment cause affectionless psychopathy?

Bowlby, J. (1946) *Forty-four juvenile thieves*. London: Bailliere, Tindall & Cox.

Aims: Bowlby believed that prolonged separation from the primary carer during the first two or three years of life could cause permanent emotional damage. One way in which this damage manifests itself is affectionless psychopathy. Bowlby aimed in this study to see whether teenage criminals who displayed affectionless psychopathy were more likely to have had early separation than those who had not.

Method: Forty-four of the teenagers referred to the Child Guidance Clinic where Bowlby worked were selected on the basis that they were involved in criminal activity, and that they were living with their biological parents. Bowlby interviewed them in order to assess whether they exhibited signs of affectionless psychopathy. This was identified by lack of affection to others, lack of guilt or shame at their actions and lack of empathy for their victims. Bowlby also interviewed the families of the adolescents in order to establish whether the children had had prolonged early separations from their primary carer in their first two years. Bowlby then matched up those young people who had been classified as affectionless psychopaths with those who had had prolonged maternal deprivation in the first two years. A control group of non-delinquent young people was established in order to see how commonly maternal deprivation occurred in the non-delinquent children.

Results: The results were striking. Of the 14 children identified as affectionless psychopaths, 12 had experienced prolonged separation from their mothers in the first two years. By contrast, only 5 of the 30 delinquent children not classified as affectionless psychopaths had experienced similar separations. Of the 44 people in the non-delinquent control group, only 2 had experienced prolonged separations.

Conclusions: The young criminals who had had a prolonged separation in their first two years were several times more likely to exhibit affectionless psychopathy than those who had no such separation. This provides strong support for Bowlby's maternal deprivation hypothesis.

Learning theory and social learning theory

The learning theory view of criminal behaviour as espoused by traditional learning theories is that it is learnt in the same way as all other learning: by classical and operant conditioning. (These are discussed in detail in Jarvis *et al.* (2000), *Angles on Psychology*.) Classical conditioning involves learning to associate one thing with another, so a child may learn to associate stealing sweets with excitement. Operant conditioning involves learning by the consequences of your actions; if you are reinforced for an action you are more likely to repeat that action in future; if you are punished, then the behaviour will decline in frequency.

When applied to the causes of criminal behaviour, the principle is quite simple and involves mainly operant conditioning – criminal behaviour is learned and maintained by the rewards it brings. For example, stealing brings obvious material rewards and may bring less obvious but equally powerful ones such as the admiration of peers, a feeling of competence, increased self-esteem and a thrill.

Bandura's approach

Social learning theory differs in significant ways from behaviourism by considering some important *cognitive* elements to learning. Bandura (1963) postulated that there are three main influences on people's behaviour. The first is external reinforcement (as in operant conditioning); the second is vicarious reinforcement; the third is self-reinforcement. Let us explain these last two terms.

Vicarious reinforcement involves learning by watching other people, rather than by receiving rewards or punishments directly. According to Bandura, one way in which children learn is by watching other people; this learning is known as *observational learning* and is very influential. Individuals, particularly children, copy other people, especially if the behaviour is rewarded. If one child sees another snatch a toy from someone and play with it without being told off (without being punished), he or she may well do the same. Conversely, a child is unlikely to copy a behaviour for which the model is punished. Some people are more likely to be imitated than others, namely significant and respected models such as parents, teachers, peers and media figures.

Self-reinforcement involves the pride you feel when you do something well. Again, direct reinforcement is not necessary – if you feel good about the way you have behaved, then this motivates you to behave similarly in the future. The converse is the feeling of shame you experience if you do something that goes against your own moral standards; this puts you off repeating such behaviour.

Social learning theory, unlike traditional learning theories, does not regard people as simply passive respondents to external stimuli but argues that their behaviour is influenced by anticipation and attitudes. Based on previous experience, people have expectations about the consequences of what they do (if you are punished for walloping your brother, you expect that this may happen again if you hit him, and this may influence whether or not you repeat the action). People also create their own environments: some people don't wait for events to happen, they seek out exciting experiences, including, in some cases, criminal ones.

A lot of Bandura's work was concerned with the observational learning of aggressive behaviour and we will return to that in Chapter 5. In the meantime we will look at theories of crime that are based on the principles of learning and which therefore differ significantly from the biological theories of crime.

The theory of differential association: a sociological learning theory

As long ago as 1939 Sutherland used social learning theory principles to advance a sociological theory of crime known as Differential Association

Theory. This theory, originally written in 1939 and slightly modified in 1947, is sociological because it postulates that it is the *social organisations* in which people are socialised that determine whether or not they will participate in criminal activities. According to Sutherland, criminal behaviour, like all behaviour, is learned through social interactions. Some subcultures within society are organised so that the norms are favourable towards criminal activities whilst others are organised so that the norms are unfavourable to such law violation. Individuals come into contact with both types of attitudes or, in Sutherland's terminology, *definitions*. If they encounter more and stronger definitions in favour of law violation than against it, then they will consider crime to be an acceptable way of life. The term *differential association* reflects the ratio of favourable to non-favourable definitions of crime. This theory therefore explains why any individual may be drawn into a life of crime and why crime rates are higher in some neighbourhoods than in others.

Sutherland advanced nine principles on which the theory of differential association is based:

- Criminal behaviour is learned rather than inherited.

- The learning of criminal behaviour takes place through association with other people in a process of communication.

- Most of such learning is through association with close family and friends, that is, intimate personal groups.

- The learning involves techniques for carrying out crimes, and also criminal motives, drives, attitudes and rationalisations (such as it being all right to steal from large shops because they overcharge in order to make excessive profits and no individual will suffer as a consequence of such minor shoplifting).

- This learning involves definitions, or norms, which may be favourable or unfavourable to breaking the law.

- If there are more definitions (attitudes) favourable to breaking the law than ones that are unfavourable then a person becomes delinquent. This is the principle of differential association.

- The learning experiences, called differential associations, will vary in frequency, intensity and importance for each individual.

- The processes by which criminal behaviour is learned are the same as those for all types of learning.

- Although criminal behaviour is an expression of general needs and values (such as the desire for material goods, the need to support one's children), the expression of these needs and values does not *explain* criminal behaviour since non-criminal behaviour is motivated by the same needs and values.

This theory, then, states that the main factors influencing behaviour are who a person associates with, for how long, how frequently and how personally meaningful the associations are. Sutherland did not propose that it was necessary to associate directly with criminals in order to learn these attitudes and methods, but that contact with people who were favourable to certain law violations or cheating was quite sufficient. For example, parents may emphasise the importance of not stealing but may falsify their tax returns or avoid buying a television licence. In this way a child may have little or no contact with deviant groups and still learn values conducive to antisocial behaviour. Sutherland, then, believed that criminal behaviour was not caused by a lack of personal fibre but by the content of what was learned. As Lilly *et al.* (1989) appositely express it: 'Those with the good fortune of growing up in a conventional neighbourhood will learn to play baseball and to attend church services; those with the misfortune of growing up in a slum will learn to rob drunks and to roam the streets looking for mischief' (page 47). This was, for its time, a very radical theory, which shifted the emphasis from individual lack of morality to problems within society.

Evaluation of Sutherland's theory

One of the most important contributions made by Sutherland's theory was to draw attention to the fact that by no means all crimes are committed by deviant psychopathic individuals from poverty-stricken backgrounds. Sutherland coined the term 'white collar crimes' to describe the illegal activities engaged in by the middle classes in the course of their professional lives. It was his belief that in the worlds of business, politics and the professions illegal practices were accepted widely as a way of doing business. This is easily accountable within his theory but not by other theories of the day, with their emphasis on abnormality, feeblemindedness and deteriorating families living in slums.

On the negative side, this theory would find it more difficult to explain crimes of passion and other impulsive offences by people who have not been raised to have deviant values. The theory has also been criticised for being vague and untestable. One point on which it is vague is that it does not specify exactly how learning takes place: is it by classical conditioning, operant conditioning or observational learning? The difficulty in testing it arises because of the problems of measuring the number and strength of an individual's various associations and the extent of the influence they may have exerted. Yet another problem is that it says nothing about individual differences in susceptibility to the influence of other people. Nevertheless, although the theory may be incomplete, there is little to suggest, as there is with some others, that it is inaccurate and it has been used as the basis of other theories, such as the differential association-reinforcement theory of Akers (1977).

Evaluation of learning theories as a whole

Learning theories as a whole have highlighted the importance of environmental influences on criminal behaviour. However, as Nietzel (1979) points out, a major problem with them is that they try to apply simple principles to very complex and varied behaviour. Moreover, the studies used to test the theory usually involve specific learning tasks in an artificial environment and therefore lack validity since they are unlikely to reflect behaviour in an everyday setting. Learning theory, like many other theories, also finds it difficult to account for the fact that many deviant adolescents abandon their life of crime in early adulthood.

for and
against

learning theory and social learning theories of crime

+ The theories are based on carefully conducted empirical research, which clearly demonstrates the influence of reinforcement and observation on behaviour.

+ They can help to explain why criminality does, to an extent, run in families. There is a considerable body of evidence indicating that in real-world situations, people do imitate those around them, especially family members.

+ Males and females are socialised very differently, with females encouraged not to be aggressive and to conform, while males are encouraged to 'stick up for themselves' and be independent. This may account for the considerable differences in crime rates of men and women.

— The studies on which these theories are based are conducted in laboratories or other artificial environments in carefully controlled conditions. They therefore lack validity in that they may not be sampling behaviour as it occurs in real life situations.

— The fact that criminal behaviour tends to run in families is not necessarily due to imitation but may be due to circumstances such as social deprivation, or to genetic propensity to behave in an antisocial way.

— There are biological differences between men and women, especially hormonal ones, and this, rather than socialisation, may account for differential rates of crime between men and women.

research
now

are violent criminals more angry and paranoid than non-violent criminals?

Katz, R.C. & Marquette, J. (1999) Psychosocial characteristics of young violent offenders: a comparative study. *Criminal Behaviour and Mental Health*, 6, 339–348

Aim: To compare a group of violent offenders (murderers), non-violent offenders and non-offenders on measures of anger, hostility, paranoid ideation and global psychopathology. The hypothesis was that those guilty of violent crimes would, compared to the other two groups, have more anger, rage or paranoid symptoms.

This hypothesis was based on several theories of crime. The psychodynamic approach sees homicidal behaviour as stemming from unconscious conflict, an ego weakness, displaced anger or repressive coping mechanisms. From a biological interactionist viewpoint, Lewis & Pincus (1989) suggest that many extremely aggressive young men have suffered from abuse and family violence resulting in damage to their central nervous system. Psychosocial variables such as poverty, family turmoil, gang involvement, excessive alcohol intake, physical abuse, educational difficulties and exposure to violent role models either within the family or through the media have also been found to be related with adolescent aggression.

Method:

Design: The method used was psychometric testing. This was an independent groups design comparing three groups of young men:

- convicted murderers

- non-violent offenders

- non-offending high school juniors and seniors.

Participants: There was a total of 77 participants, all males from Stockton in California, ranging in age from 16 to 23 with a mean age of 19. All were volunteers who were told that the purpose of the study was to assess various attitudes and beliefs in young people; they all received $5 for participating. There were 29 convicted murderers; 15 non-violent offenders imprisoned for repeated robbery and similar acquisitive crimes or for violation of probation; 33 junior and senior school students from a state school, all studying psychology.

All three groups were ethnically diverse and consisted of roughly equal numbers of Caucasians, Blacks, Hispanics and Asians. The two offender groups had a somewhat larger number of Blacks and Hispanics.

The psychometric tests: Three tests were used:

- MMPI-A: a revision of the MMPI for use with adolescents. This is a personality test which measures adolescent anger, family problems, alienation and conduct problems.

- SCL-90-R: used in this study to measure hostility, paranoid ideation, interpersonal sensitivity and level of distress.

- State–Trait Anger Scale: a self-report measure that assesses anger in two ways: as a relatively stable personality trait (trait anger) and as a current emotional state (state anger) reflected in feelings of tension, annoyance, irritation or rage.

The participants were also asked to complete a questionnaire asking the number of times they had been arrested, the number of times they had been arrested for a violent crime, whether they had ever been a gang member and whether anyone in their family had ever been imprisoned. In order to encourage honest responses, they were asked not to put their names on the tests.

Results: The prediction that young murderers would show increased levels of anger, hostility, paranoid ideation, feelings of alienation and global psychopathology was not supported. There was no significant difference here between any of the three groups.

However, there were some differences between the groups. Compared with the school students, a significantly higher proportion of the offenders had grown up in families where at least one other family member had spent time in jail or prison.

Murderers were more likely to be gang members and more inclined to express feelings of self-consciousness, inferiority and inadequacy.

Compared with school students, young offenders expressed *less* global distress and were *less* troubled by feelings of anger and hostility; they were more likely to have been gang members or to have come from a family where antisocial behaviour was a problem.

Conclusion: There was no evidence for differences in anger, hostility and psychopathology between violent offenders, non-violent offenders and non-offenders. A history of gang membership was more likely to distinguish between the three groups. This supports a report from the US Department of Justice (Blumstein, 1995; Snyder & Sickman, 1995) that sociocultural variables are the driving force behind the considerable and steady increase in the amount of juvenile crime and violence in the US.

Social and familial correlates of crime

Factors that correlate with crime are those variables, such as economic deprivation, that demonstrate a relationship with the incidence of criminal behaviour. It is crucial to remember that correlations only tell us that there is a relationship between one variable and another; they do *not* tell us what is causing what. For example, there is a relationship between poor school performance and juvenile delinquency but we cannot say that low school achievement necessarily *causes* delinquency. It is equally plausible that once an individual becomes involved in delinquent behaviour, their school work suffers and exam results fall.

Alternatively, there may be a third factor – perhaps the attitude of the family towards school work and offending – that causes both of the other factors. It is important, though, to recognise that a relationship does have a cause and this is what researchers are trying to uncover, but we should not jump to superficial conclusions about the exact direction of the cause.

There is a myriad of individual, familial and social correlates of crime: we will consider research on some of the more salient ones but before doing so we will take a look in Research Now at a longitudinal study based in Cambridge which looks at many factors associated with crime. The study began in 1961–62 and was originally under the directorship of West, whose interim findings were published in 1982, so references made later to West (1982) refer to this study.

research now

the Cambridge Study: problem families produce problem children

Farrington, D.P. (1996) The Development of Offending and Antisocial Behaviour from Childhood to Adulthood. In Cordella, P. & Siegel, L. (eds) *Readings in Contemporary Criminological Theory*. Boston: Northeast University Press.

Aim: To describe the development of delinquent and criminal behaviour in inner-city males, to investigate how far it could be predicted in advance, and to explain why juvenile delinquency began. The original study was begun in 1961–62; this is a follow-up study of 411 London boys, born mostly in 1953.

Method:

Design: This is a longitudinal study based on interviews and tests conducted at various ages over, to date, 24 years.

Participants: The great majority of the sample were chosen by taking all the boys who were then 8–9 years old and on the registers of six state primary schools in one location in London. The boys were almost all white and predominantly from working-class families.

Measures used:

1   Tests and interviews at school at ages 8, 10 and 14 years. Interviews in the research office at about 16, 18 and 21 and in homes at about 25 and 31. The tests in schools measured intelligence, attainment, personality and psychomotor skills. The interviews collected information concerning employment history, relationships with females, leisure activities such as drinking and fighting, and offending behaviour.

2   Interviews with the parents about once a year from when the study began (when the boys were about 8) to when they were 14 or 15 years old. It was mainly the mothers who were interviewed. The parents provided information on family size, employment history, child-rearing practices, degree of supervision and whether there had been any temporary separations.

3   Questionnaires completed by the boys' teachers when the boys were 8, 10, 12 and 14. These concerned troublesome and aggressive behaviour, attainment, and truancy. Peers

provided information on popularity, daring, dishonesty and troublesomeness.

4   Records from the Criminal Record Office to gain information on convictions of the boys, their parents, their siblings and, later, their wives or cohabitees. Minor offences such as common assault, traffic offences and drunkenness were not included in these statistics.

Results:

Statistics on crimes committed:

1   By the age of 32, 37 per cent of the males had committed criminal offences. The peak age was 17. Nearly three quarters of those convicted as juveniles were reconvicted between the ages of 17 and 24, and nearly half of the juvenile offenders were reconvicted between the ages of 25 and 32.

2   Offending was very much concentrated in families. Just 4 per cent of the 400 families accounted for 50 per cent of all convictions of all family members.

3   The worst offenders tended to be from large-sized, multiproblem families.

4   Most juvenile and young adult offences occurred with other people, but this co-offending declined with age. Co-offending with brothers was not uncommon when the siblings were close in age but co-offending with fathers (or mothers) was very rare.

5   The most common crimes in late teens were burglary, shoplifting, theft of and from vehicles, and vandalism. All of these declined in the twenties, but theft from work increased.

6   Self reports showed that 96 per cent of the males had committed at least one crime that might have led to conviction, so criminal behaviour was not deviant.

Predictors of crime at age 8–10:

1   Antisocial child behaviour including troublesomeness, dishonesty and aggression.

2   Hyperactivity-impulsivity-attention deficit.

3   Low intelligence and poor school attainment.

4   Family criminality.

5   Family poverty, including low family income, large family size and poor housing.

6   Poor parental child-rearing techniques, poor supervision, parental conflict and separation from parents.

Conclusion: Any one of these factors independently predicts offending and the following suggestions are made as to the reasons for this. Children from poorer families are more likely to offend because, due to poor school attainment and an inability to manipulate abstract concepts, they are less able to achieve their goals legally. Impulsive children cannot see the consequences of their actions and desire immediate gratification. Children who are exposed to poor child-rearing practices, conflict or separation do not build up inhibitions against antisocial behaviour. Lastly, children from criminal families and those with delinquent friends develop anti-establishment attitudes and the belief that it is justifiable to offend. This research demonstrates that problem children grow into problem adults who in turn produce problem children. Sooner or later serious measures must be taken to break this cycle.

Poverty

Crime has often been perceived as more common amongst the poor than among the more affluent but the evidence is equivocal. Ehrlich (1974) found a positive correlation between rates of property crime in America and the percentage of homes receiving half the average income. In the Cambridge study low family income was found to be related to later delinquency, regardless of other factors (West, 1982). Several studies have also demonstrated a link between dependence on welfare and delinquency (e.g. Offord, 1982; Ouston, 1984). However, no such relationship was found by Jacobs (1981) when looking at levels of burglary, robbery and theft.

It is necessary to use several measures of poverty, rather than simply income, in order to gain a more complete picture. Messner (1988) used 'structural poverty' as a measure, that is an assessment based on income, one-parent families, poor education and high infant mortality, and found a stronger relationship between these measures and crime rates.

Poverty due to unemployment has also been implicated in the incidence of crime. Benyan (1994) reviewed a number of studies of offenders and concluded that unemployment was one of the principal causes of crime and disorder in Britain. Similarly, Wells (1995) commented, with reference to Britain, that a society that had such large numbers of children in poverty ran a high risk of widespread delinquency. However, unemployment has a large number of effects other than poverty, including a loss of status and self-esteem, boredom and alienation, and it would therefore be misleading to imply that it is the poverty resulting from unemployment that is implicated in criminal behaviour. Given that the relationship between unemployment and crime is fairly clear, society cannot afford to be complacent about the social consequences of unemployment.

Sociologists draw our attention to the importance of economic inequality rather than poverty as an important influence on much social behaviour, including crime. Economic inequality entails a comparison of the levels of material wealth between different groups within society. Goodman *et al.* (1997), in an analysis for the Institute for Fiscal Studies, reported that the level of economic inequality has risen massively in the last 20 years: the combined income of the top 10 per cent of earners was equal to that of the bottom 50 per cent of all earners. It has been suggested by several theorists (e.g. Stack, 1984) that there is a relationship between crime and inequality. From an analysis of 16 studies of crime and economic inequality between 1974 and 1985, Box (1987) found that eleven showed a positive correlation between economic inequality and crime and he hypothesised that this inequality was responsible for the rise in crime during periods of recession, especially amongst the poorest – the young, women, and ethnic minorities. From an analysis of the situation in the US, Hagan (1994) suggested that the increasing inability of the poorest citizens to attain any upward social mobility is likely to lead to increasing competition and violence in the underworld of vice and racketeering. Ironically, this is liable to give the wealthier more opportunity to exploit the poor, both by legal and illegal means.

In conclusion, it would be misleading to equate crime with absolute poverty. The great majority of poor people are law-abiding citizens and the poor do not steal solely because they lack food or clothing. There is more evidence for a relationship between economic inequality and crime. Nevertheless it is important to recognise the possibility that the poor are more likely than the wealthy to be apprehended. It is widely recognised that some of the wealthiest people in society engage in all manner of acquisitive illegal acts such as tax evasion and fraud, and they get away with it.

Family background

Certain patterns of family life have consistently been shown to be related to crime, as evidenced by the finding that a small minority of families accounts for a large proportion of offences. For example, in the Cambridge study 4.6 per cent of families accounted for 48 per cent of all convictions (West, 1982). There is an abundant amount of folk wisdom as to what aspects of the family environment are conducive to criminal or delinquent behaviour, with the blame at various times being placed on parental irresponsibility, physical abuse, broken homes and lack of affectionate parenting, to name but a few. We will take a look at research which has investigated some of these variables.

Many studies indicate that delinquents are more likely to come from broken rather than intact homes (Glueck & Glueck, 1950; Flynn, 1983). As we saw earlier in Classic Research, Bowlby's research supports this idea. This has often led to statements by politicians and other high profile groups that divorce and separation are directly responsible for delinquency. This superficial conclusion has been repeatedly questioned by those who analyse data in greater depth. There are many variables that are associated with the broken home and may therefore have an influence on the child. For example, the divorced are more likely to belong to the lower socioeconomic groups (Belsky et al., 1964). It is quite possible that factors associated with socioeconomic status, such as poverty and poor educational opportunities, are more closely correlated with delinquency than the number of parents raising the children. Another factor that may be influential is the amount of conflict in the home. There is evidence that children from broken but harmonious homes are less likely to be delinquent than those brought up in intact but conflict-ridden families (Gove & Crutchfield, 1982).

Certain styles of parental discipline are also related to delinquency. Harsh physical punishment is more likely to result in more delinquency than reasoning with the child. This is especially true if the corporal punishment is inconsistent and dependent more on the mood of the parent than on the transgression of the child (McCord *et al.* 1959; Glueck & Glueck, 1956). Other forms of abuse such as neglect or emotional abuse (for example, screaming, constantly criticising and frequently insulting a child) may also play their part in later delinquency; indeed some researchers suggest that this can be more devastating than physical punishment (Brown, 1984).

Large family size is also related to delinquency. Farrington (1996) found in the Cambridge study that delinquents were more likely to come from families with four or more children. Recidivists, that is criminals who relapse into crime, also come from larger families (Buikhuisen *et al.*, 1974). Again, explanations are complicated by the presence of other variables: larger families tend to be poorer and live in more overcrowded accommodation, so stress may be a causal factor. However, when large families are matched with smaller ones on family income and socioeconomic status the difference in delinquency rates still persists, so it is possible that lack of attention, difficulties with discipline and/or lack of parental supervision have an effect.

Any single one of the aforementioned family variables (with perhaps the exception of harsh physical punishment) is unlikely to be a strong predictor of delinquency, but the more of such factors that are present in a family, the stronger the relationship. In the Cambridge study, 73 per cent of boys reared in homes showing three or more of these factors had convictions by the age of 32 compared with just over 30 per cent of the remainder. However, a very important rider is necessary here. Both in the Cambridge study and in others (e.g. Kolvin *et al.*, 1988), a large percentage of the offenders (more than two-thirds) had not been reared in deprived families. We need, therefore, to be very careful about the contribution that family variables make to delinquency and to remember that correlation is not causation. Poor parenting and conflict in the home may well be the result of poverty and poor housing which may be more of a direct influence on delinquency.

School and peer group

Children who become delinquent do not do well in the school system. Some sociologists maintain that the educational system, with its emphasis on middle-class values, alienates some working-class children and eventually drives them towards delinquency (Cohen, 1955). An alternative explanation is that the problem lies not so much with the educational system but with the individuals whose intellectual ability is so limited that they fail and become alienated (Hirschi & Hindelang, 1977), or who lack the necessary skills to cope with the demands of the classroom and playground (Dishion *et al.*, 1991). Most analyses of educational establishments seem to assume that all schools are the same but, as pointed out by Blackburn (1993), schools vary in their educational philosophies and social organisation which in turn may influence whether they inhibit or facilitate antisocial behaviour.

A major predictor of delinquency among adolescents is the delinquency of close friends; few youngsters engage in solitary offending, most work in groups of two or three (Aultman, 1980). Hargreaves (1980) argues that 'status deprivation' of those who fail in the school system leads to both negative attitudes towards education and the motivation to join delinquent groups. Gold (1978), however, argues that different processes are acting in the two situations. School failure results in lowered self-esteem whilst antisocial behaviour amongst peers helps to present an attitude of defiance which is rewarded by peer admiration. When boys are unloved and maltreated at home and have been made to feel a failure at school, it is not surprising that they turn to a group who provides friendship, admiration and a sense of belonging, as well as excitement and some material rewards.

There is disagreement amongst theorists about the extent to which certain adolescents are passively recruited into delinquent groups and how much they seek out those who they perceive as similar to themselves. It would appear that unsocialised youths tend to seek out similar partners for friendship (Bandura & Walters 1963; Dishion et al., 1991) and that once these alliances are formed, the associates tend to become more alike over time, suggesting that they influence each other. This is consistent with research on interpersonal attraction showing that people form relationships with those who share their attitudes and that stable friendships are maintained by mutual influence (Dwyer, 2000).

Others argue that the peer group is a relatively unimportant influence in delinquency and occurs only after early life experiences in the family and school have led the adolescent towards a life of delinquency. Finding friends with whom to commit crimes is incidental to this process. However Hirschi (1969), who originally espoused this view, later acknowledged that association with delinquents could influence even those boys who had strong family ties. The strength of peer group influence is as yet still not established. The evidence does suggest that whilst the peer group may facilitate criminal behaviour, a propensity for delinquency is already present in individuals who join such groups (Gottfredson & Hirschi, 1990).

Finally, we need to note that not all delinquents work in gangs or are influenced by peer group pressure. A considerable number make solitary rational choices to engage in criminal behaviour for financial gain or as a means of venting their anger and seeking revenge (Agnew, 1990).

Ethnicity

In Britain and the USA the proportion of certain ethnic minority groups convicted of offences is much larger than their proportion in the population as a whole. This applies particularly to people of Afro-Caribbean and black African origin. For example, in June 1998, the rate of incarceration in Britain per 100,000 of the general population was 1,245 for black people, 185 for whites and 168 for Asians (from Dodd, 2000). There has been huge high-profile media coverage of this issue, often very emotive in tone. The argument centres on the extent to which these statistics reflect discrimination within the criminal justice system or are a true reflection of the rates of crime among these groups.

It is extremely difficult to ascertain whether black youths do offend to a greater extent than their white counterparts but, if this so, it is probably a reflection of the factors already considered, that is, alienation and economic deprivation. Black people are also significantly more likely than whites to be the victims of crime.

Certainly there is evidence that discrimination does exist in the criminal justice system. Crawford (2000) explored the effects of race on over 1,100 habitual female offenders in Florida and found that African-American women were given harsher sentences than their white counterparts. Similarly, when crime seriousness, crime type and prior record are controlled for, black males receive harsher sentences than white males do (Crawford *et al.*, 1998).

The Macpherson Report, commissioned to address concerns about police racism in Britain, identified unequal treatment of the black community at the hands of the police and a report by the Howard League for Penal Reform (2000) similarly identified discrimination against ethnic minorities, ranging from the disproportionately high rates at which the notorious 'stop-and-search' is applied to young blacks right through to the sentencing procedures and even beyond. Dodd (2000), a reporter, writes that

> '*Every key stage of the criminal justice system is riddled with racism, leaving black people with a greater prospect of being arrested and jailed than whites, according to a study by a penal reform group.*
>
> *British Afro-Caribbean people are seven times more likely to be in jail despite being no more likely to commit crimes, says the Howard League.*' (The Guardian, 20 March 2000)

The British Crime Survey, mentioned in Chapter 1, asks people about crimes they have experienced in the last year and about their contacts with the police. Bucke (1997), reflecting BCS findings of 1994 and 1996, reported that Afro-Caribbeans were more likely to be stopped by the police while on foot or in a car and were also more likely to experience multiple stops. The rate for Asians was no greater than that for whites. Afro-Caribbeans were also more than twice as likely as whites to be searched when stopped and four times more likely to be arrested.

Racial discrimination is, of course, not confined to the criminal justice system but extends across the whole of society. This limits the educational and employment opportunities of ethnic minority groups and, as we have seen, increases the likelihood that they will participate in crime. These wider issues, as well as the specific problems within the justice system, need to be addressed if any real justice is to be achieved.

Gender

Women are, on the whole, a law-abiding lot: they are consistently convicted of crimes to a far lesser extent than men and this pattern seems to hold true across the world. Despite the fact that this difference is far larger than any other, it is only since the 1970s that criminologists have paid it much attention at all. Studies from a variety of countries show that approximately 80 per cent of crimes are committed by men (Heidensohn, 1991 in France & Germany; FBI, 1991 in the USA: Harvey et al., 1992 for the United Nations). In Britain, around 1 in 3 men will have a conviction for a serious offence by the age of 31 (a staggering statistic), while this applies to only 1 in 13 women (Home Office, 1992). Moreover, women are usually convicted of less serious offences than men (UN statistic, 1975–1985; 1996 Criminal Statistics for England and Wales). The general pattern is that although men and women commit similar crimes, they do so at very different rates; for example, women are far less likely to commit robbery, sexual offences or murder. Some criminologists argue that women are under-represented in crime statistics but others (e.g. Box, 1983) argue that they may even be over-represented since they seldom have the opportunity to be involved in organised and corporate crime of which many men are guilty but not convicted.

Traditionally the explanation for the relative infrequency of female criminality is that girls are socialised to be more conforming, are more strictly supervised by parents and are shown greater disapproval for breaking society's rules than are boys (Hagan et al., 1979). In a study of high school children in Toronto, these researchers found that girls were subject to more control within the family than boys were. The effects of early socialisation are carried through life. It has also been suggested that because most adult women have part-time and low-level jobs they are reluctant to risk them by engaging in criminal activity (Heidensohn, 1996). They are also controlled by the threat of violence on the street which makes them more likely to stay out of harm's way.

These are some of the reasons why women do not get involved in crime. Looking at the other side of the coin, various theories have been advanced to account for why some women do get involved in criminal activity. Lombroso believed that women were evolutionarily inferior to men, a lower form of life. Having, as we saw earlier in the chapter, hypothesised that the criminal male was an evolutionary throwback, his ideas about women made it difficult for him to account for their relative lack of offending. He suggested that the 'natural' female criminal was so physically unattractive that natural selection had operated to make her unlikely to breed. Those who remained were among the few not 'neutralised by maternity' and were likely to be even more horrific and monstrous than their male counterparts (Lombroso & Ferrero, 1895).

Freud (1925) offered an explanation of female crime. He believed that women, who universally are not able to fully resolve the Oedipus complex, have a great deal of need for the approval of men, so as a rule they do not risk upsetting them by committing crimes. The exceptional female who does offend is seen as suffering from extreme penis envy and, in a desire to be a man, takes an aggressive, non-conforming attitude that may result in criminal behaviour. As Jones (1998) comments, 'If anything, this explanation of female crime is likely to induce more ridicule and mirth than that of Lombroso' (page 276).

Box (1987) explains female crime in terms of poverty and unemployment. Women's usual response to lack of opportunity and school failure, he argues, is to blame themselves rather than society so they are less likely to turn to crime. When they do, it is as a desperate attempt to escape from poverty rather than, as in the case of many men, an aggressive response to their social situation. Carlen (1988) conducted in-depth interviews with criminal women and concluded that many crimes were an attempt to escape financial hardship.

A rather different approach to the issue of gender and crime is taken by Messerschmidt (1993) who argues that it is society's concept of masculinity that leads to criminal behaviour in boys and men. To be masculine means, he argues, to assert authority and control over others, to be individualistic, aggressive and independent. If legitimate male outlets are unavailable, the only way to assert one's masculinity is to turn to crime. This is very different from the biological view that because 'boys will be boys' a certain level of violence and antisocial behaviour is inevitable. Messerschmidt has considered in detail how masculinity is asserted by different groups but he has not provided a detailed analysis of why some men assert their masculinity by behaving in a deviant fashion whilst others use alternatives such as sport.

Although a start has been made on investigating the relationship between gender and crime, there is a long way to go. Most research on female crime has focused on minor offences, such as under-age drinking and truancy, carried out by young girls. The study of older women convicted of serious crimes has received little attention so as yet we know little about it (Jones, 1998). If society has a commitment to reducing crime rates, then taking a serious look at the processes that result in so few women offending may be very productive, for, as Wootton (1959) commented '… if men behaved like women, the courts would be idle and the prisons empty.'

where to now?

The following are good sources of further information on explanations of criminal behaviour:

▶ **Newburn, T. & Stanko, E. (eds.) (1994).** *Just Boys Doing Business?* **London: Routledge** – the study of the relationship between masculinity and crime is new and fascinating. This book looks at the implications of such a perspective.

▶ **Blackburn, R. (1993).** *The Psychology of Criminal Conduct: Theory, Research and Practice.* **England: Wiley** – this book looks in detail at some of the factors associated with crime and discusses how each relates to the theories discussed in the first part of the chapter.

Conclusion

Crime, like all behaviour, is complex and varied, and there are no simple answers regarding its causes. This is hardly surprising considering the great variety of crimes and offenders. Different theories put the emphasis on different causal factors: biology, personality, unconscious conflict, social learning, to name but a few. It is still by no means clear whether or not biological factors are implicated in antisocial behaviour but, even if they are, most researchers acknowledge that the environment in which children are reared can either stimulate or inhibit any inborn tendency to criminality. The type of environment most conducive to delinquency is one of poverty, deprivation, a stressful family life and lack of educational opportunities. These factors are inextricably inter-related and the more of these that a child endures, the greater the likelihood of them committing criminal acts. Nevertheless, many individuals exposed to all of these risk factors do not embrace a life of crime. Perhaps we need to take a more careful look at protective factors such as personal disposition, loving relationships, social support systems and, indeed, gender, in order to more successfully address the problem of crime.

what do you know?

1 Compare and contrast two biological theories of crime.

2 Evaluate Freud's theory of crime in terms of two contributions and two limitations.

3 Outline Sutherland's theory of differential association.

4 Describe and discuss a study into social factors associated with delinquency.

5 Outline and discuss three characteristics of family life that may lead to delinquency.

6 Describe and discuss statistics showing that the proportion of certain ethnic groups convicted of offences is much larger than their proportion in the population as a whole.

7 Discuss three possible reasons why women commit fewer crimes than men do.

3

Offender Profiling

what's
ahead?

The concept of offender profiling has attracted a great deal of attention in recent years but our fascination with the subject is not new; long ago fictional detectives such as Sherlock Holmes and Charlie Chan established its popularity. What is relatively recent is that police forces the world over have begun to recognise its potential. In this chapter we will look at what is meant by profiling and at two very different approaches to it – the American and British methods. A real life case study of the profiling of a serial rapist and murderer in London will be outlined before we go on to consider the very important issue of the extent to which profiling actually works – is it a misleading fiction or an indispensable tool in the apprehension of serious criminals? Or, indeed, is it neither, but simply one of many useful aids to the apprehension of criminals?

Introduction

'Offender Profiling', a term coined by the Federal Bureau of Investigation (FBI), has been defined in many ways but the underlying concept is the same: profiling entails providing a description of the offender based on an analysis of the crime scene, the victim and any other available evidence.

Offender Profiling is one of the most controversial and misunderstood areas of criminal detection. As Davies (1997) comments:

> 'The public perception of the profiler, fuelled no doubt by public portrayals in television series like Cracker and films such as The Silence of the Lambs, is of the brilliant loner, the gifted psychologist, whose unique insights into the criminal mind lead the police unerringly to the most likely suspect. There is a wealth of anecdote which seems to support this view. One thinks of the fascinating case of the American psychiatrist James Brussel, who pinpointed the "mad bomber of New York" after a decade of

fruitless police work, or the insights of David Canter into the likely background of the "railway rapist", which brought an end to the criminal career of John Duffy and introduced profiling to the British police in 1986. However ... every individual triumph can be balanced with another investigative disaster, where police resources have been wasted pursuing a mythical fugitive who, it subsequently emerges, bears little or no resemblance to the true perpetrator.' (page xi)

This last point is brought home by Holmes (1989) who cites FBI data from 1981 indicating that in 192 cases of profiling, arrests were made in 88 but the profile only contributed to 17 per cent of the arrests. These reservations aside, offender profiling is an area of criminology in which psychologists have contributed to assisting in the detection of offenders, mainly those who committed serious crimes such as serial rape or serial murder.

The goals of profiling

According to Holmes & Holmes (1996) there are three major goals of profiling, viz:

1 *Social and psychological assessments*: the profile should contain basic information about the offender's personality, age, race, type of employment (if any), religion, marital status and level of education. The personality aspects of the profile may help the police to predict possible future attacks.

2 *Psychological evaluation of belongings*: once a main suspect has been identified, the profile should provide suggestions as to any possessions the offender may have that would associate him with the crime scene. These may include scene souvenirs, photos or items of pornography. Such physical evidence could be listed on a search warrant so the police take particular care to look for them.

3 *Interviewing suggestions and strategies*: even when people have committed similar crimes, they do not respond to questioning in the same way because their motives are different. A good profile can provide the police with strategies that may be effective for a particular offender. An example cited by Holmes & Holmes (1996) was the murder of a young girl and her boyfriend in which the stepfather was the main suspect but there was no forensic evidence to tie him to it. When questioned in a conventional way, he denied any involvement. The profiler suggested that as he was a man who had a great need for control, it would be good tactics to appear to solicit his help in solving the crime. Under the guise of doing this, the suspect was surrounded by photographs of the crime scene and, believing himself in control of

the investigation, became so engrossed in talking about the case that he revealed more and more his familiarity with the crime until he eventually broke down and confessed.

The obvious starting point of any investigation of a crime is the analysis of 'hard' evidence such as blood stains and fibre samples but *behavioural information* from the crime scene may offer additional information that aids the investigation. Such information may be gleaned from various sources: in the case of rape of a woman by a man, for example, it may include how the perpetrator talked to his victim, how he treated her and whether or not he showed remorse. This behavioural information then provides insights into the thinking patterns and personal habits of the offender which may offer clues as to how they behave in their everyday life: their lifestyle, motivations, personal needs and past history. Offender profiles do not solve crimes, they simply provide a way of narrowing down the range of potential suspects by providing information about the possible personal characteristics of the perpetrator of the crime.

There is no single established method by which profiling is conducted; the approach used by the FBI is rather more systematic than that used in Britain. We will take a look at two different techniques, one practised in America and the other in Britain.

The American method – a 'top-down' approach

The initial approach adopted by the FBI was two-pronged. One was a series of in-depth interviews with 36 convicted sexually orientated murderers, including Ted Bundy and Charles Manson. The second was the collection of detailed information from members of their Behavioural Science Unit who were experienced in the area of sexual crime and homicide. They then combined this information with detailed examination of the crime scene, the nature of the attacks, forensic evidence and any information relating to the victim to develop models that would result in a profile of the offender.

On the basis of this evidence, the FBI developed a classification system for several serious crimes, including murder and rape. Murderers were classified as 'organised' or 'disorganised' and the two types were believed to demonstrate quite different characteristics. Organised criminals plan their crimes, show self control at the crime scene, are careful to cover their tracks and leave few or no clues; their victim is likely to be a stranger who they have deliberately targeted. Disorganised murderers, in contrast, act in an unplanned and haphazard manner and are likely to leave more clues. Organised offenders are likely to be intelligent, in a skilled occupation, socially and sexually competent and married or cohabiting. At the time of the murder, they would have been angry and depressed; they would also be likely to follow reports of the crime in the media. Disorganised offenders are likely to be socially inadequate individuals, a first or last-born child, in an unskilled occupation. They would probably have sexual problems in relation to their mother and be frightened and confused at the time of the murder. They are likely to live alone and to know the victim and be familiar with the crime scene. By use of this classification system, an analysis of the crime scene has obvious implications in suggesting possible characteristics of offenders.

Having established a classification system, the FBI then went on to detail what should happen once a very serious crime occurred. Jackson & Bekerian (1997) describe the series of stages the FBI has developed in their crime analysis as follows:

- Stage 1: **data assimilation** – the collection of all available information from as many sources as possible, such as photographs of the crime scene and autopsy of the victim.

- Stage 2: **crime classification** – putting the crime into a particular category based on the data collected.

- Stage 3: **crime reconstruction** – the development of hypotheses about the behaviour of victims and the modus operandi of the criminal based on reconstruction of the crime.

- Stage 4: **profile generation** – the development of a profile which includes suggestions about the perpetrator's physical appearance, their demographic characteristics (for example, the age range, race, socioeconomic status), habits and personality.

This type of profiling is best suited to crime scenes that reveal important details about the suspect, those such as rape, arson and cult killings that involve such macabre practices as sadistic torture, dissection of the body and acting out of fantasy. According to the FBI, crimes such as murder or assault in the course of a robbery and destruction of property do not lend themselves to profiling because the crime scene reveals little about the offender.

The FBI approach has been subject to criticism on several fronts. Firstly, the samples of serious offenders interviewed in order to draw up the classification system were quite small. Secondly, the crime classifications for murderers and rapists were crude and not very helpful in terms of detection. Thirdly, details of the development and efficiency of the methods were not published.

The British method – a 'bottom-up' approach

Whereas the FBI had put the use of offender profiling onto a fairly systematic footing by the late 1970s, profiling in Britain was both later in its inception and has never been uniform. After a fairly reluctant start, profiling in Britain was given a kick start in the mid 1980s by the work of Canter when he produced an astonishingly accurate profile of John Duffy, an account of which is provided in the next section (Canter, 1994). Bearing in mind that the British approach is essentially idiosyncratic, we will consider the approach used by Canter since this probably best typifies the British approach.

Canter's approach to profiling is more scientific than that of the FBI because it is based more on psychological theories and methodologies. It attempts to formulate psychological theories that will show how and why variations in criminal behaviour occur. Central to this theory building is the need to demonstrate consistencies *within* the actions of offenders and identifiable differences *between* them.

Canter (1989) has outlined several aspects of criminal behaviour which may provide clues to other aspects of the criminal's everyday life and which may reflect the sub-group to which he belongs. (In Canter's 1989 paper, he uses the masculine pronoun with a footnote explaining that this is because most criminals are male and that the material on which his paper is based has not included women criminals. This pronoun, therefore, is not generic – it applies only to men.) The salient factors include the following.

Interpersonal coherence

The degree of violence and control used in serious crimes, especially rape, varies widely between perpetrators but any single individual will tend to be consistent in his treatment of the victim. For example, with respect to rape, some offenders will be very abusive and controlling, maximising the amount of humiliation they heap on the victim; others may be far less violent, even apologetic. This may reflect the way the criminal treats other women in his non-criminal life.

The type of victim may also reflect the sub-group to which the criminal belongs. Canter gives the example of Theodore Bundy who killed over 30 students when he himself was a student. On a psychologically deeper level, the choice of victims, if they are a homogeneous group, may reflect the group against which the offender has a particular grudge.

Knowledge of the victims may therefore make it possible to ascertain something about the assailant, his sub-class or his associates.

Significance of time and place

When and where a crime takes place may also furnish clues about the offender. Both the precise location and the map of the relationship between the places in which a series of offences took place may relate to where the offender is living and to his previous experience.

Forensic awareness

If criminals have previously been questioned by the police their subsequent crimes may leave indications of this. Some rapists, for example, make their victims bathe in order to remove significant evidence. In such cases, a check of people who are on police records may well be worthwhile.

Comparing the two approaches

As you can see, the British approach to profiling is rather different from the American one (although it draws on practices originated by the FBI). Boon & Davies (1992) refer to the British style as 'bottom up' and the American one as 'top down' (concepts with which you may be familiar from the study of perception). In general terms a 'bottom-up' approach is one in which a person starts with all the raw data and works their way up to a conclusion that makes sense of this data. In terms of a criminal investigation, you collect all the different pieces of evidence and then piece them together to try and infer the state of mind of the perpetrator (if it was a murder, were there signs of loss of temper or was it cold and calculated?) and from that, their personality, whether or not they had committed such a crime before and so on. A top-down approach looks at the evidence, or data, in light of certain theories or general principles and uses these theories to make sense of the data. In terms of a murder, a theory might state that only people with a particular sexual deviance commit certain crimes, so when such a crime occurs, the investigators look for a person with this particular depravity.

The British approach starts from all the available evidence and then looks for links and associations between them (such as consistency in their treatment of the victim or their choice of location). It then tries to draw up a profile based on these relationships. The American approach looked originally at the experience of a group of convicted criminals (such as serial killers like Charles Manson) and the knowledge gained by experienced investigators in the field and used this to devise a *classification system* into which subsequent crimes could be placed in order to ascertain the type of person who would have committed this variety of crime in that particular fashion. In this way, as mentioned earlier, they drew up the distinction between organised and disorganised crimes and the characteristics of an individual who is likely to operate in this way. These two styles of profiling, therefore, are quite distinct.

Applying profiling: a case study of profiling (Canter, 1994)

The following case study is based on the account by Canter (1994) of the profiling of the so-called 'Railway Rapist'. Canter first became involved in this case when he bought a copy of the *Evening Standard* (a London daily paper) on 9 January 1986, whose front page contained details of a series of 24 sexual assaults in London over the previous four years. All the assaults were assumed to be by the same man, sometimes working alone, sometimes with another person. Canter drew up a table and attempted to see if there was any obvious pattern to the rapes.

Canter made two assumptions based on psychological principles: firstly, that people influence each other's actions and that any differences between the attacks involving one man and those in which they were both involved might offer clues; secondly, that people's behaviour changes over time and that looking at the changes that took place over the four-year period could provide clues to the offenders.

In December 1985 and Spring 1986 two murders took place. Information linking the two murders was discovered by accident when a police officer investigating one saw a *Crimewatch* programme about the second one and realised that they had certain features in common. On analysing the details of these murders, it became apparent that they had been perpetrated by the man responsible for the rapes and a major manhunt was begun in the hope of apprehending him before he murdered again.

Although the police had gathered a wealth of evidence, with every detail of every rape carefully documented, there was so little co-ordination that despite enormous dedication and hard work on the part of the police, the overall impression was described by Canter as one of 'great confusion'. This was hardly surprising given the lack of theoretical underpinning but the detectives were intent on a change of plan. 'At the senior levels of the police force, at least, there was an attempt to move beyond a craft, based solely on experience and knowledge of the law, to something more professional, using scientific procedures, methods and theories as central to their investigations rather than as an optional extra.' (page 34)

They began looking in greater detail at the assailant's behaviour during each rape:

- What exactly was said to the victim before the assault?

- Were the victims' clothes pulled off, torn off or cut off?

- What sort of threats were made?

- What sort of sexual activity took place?

- How did the assailant deal with the victim after the assault?

All these details were fed into a computer (an innovation, since all previous documentation had been done by hand) in order to indicate the degree of similarity and difference between the crimes. Two lines of investigation were then taken: looking at each individual attack and looking at the changes that had occurred over time.

With respect to the behaviour shown at the scene of each rape, Canter used two principles from social psychology in his investigation. Firstly, the concept that the type of 'relationship' (if any) that the assailant tried to form with the victim might reflect his relationships with others. In this case a relationship had been made: the rapist talked to his victims, asking them questions about their personal life, and even showed some consideration to them. Secondly, the degree of domination he exercised over the victims would also provide clues. He had only used enough control to rape and was therefore probably not a very powerful or secure individual.

The investigation into the way in which the assaults had changed over time indicated that the assailant had learned directly from his own experience of the crimes and that this had made him more subtle and sophisticated. There was an indication that he was familiar with police procedures: on one occasion he combed the pubic hair of his victim in order to remove his own hairs. This implied that he had at least been questioned by the police, if not charged.

On 28 July 1986, Canter produced the following preliminary profile (Canter, 1994, pages 50–52):

- *Residence*: has lived in the area circumscribed by the first three cases since 1983.

- *Marital status*: probably lives with wife/girlfriend, quite possibly without children.

- *Age etc*: mid to late 20s; light hair, about 5'9".

- *Occupation*: probably semi-skilled job, involving weekend work or casual labour from June 1984 onwards. Job does not bring him into a lot of contact with public, in all probability.

- *Character*: keeps to himself but has one or two very close men friends. Probably very little contact with women, especially in work situation. Has knowledge of the railway system along which attacks happened.

- *Sexual activity*: the variety and mixture of his sexual actions suggest considerable sexual experience.

- *Criminal record*: was probably under arrest at some time between 24 October 1982 and January 1984. His arrest may not have been a sex-related crime at all but an aggressive attack, possibly under the influence of alcohol (or drugs?).

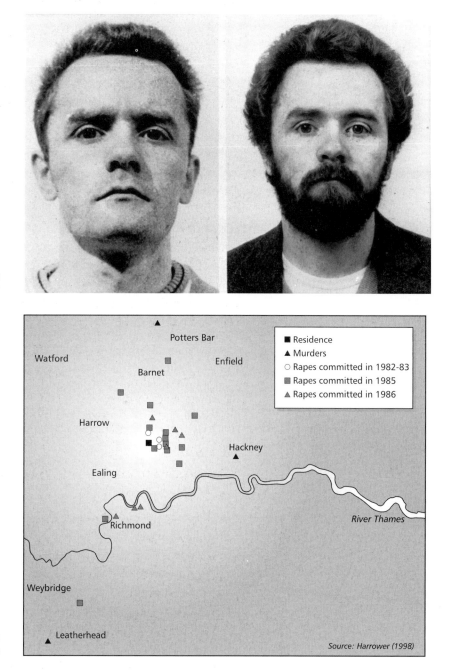

Two photos of John Duffy, the 'Railway Rapist'

The 'map' of Duffy's offences, which enabled David Canter to compile an offender profile

What factors led to this particular profile? It was the result of an enormous amount of information; let us consider just one aspect – that he was in a sexual relationship, married or cohabiting. More of the men who are convicted of rape are unmarried than are married, so why was a different conclusion drawn in this case? The rapist was sexually experienced as shown by the variety of sexual practices used in the rapes. He approached the women beforehand, often asking for directions or using a similar subterfuge. He was at ease with approaching strange women without fear of rebuff, interested enough to ask them questions about their own relationships and felt comfortable about being in control of them. All of this could be used to hypothesise that he was, or had been, in a sexual relationship. This relationship was likely to have been abusive; by the time the rapes were happening, this relationship may have broken up completely (this was later found to be the case). This single example serves to illustrate how every aspect of the profile is the result of painstaking analysis of the minute details of the crimes, not the result of 'flashes of inspiration' that provide the sudden 'turnabout' in the investigation so beloved of fiction.

In November 1986 John Duffy was arrested and later convicted; he was sentenced to life imprisonment. Duffy was initially on a list of 2,000 suspects but not a prominent one, placed as 1,505th on the list. His arrest was the result of the fact that he so closely fitted the profile that the police had mounted a large-scale surveillance operation to watch him; his activities convinced police that he was the rapist and murderer responsible for this series of crimes.

How close was the profile? Duffy lived in Kilburn (which fitted the area mentioned in the profile); he was 29 years old; he was separated from his wife with whom, in the later stages of the relationship, he had had an abusive relationship; he was a travelling carpenter for British Rail; he had a prior criminal record (for stealing; he had also been accused of raping his wife at knife point). The analysis had been extraordinarily accurate.

It is worth noting two further points from this case study. Canter was able to use not only the successes in this profile but also the inaccuracies in order to further theories of how to draw up profiles. Secondly, some very important clues were gained about the accuracy of eye-witness testimony (discussed in Chapter 4), one of which is that rape victims are not always accurate in their physical description of the assailant but they are very good indeed at accurately recalling the actions that took place.

where to now?

The following is a good source of further information regarding this particular case of offender profiling:

▶ **Canter, D. (1994) *Criminal Shadows*. London: Harper** – this is the personal account of the profiling of the 'Railway Rapist' and the scientific principles underlying profiling. It's a very intriguing read.

media watch

Murder on his mind

Britain's prisons abound with killers who thought they could outwit Paul Britton. From seemingly inconsequential details of a murder scene, Britton can construct a character sketch that gives an insight into the mind of the killer. He pioneered offender profiling in this country and has been called in to more than 100 cases.

Television's Cracker was inspired by his work (though Robbie Coltrane's rambling, fumbling, gambling addict is a world away from Britton). His subjects have included Fred and Rosemary West, James Bulger's killers and Colin Ireland, who murdered five gay men in London in 1993.

Behind the public profile, however, there has been a long career as a clinical forensic psychologist, working with patients who pose a danger to society. His book about offender profiling, The Jigsaw Man, was a bestseller. Now retired from the NHS, he has written a new book, Picking Up the Pieces, based on his clinical casebook. It is a chilling read.

"If you are looking at a murder you have to understand fully the destruction of another human being. The idea of anyone getting a buzz out of it leaves me very uneasy.

"You have to get to know the victim in order to find out what you need to know about the killer. It's more personal than 'she was a woman, 5ft 6in, fair hair'. You have to get to know how she responded to her killer.

"And when you get to know someone that well, the pain they endured touches you. In each case you leave a bit of yourself behind. It erodes you."

The Sunday Times, 12 November 2000

Discussion points

1 What kind of 'inconsequential details' from a crime scene might help to give clues to the character of the offender?

2 Why do you have to understand the victim in order to understand the perpetrator?

Evaluating offender profiling

Earlier, we briefly considered some criticisms of specific profiling methods; now we will look in more detail at evaluating profiling.

Limitations

The main limitation of profiling is that it is only appropriate for a small number of highly specific types of crimes, mainly those stemming from psychopathology. Holmes & Holmes (1996) list the types of crimes most appropriate to psychological profiling as follows:

- sadistic torture in sexual assaults

- evisceration (tearing out of the gut/bowels)

- postmortem slashing and cutting

- motiveless fire setting

- lust and mutilation murder

- rape

- satanic and ritualistic crime

- paedophilia.

Limited though this list may be, such crimes, although comparatively rare, are so horrific that the need to apprehend the offender is of paramount importance. This leads, however, to another problem, namely that when attempting to assess whether profiling works, there are so few real life cases that it can be difficult to effectively analyse its contribution.

Does profiling work?

Some researchers believe that profiling is ineffective, unnecessary and unhelpful. Campbell (1976) maintains that profiles offer no more information than could be obtained from the local bartender; that they are so vague and ambiguous as to be no more than common sense and the only reason the police take any notice of them is that they are impressed by the qualifications of academics. His comment that 'psychologists confronted with real-life murder mystery can't do any better than a college student could do with the same materials put in front of him' (page 119) is now over 25 years old but is still being quoted, for example by Oleson (1996). Despite this, there has been a steady increase in the demand for offender profiling advice (Copson, 1996). Let us take a look at some of the attempts to assess its usefulness, first by looking at satisfaction surveys and then at one piece of direct research on its effectiveness.

Satisfaction surveys

Douglas (1981) (whose study is often attributed to Pinizzotto (1984) who reported on it) conducted an internal review for the FBI on the costs and benefits of profiling. His findings reflect those of many other such studies – that profiling does not often lead to the direct identification of the suspect but that the peripheral benefits are considerable and far outweigh the costs. In the 192 cases considered in this review, profiling identified the suspect in only 15 cases but in 77 per cent it helped to focus the investigation. In general, the procedures used in profiling often helped to ensure that the investigation was thorough. Investigators estimated that it saved many days' work and all users agreed that the service should continue.

Britton (1992) conducted a review evaluating British initiatives in offender profiling. Questionnaires were sent to Heads of CID and focused on establishing how far profiling advice had led to the arrest of suspects. Judged on these criteria, the responses appeared to paint a very negative picture: there was very little evidence that profiles were either accurate or had contributed to any arrests. Nevertheless, most respondents expressed the view that their experience of profiling led them to believe that it had potential which, as long as it was done with caution, was worth developing.

Jackson *et al.* (1993) conducted a survey to assess the satisfaction of officers of the criminal justice system in the Netherlands for whom profiles had been compiled. Since there were only 20 respondents, interviews rather than questionnaires were used. Overall, there was a high level of satisfaction but, as in previous studies, the profilers appeared to be better at offering advice on how the investigation should be conducted than on generating profiles. The researchers commented that this is an important type of success but is extremely difficult to measure.

In Britain, Copson (1996) produced a report for the Home Office on the effectiveness of profiling. This is documented below in Research Now.

research now

is offender profiling really necessary?

Copson, G. (1995) Coals to Newcastle? Part 1: a study of offender profiling. Police Research Group. Special Interest Series: Paper no. 7. London: Home Office Police Department.

Aim: There is no systematic approach to offender profiling in Britain, rather there are many individual approaches which have resulted in arguments about the nature of the process and how far it is or can be developed as a science. Although many profiles have been used by British police, no independent scientific assessment has been conducted to evaluate its usefulness.

This paper is part of a wider programme of research into offender profiling by the Home Office Police Research Group (PRG). The objectives of this PRG research programme are twofold:

- to establish whether offender profiling can significantly improve the proficiency of the experienced detective

- to devise appropriate ways of delivering any benefits of offender profiling to the police service.

Method: A survey using a questionnaire. A questionnaire was considered the most appropriate method for two main reasons. There were too many respondents to use interviews and it was considered that the impersonal questionnaire would minimise the risk of bias being introduced that might influence police officers' responses. Great care was taken not to invite opinions (since these are contaminated by prejudice, misconception, pride and other such factors). What was sought was the professional judgements on the service provided by the profilers.

Questionnaires were sent to police officers who had used profilers.

Results: The response rate was 81 per cent. There were 184 returned questionnaires, just over 60 per cent of which concerned murder investigations; the majority of these murder investigations (at least 60 per cent) did not involve any secondary sexual motive. The study's main interest, as indicated by the title 'Coals to Newcastle', was whether or not profilers provided any information that was not already available. This proved a difficult question to answer since there are so many complex variables, but over 50 per cent of respondents felt that the profilers had provided something extra and over 80 per cent reported that the advice given by the profiler had been useful – on the face of it a very positive statistic. However, only 14 per cent of respondents reported that it had assisted in solving the case. In less than 3 per cent of cases had it led to the identification of the offender. How, then, had it been useful? The main way was that it furthered the understanding of the case and/or of the offender or it provided expert reassurance from the profiler that the judgements of the investigating team were sound. The benefits of offender profiling were seen mainly not so much in identifying the offender but in having an intelligent second opinion that may provide new ways of approaching the case, thereby enabling the officers involved to look at it from a new angle. It seems that profiling does assist in solving crimes but its effect is indirect rather than direct.

Conclusion: One important finding from this particular survey was that profilers are all very different in their approach and that satisfaction or otherwise depended very much on the individual profiler. At present in Britain at least there is little consistency of approach, therefore overall assessment of usefulness is extremely difficult if not impossible.

Direct research into the effectiveness of profilers

In an interesting study, Pinizzotto & Finkel (1990) compared five groups on their ability to write profiles of a homicide and a sex offence; both cases that had been closed. The groups were expert profilers, detectives with profiling experience, detectives without profiling experience, clinical psychologists and undergraduates. Profilers were significantly more accurate than non-profilers on the sex offence but not as accurate as detectives without profiling experience on the homicide case. This suggests that 'old fashioned experience may be far more important in profiling a case than training in psychological profiling' (Oleson, 1996, page 13).

Conclusion

There is no magic to profiling. Building up a picture of an offender requires painstaking systematic evidence gathering in order to work out how he thinks and behaves. The television character Cracker may be able to depend on seemingly brilliant insightful hunches but the real world does not operate in such a manner. There are enormous problems with trying to assess the usefulness of offender profiling, especially when the profiling methods of investigators are so idiosyncratic. What is essential is a detailed analysis of the factors that are and are not useful in profiling in order to provide a uniform, effective theoretical structure to advise on how it should be conducted. As Canter (1989) comments:

> 'It is ... essential that psychologists involved in this work seize the initiative by developing and testing explanatory frameworks for the advice they give. If they do not they will soon rejoin the ranks of the astrologers and numerologists, whose contributions are found to be of value on some occasions, but whose lack of scientific discipline precludes the evolution of cumulative principles that will improve the effectiveness of their contribution.' (page 16)

where to now?

The following is a good source of further information on offender profiling:

Holmes, R.M. & Holmes, S.T. (1996) *Profiling violent crimes: An Investigative Tool* (2nd edition). California: Sage Publications – this is a very accessible, interesting, up-to-date book on all aspects of profiling, including that of fictional characters. The authors use many fascinating case studies to illustrate virtually every point made. An excellent, effortless read.

what do you know?

1 Outline three goals of offender profiling.

2 Describe what is meant by the expressions 'bottom up' and 'top down' when applied to offender profiling. Compare and contrast these two approaches.

3 Discuss research that investigates the usefulness and limitations of offender profiling.

4

Witness Testimony

When someone is a witness to a crime they may be required to do a considerable amount of testifying. They will probably be asked to describe what happened, they may be asked to identify a suspect from an identikit picture and/or an identity parade and if a criminal trial takes place, they may be called to the stand to recount events that they have witnessed. The evidence they present at the trial is crucial for the judge and/or jury in reaching a verdict on the guilt or innocence of the defendant. Obviously if the testimony these witnesses provide is inaccurate then verdicts are unlikely to be fair – the guilty may go free and the innocent may be prosecuted. Accurate witness testimony is essential to the criminal justice system.

In this chapter we first take a look at research into the accuracy of eyewitness testimony and of the less well-researched realm of earwitness testimony. We will also consider whether the use of hypnosis is advisable in criminal investigations.

There has been much concern about how children who are witnesses in criminal actions are questioned, especially in sensitive cases involving abuse. We will take a look at recent developments in this area.

Finally, having discovered how selective, fragile and fallible witness memory can be, we look at the positive advice and guidance that psychologists offer to improve the reliability of witness testimony by advising on the construction of identification parades and photofit resemblances, and by improving the interviewing of witnesses.

The accuracy of witness testimony

When someone who has witnessed a crime recounts what they have seen 'with their own eyes' they tend to be believed. A leading researcher in this area, Elizabeth Loftus, reported that jury members tend to trust eyewitness reports more than they do fingerprint experts. However, there is a considerable body of evidence which indicates that eyewitness testimony is disconcertingly unreliable and it is likely that there are many wrongful convictions every year as a result of faulty eyewitness testimony (Loftus, 1986). In the USA some of the cases of people convicted of serious crimes before the advent of DNA testing, introduced in 1990, have been reanalysed using this new forensic technique. By March 1994, 40 people were found to have been wrongfully convicted, some of them having been sentenced to death. In 36 of these cases, mistaken eyewitness testimony was the major evidence presented against them (Wells *et al.*, 1998).

General errors in memory

One of the reasons why eyewitness testimony may be inexact is because memory under any circumstances is subject to inaccuracy. In everyday life we often remember things differently from what was experienced. We organise material to make it meaningful, we add details to make sense of events, we change it in the light of subsequent information. Memory does not provide an accurate record of an event but an *interpretation* of it.

There is therefore a host of reasons why memory may be unreliable; we will concentrate on those aspects that apply particularly to eyewitness testimony.

Estimator variables and system variables in eyewitness testimony

Wells (1978) distinguishes two types of errors that are liable to occur in eyewitness testimony.

- **Estimator variables** are factors which affect the accuracy of witness testimony over which the justice system has no control, for example how much attention the witness was paying at the time of the incident or how much stress the witness experienced. Wells labelled them estimator variables because they cannot be controlled in real life criminal situations so their effect can only be guessed (estimated) after the event.

- **System variables** are those which affect the accuracy of witness testimony and over which the justice system has some control (hence *system* variables), such as the way in which questions asked of the witness are worded or the way in which a line-up is constructed and conducted.

There are many variables in each of these categories; we will consider a few of the most important ones.

Estimator variables

The amount of stress and arousal

Common sense would infer that being a witness to a criminal event, especially a serious event, would put that witness under considerable stress. The numerous studies conducted on the effect of arousal levels on performance indicate that we perform poorly when we are at both low and high levels of arousal (when we are very relaxed or extremely nervous) and that we perform best at medium levels of arousal. This rule is expressed in the *Yerkes-Dodson law*.

If this law is applied when people are witnesses to crime, we may expect their recall of events to be poor since it involves high levels of arousal. Any attempt to conduct simulated research into the effect of such stress on eyewitness testimony is extremely difficult for obvious practical and ethical reasons. However, field studies of witness accuracy in real life incidents indicate that the Yerkes-Dodson law does not necessarily apply. MacLeod *et al.* (1986) studied 379 reports of eyewitnesses to assaults and compared the accuracy of those in which no physical injury occurred with those in which people were hurt. There were no overall differences in the degree of accuracy. A different finding, but one that also contradicts this law, was demonstrated by Yuille *et al.* (1986) who found that the greater the reported level of arousal, the more accurate the testimony.

One problem with trying to ascertain the relationship between stress and memory is that many witnesses to really dramatic events believe that they will never forget them because they are so deeply ingrained in their memory. Brown & Kulik (1977) use the term *flashbulb memory* to describe what they believe happens when we witness something that has a huge emotional impact on us – it is as if our mind has taken a flashbulb photograph of it. These researchers believe that this type of memory is qualitatively different from ordinary memories and leaves an unusually clear, long-lasting, detailed and *accurate* memory trace. However, various studies have challenged the idea that flashbulb memories are more accurate than other types of memory. Neisser *et al.* (1992) asked a group of Americans to complete a questionnaire concerning the circumstances under which they heard about the Challenger disaster the day after it occurred and then repeated the experiment three years later. The findings indicated that the accounts had changed considerably over that period of time. The real problem in such cases is that people sincerely believe that intense emotional experiences cannot be forgotten and that they remember it 'as if it were yesterday'. In other words, people think they recall things especially well in such circumstances and therefore may be especially convincing. But, as Neisser *et al.* (1992) found, confidence is in no way related to correctness. As Wells *et al.* (1999) neatly express it: 'It might be more appropriate to conclude that significant events leave an impression of indelibility but not an indelible impression' (page 65).

In conclusion, all we can say about the relationship between stress and accuracy of testimony is that it is a very complex one. The fact that stress interacts with very many other factors means that there are no simple answers but it is a factor that cannot be ignored, especially when people witness a very serious crime.

Weapon focus

Many experimental and field studies indicate that if a witness to a crime sees the perpetrator wielding a weapon, such as a gun or a knife, they will tend to remember details of the weapon but be less accurate on other aspects of the scene, including the perpetrator's face (e.g. Loftus *et al.*, 1987; Kramer *et al.*, 1990). This tendency to notice the weapon is known as the *weapon focus effect*.

Loftus *et al.* (1987) suggest that the weapon focus effect occurs because the presence of a weapon focuses attention away from less dramatic visual images, such as the face of the perpetrator. Support for this hypothesis was demonstrated by Loftus *et al.* who found that witnesses looked longer and more often at a gun in a slide sequence than at a neutral object.

One suggestion as to why weapons attract attention is that the threat they pose may cause emotional arousal which then causes the witness to process and remember accurately central information (the weapon itself) while being less able to encode other visual information, such as the perpetrator's face. However, Pickel (1998) questions the validity of such a suggestion, arguing that this effect has been found in simulated situations in which participants looked at pictures or videotapes of a scenario in which there is little if any threat. Furthermore, Kramer *et al.* (1990) found that the weapon focus effect can occur even when witnesses' self-reported arousal is low.

Pickel argues that it is *unusualness* rather than the degree of threat that is the key variable producing the weapon focus effect; this is supported by two experiments he conducted (Pickel, 1999). In the first it was found that undergraduates who watched a videotape showing an armed man provided less accurate descriptions of him if the setting was one in which a gun would not be expected (such as at a baseball game) than if it was quite usual (such as at a shooting range). The second study showed that witnesses gave poorer descriptions of an individual if they were carrying an object that did not fit with their occupation (such as a Catholic priest carrying a gun) and better if the object carried was not unexpected (such as a police officer carrying a gun). These results indicate that weapon focus occurs not because of the presence of weapons per se but because weapons are surprising and unexpected in many situations.

Confidence of the witness

One of the most disturbing aspects of eyewitness testimony is that although jurors understandably believe those who express confidence in what they saw, there is little or no relationship between confidence and accuracy. Someone who asserts that 'I'm absolutely certain that he was wearing black trousers' is only slightly more likely to be accurate than someone who comments that 'I can't swear to it, I may be wrong, but I'd say that he was wearing a blue shirt.' Several researchers have found that confidence is not related to accuracy. Recently, however, Sporer *et al.* (1998) did find some relationship in that the more confident were more likely to be accurate, but the relationship was not strong.

Research also demonstrates that if a person who makes a false identification from photospreads is told that a co-witness has identified the same individual their confidence increases dramatically. Conversely, if they believe that the co-witness has identified someone else, or not been able to select anyone, then their confidence drops profoundly (Luus & Wells, 1994). In real life, once an eyewitness has made an identification, there is nothing to stop the police or prosecutors telling them about co-witnesses. This means that once they are on the witness stand, their confidence may be due as much to information from others as it is to their own memories even though they may not be aware of this.

Even more convincing evidence that it is easy to manipulate the confidence of witnesses was shown in a study by Wells & Bradfield (1998) described below in Research Now. This paper begins with the following quotation from a real life case:

> *Eyewitness to a crime on viewing a lineup: "Oh, my God ... I don't know ... It's one of those two ... but I don't know ... Oh man ... the guy a little bit taller than number two ... It's one of those two, but I don't know."*

> *Eyewitness 30 min later, still viewing the lineup and having difficulty making a decision: "I don't know ... number two?"*

> *Officer administrating lineup: "Okay."*

> *Months later ... at the trial: "You were positive it was number two? It wasn't a maybe?"*

> *Answer from eyewitness: "There was no maybe about it ... I was absolutely positive." (Missouri v. Huchting, 1996, p. 202)*

(Wells & Bradfield, 1998, page 360)

Notice particularly that Wells & Bradfield showed that not only is people's confidence increased significantly by being told they are correct but it distorts their memory in other ways. They reported having had a better view of the perpetrator, having paid more attention to the event and having more easily made their identification decision than did those who believed themselves to be incorrect.

research
now

does feedback distort eyewitness testimony?

Wells, G.L. & Bradfield, A.L. (1998) 'Good, You Identified the Suspect': Feedback to Eyewitnesses Distorts Their Reports of the Witnessing Experience. *Journal of Applied Psychology*, 83(3), 360–376.

Aims:

a) To test the hypothesis that confirming post-identification feedback (telling the witness they had made the correct identification) would lead eyewitnesses to recall having been more confident in their line-up identification than they really were at the time.

b) To test the hypothesis that the effects of such feedback are quite broad, influencing not only confidence but also leading them to falsely recall other qualities of the witnessing experience.

Method: This is an experiment using an independent groups design, with three groups:

1 a group told they had made a correct identification

2 a group told they had made an incorrect identification

3 a group given no feedback (a control group).

One hundred and seventy-two student participants watched a grainy (poor quality) *real* shop video showing a man entering the store. Participants were told to pay particular attention to the man as they would be asked questions about him later. After watching the brief video, they were informed that the man murdered a security guard moments later (*Iowa v. Chidester*, 1995). Participants did not see the murder itself on video.

The participants were then asked to identify the gunman from a photospread of five faces. This was the same photospread as used in the actual criminal case, except that the actual gunman was removed, *so any identifications were false*.

After the participants had made their choice they received one of the following feedbacks, depending on the condition they were in:

a) 'Good, you've identified the suspect' – the confirming feedback condition.

b) 'Actually the suspect was number ...' – the disconfirming feedback condition.

c) No feedback – the control condition.

This feedback was given in a very casual manner with no embellishment.

After this the participants were asked a series of questions, including

1   How certain were you that the person you identified from the photos was the gunman that you saw in the video?

2   How good a view did you get of the gunman?

3   How well were you able to make out specific features of the gunman's face from the video?

4   How much attention were you paying to the gunman's face while viewing the video?

5   How easy or difficult was it for you to figure out which person in the photos was the gunman?

6   On the basis of your memory of the gunman, how willing would you be to testify in court that the person you identified was the person you saw in the video?

To each of these questions the witnesses were asked to answer on a scale of 1 to 7; 1 being, for example, a poor view, and 7 being a good one.

Experimenters were kept blind to the feedback condition until after the eyewitness had made an identification.

Results: The participants in the confirming-feedback condition, compared to the disconfirming-feedback condition

●   were more certain of the accuracy of their identification

●   thought they had had a better view of the culprit

●   believed they could make out more details of the face of the culprit

●   thought they had paid more attention to the event

●   considered the identification easier to make

●   said they would be more willing to testify

●   provided more details in their description of the gunman.

(The control condition fell between the two other conditions, always showing a significant difference compared to the confirming-feedback group.)

Conclusion: These results are alarming. In real life cases the effect may be even greater since the feedback in this study was a very casual comment. Consider how much greater they might have been if the feedback had been stronger, such as 'That's the guy!'; 'You got em!'; 'We knew this was the guy, but we couldn't use what we had as evidence. This will allow us to finally get this guy off the street.' In general the researchers consider that there is good reason to believe these effects do occur in real life. They strongly advocate double-blind testing and asking eyewitnesses about their confidence at the time of the identification rather than after there has been an opportunity to influence the eyewitnesses' confidence and other judgements.

In summary then, confident witnesses are very convincing to jurors but they are not necessarily accurate and reliable. Yet when jurors try to decide on the accuracy of eyewitness testimony, they rely quite heavily on how confident the witness appears to be.

System variables

The effects of leading questions

A real life example of the inaccuracy of eyewitnesses was graphically demonstrated by Crombag *et al.* (1996). They studied people's memory of an accident in which a Boeing 747 crashed into a high-rise apartment in Amsterdam in October 1992, news of which was extensively reported over two days on Dutch television with scenes of the fire brigade rescuing people from the burning, collapsing building. Despite the fact that no scenes were shown of the actual crash, two thirds of the 93 students who participated in the study answered 'yes' to the question, 'Did you see the television film of the moment the plane hit the apartment building?' Many of them felt able to elaborate on what they had supposedly seen; for example, 14 students 'remembered' seeing that the plane was already on fire when it crashed into the building. When witnesses are interviewed by the police, it is possible that even subtle differences in the wording of questions can affect the witnesses' responses as the Classic Research study below demonstrates.

classic research

does the wording of questions influence recall?

Loftus, E.F. & Palmer, J.C. (1974). Reconstruction of auto-mobile destruction: An example of the interaction between language and memory. *Journal of Verbal Learning and Verbal Behaviour,* 13, 585–589.

Aim: To see if the wording of questions influences recall. The particular questions used are leading questions, that is questions which, because of their content or the way they are expressed, suggest to witnesses what answer should be given.

Method: There were two studies which both used the experimental method with an independent groups design.

Study 1: 45 student participants were shown seven film clips of traffic accidents and after each one were asked to write an account of what they had seen. They were then asked specific questions, identical for all participants except one about the speed of the vehicles involved in a collision. This key question was: 'About how fast were the cars going when they … each other?'

There were five groups; each group of nine participants was given a different word or phrase to describe the impact. These were:

collided   smashed   bumped   hit   contacted

The independent variable was the verb used to describe the collision. The dependent variable was the estimated speed.

Study 2: 150 student participants were shown a one-minute film in which there was a four-second scene of a multiple car accident.

The procedure was similar to the previous one: there were two experimental conditions in which the wording of a key question was varied and a control condition in which the participants were not asked a question about the speed of the cars. There were 50 participants in each condition. The questions asked in the two experimental conditions were:

● How fast were the cars going when they *hit* each other?

● How fast were the cars going when they *smashed into* each other?

A week later all the participants, without seeing the film clips again, were asked further questions about the car accident, including the key question, 'Did you see any broken glass?' There was no broken glass in the film.

Results:
Study 1: The estimated speed varied depending on the wording of the question. The mean speed in each condition (rounded to whole numbers) was as follows:

Verb used	Estimated speed
smashed	41 mph
collided	39 mph
bumped	38 mph
hit	34 mph
contacted	32 mph

Thus there was a full nine miles per hour difference between the 'smashed' and 'contacted' groups.

Study 2: The table below summarises the main findings:

Condition	Percentage of 'yes' responses
smashed	32
hit	14
control	12

It can be seen from the table that the wording of the question had a significant effect on whether participants mis-perceived broken glass.

Conclusion: Study 1 shows that the wording of a question can have a significant effect on people's memory of events. This may be because the participant, being unsure of the speed, adjusts it to suit what the questioner wants and is therefore influenced by *demand characteristics*. Alternatively, the memory may have been affected by the way in which the crash was labelled.

Study 2 shows that the change of a single word a week earlier had had a dramatic effect on memory.

The classic study is one of a series of such studies conducted by Loftus and her colleagues. For example, Loftus & Zanni (1975) asked some of the witnesses 'Did you see **a** broken headlight?', and asked other witnesses 'Did you see **the** broken headlight?' Just 7 per cent of those asked about **a** broken headlight reported seeing one (there wasn't one in the film), compared to 17 per cent of those people asked about **the** broken headlight. These studies show how *post-event information* can result in information being added to an earlier memory. Loftus believed such information is incorporated into the original memory, so once such questions have been posed there is no going back.

There are likely to be some important differences between the way we respond in a contrived situation such as this one and the way in which we react when we have witnessed a real event. In the former we are fairly detached and have no vested interest in the estimation of speed. In contrast, when we actually see an accident we inevitably become personally involved in it and that may change our perception. In addition to this, watching a video or film clip of an emotionally disturbing situation does not equate to the real life situation in terms of the fear and stress that are experienced. Loftus's research has therefore been criticised for its lack of ecological validity. However, given the ethical and practical constraints under which psychologists work, it would be difficult to make it more realistic. Although we need to be aware of the limitations of such studies, the findings are of considerable value.

Earwitness testimony

Compared with eyewitness testimony very little research has been conducted on the accuracy of 'earwitness' testimony, the identification of an individual by voice. Nevertheless, this type of testimony has been used to convict people of very serious crimes. For example, in 1935 Hauptmann was convicted of kidnapping and murdering the baby son of Charles Lindbergh. The testimony against him included the fact that Lindbergh believed that the voice of the man accused of the murder was the same as the one who had spoken six words ('Hey doctor, over here, over here') while collecting the ransom three years earlier. Despite the lack of research, earwitness identification has been increasingly used in recent times, so much so that in 1997 judges asked for guidance on the extent of its reliability.

In Britain three researchers, John Wilding, Susan Cook and Josh Davis, have been prominent in trying to redress the balance in an area in which they describe research so far as meagre and unsystematic. The evidence presented here is based on a recent paper by these researchers (Wilding *et al.*, 2000).

Let us start by considering some rather unsurprising but important findings with respect to earwitness testimony:

1 The longer a person speaks, the easier it is to identify them by voice later (although the reasons for this are complex).

2 The more the voice is disguised by whispering and similar techniques, the more difficult the identification.

3 Changes in voice quality and tone due to the emotion of the speaker reduce the likelihood of accurate identification.

4 What is actually said has no effect.

Now let us consider the other evidence. Emotional stress caused by the situation is also liable to affect the reliability of the witness although, just as in eyewitness testimony, the exact effects are unclear. It is difficult to test this in the laboratory both for practical and ethical reasons. What is worrying is that an American survey by Deffenbacher (1983) showed that 82 per cent of defence attorneys but only 32 per cent of prosecution attorneys believed that high arousal reduces identification – they cannot both be right.

There are some intriguing gender differences in earwitnessing. Roebuck & Wilding (1993) found that although there were no differences between men and women in their accuracy of identification of male voices, women were superior to men in identifying female ones. This finding is fairly robust: it was replicated across five studies involving over 700 participants (reported by Cook, 1998). No obvious reason was proposed; it is possible, based on work in interpersonal relationships, that because women spend more time in conversation with their own sex than do men with either sex, they have become adept at female voice recognition.

It would appear that there are important differences between eyewitness and earwitness testimony. The cognitive interview (see What's New?, pages 88–90) in which witnesses try to imagine themselves back in the original situation significantly improves eyewitness testimony but does not improve memory for voices (Memon & Yarmey, 1999).

Of considerable significance in the criminal context is the fact that if suspects are seen as well as heard, it is much more difficult for most people to identify them by voice than if they remain out of sight (Cook & Wilding, 1997). Wilding, Cook and Davis have labelled this phenomenon the *face overshadowing effect*, which they suggest exists because when faces are available they are the principal means by which we identify someone. Only when they can be heard and not seen do we use their voice as a way of identifying them.

Cook (1998), in a witnessing study, asked participants to pay particular attention to the voice of people they could see as this would be used as a means of identifying them, but this had no influence on the face overshadowing effect. Only when the face was seen before the person spoke or the person spoke for a longer time, was voice identification improved, implying that perhaps we need to get used to a face before we can concentrate on the voice.

An interesting variation was introduced by Abbott (1999) who placed a stocking mask over the 'suspects' so that they appeared as they might in certain crimes, but even this did not reduce the face overshadowing effect, perhaps because certain facial features could still be seen.

In theoretical terms, Wilding *et al.* suggest that in essence people do not use voices in the same way as they use faces as a means of identifying people. Faces, not voices, are our primary means of identification. The particular characteristics of a speaker's voice are used to help understand what is said rather than to identify the individual. Research on earwitnessing cannot therefore use eyewitness research as its theoretical model – the processes are quite distinct.

In conclusion, earwitness testimony, like eyewitness testimony, can be unreliable. After considerable recent research Wilding *et al.* (2000) comment that 'From the legal point of view, our results suggest that extreme caution is needed when using voice identification by witnesses in legal contexts, unless the voice is already familiar or a fairly long utterance occurs.'

The use of hypnosis in criminal investigations

Several years ago a woman in the United States disappeared without trace and when no one had heard from her for several weeks the police hypnotised her son in order to try to ascertain whether he could shed light on her fate. Under hypnosis the son reported that he had seen his father murder his mother and chop up her body. Although there was no other evidence, the father was sentenced to life imprisonment for her murder. Some months after the conviction the women turned up in another state (reported by Kalat, 1993). Little wonder that psychologists have long been dubious about the use of hypnosis to supposedly uncover lost memories.

In the US, the FBI has been using hypnosis since 1968 and although few other countries are known to use it, interest has been expressed by other police forces including those in Britain (Gibson, 1982).

In his 1982 paper, Gibson criticises the use of hypnosis in criminal investigations. The main points he makes are as follows:

● *Increased recall but more errors*: during interrogation, hypnotised witnesses are assured that they can remember details of certain events and this leads to recall of false memories. In a classic study, Stalnaker

& Riddle (1932) asked participants to remember various pieces of prose and poetry. A year later they were tested for recall in the normal and the hypnotised state. In comparison to their recall in the normal state, they produced more accurate but also more confabulated information. This finding has been repeated in more recent studies. For example, Dwyman & Bowers (1983) showed people photos and asked them to recall as much detail as possible, first in a normal state, then under hypnosis. More items were recalled under hypnosis but most of the additional items were incorrect. The increased error rate may be due to the tendency of hypnotised people to guess or to mistake vividly imagined possibilities for actual memories. What is a cause of concern is that participants are just as convinced of their accuracy on the wrong items as on additional correct ones. Witnesses in court who have been previously hypnotised will innocently but confidently retail confabulated events as if they are real ones.

- *Alteration of existing true memories*: hypnotised people are highly suggestible and incorporate fantasies into their memories. Witnesses who have undergone hypnosis become unable to differentiate between real and imagined events, and moreover, neither can anyone else, however expert. Based on these findings, Diamond (1980), quoted by Gibson, comments that 'the use of hypnosis by police on a potential witness is tantamount to the destruction or fabrication of evidence.' (Diamond, 1980, page 314).

- *Implanting of false information*: it is quite possible for a hypnotist to implant false memories into a hypnotised person's mind, even if unwittingly. Some psychoanalytic psychiatrists, hypnotists and members of the police force tend to think of memory in terms of an 'exact copy' of what actually occurred, an indelible engram that cannot be altered by leading questions or other suggestions. Memory does not operate in such a way and however detached a hypnotist may try to be, he or she will invariably provide clues to the hypnotised person and influence their recall. Indeed, an attitude of complete detachment is likely to yield no useful material from hypnosis.

- *The facility to lie*: there are occasions when witnesses, victims and suspects wish to lie. Hypnosis offers them an ideal opportunity to do this. If evidence is later found to be false, the individual can then plead ignorance of information that was supposedly produced in good faith under hypnosis.

Vingoe (1991) argues that if hypnosis is used in police investigations, we need to consider carefully who does the hypnotising. Even well trained senior police officers should not operate without psychological or medical training. A major problem is that investigators are not trained in mental health and mental health professionals are not trained in investigative procedures.

Orne (1979) argues that if hypnosis is used in criminal investigations, the following guidelines should be followed:

- hypnosis should only be carried out by an appropriately trained psychologist or psychiatrist

- the whole procedure should be videotaped

- no one other than the hypnotist and the person to be hypnotised should be present

- interrogations conducted prior to hypnosis should be tape-recorded so that it is possible to ascertain which of the information produced under hypnosis is new.

Many official bodies have been less than positive about the use of hypnosis in criminal investigations. In 1979 the International Society of Hypnosis condemned the training of police officers by non-psychologists in the techniques of inducing hypnosis for use in interrogations. The American Medical Association (1986) advised that testimony elicited under hypnosis should not be used in courts of law. In Britain the Home Office has produced several circulars (see Where to Now?) on the use of forensic hypnosis, all of which urge extreme caution in its use and some of which suggest that hypnosis risks causing actual harm to the individual (Home Office Circular No. 66 1988).

Perhaps the safest way forward, as suggested by several researchers (e.g. Gibson, 1989; Smith, 1983), is to increase research into non-hypnotic ways to facilitate witness memory, such as contextual reinstatement and repeated testing.

where to now?

The following are good sources of further information on hypnosis, both providing accessible and useful insight into its use in criminal investigations:

▶ Gibson, H.B. (1982). The use of hypnosis in police investigations. *Bulletin of the British Psychological Society*, 35, 138–142.

▶ Vingoe, F.J. (1991). The truth and nothing but the truth about forensic hypnosis. *The Psychologist* 14(9), 395–397.

The Home Office has also produced several papers on the use of forensic hypnosis (for example, Gibson, 1989; Orne *et al.*, 1989). These can be obtained from the Home Office website (see References). For the no. 66/1988 paper mentioned in the text see the *British Journal of Experimental and Clinical Hypnosis*, 1989 vol. 6.

Children as witnesses

Until the late 1980s almost no systematic and ecologically valid research had been conducted on the accuracy of children's witness testimony and the whole field was riddled with misperception, bias and prejudice. The popular view of children as witnesses was that since they were unable to distinguish fact from fantasy and were susceptible to coaching by powerful authority figures, then their evidence would inevitably be flawed and unreliable (e.g. Underwager & Wakefield, 1990). It is perhaps ironic that while we tend to credit adults with excellent recall when, as we have seen, it can be highly suspect, we tend to underestimate a child's ability to recount the truth.

Following several well publicised and very disturbing incidents of alleged child sexual abuse, such as Cleveland and the Orkney Islands, the urgent need for well conducted realistic empirical research into the accuracy of children's testimony became obvious. Before the 1980s people seemed unaware that child abuse was a fairly common occurrence (Spencer & Flin, 1993); unfortunately, we now know that a significant proportion of children are abused physically or sexually or both. Child sexual abuse is such a heinous crime that letting the guilty go free (perhaps in the knowledge that they can continue because their tiny victims will never be believed) or accusing and convicting the innocent both have the most serious of consequences. Psychologists rose to the challenge of conducting valid research and now the literature is so large that several books have been devoted to it (e.g. Ceci, 1989; Dent & Flin, 1992; Goodman & Bottoms, 1993). The picture is by no means a simple one and what follows only touches on the major findings of this very complex and sensitive area.

Accuracy and completeness

Hedderman (1987), in a review of evidence on child witnesses produced for the Home Office, concluded that although young children had the same memory *capacity* as older ones, their ability to recall *accurately* depended on them having a certain level of cognitive maturity. This implies that very young children may be able to recall accurately what has happened to them but only if they are very skilfully interviewed, a point to which we will return later.

The work of Freud and Piaget had led to the belief among some investigators that children have problems distinguishing fact from fantasy (see Freud, 1966 (originally published 1933) and Piaget, 1926). However, Freud did not conduct empirical research on this hypothesis and the children interviewed by Piaget may not have understood what was expected of them, so any findings may have underestimated their abilities. Once newer research was conducted it was concluded that even young children are able to distinguish between reality and fantasy (Ceci & Bruck, 1993). For example, Morison & Gardner (1978) presented children aged 5 to 12 years with three toys and asked them to group them in terms of fantasy figures (such as an elf or dragon) and real figures (such as a frog). Although the older children were better at this task than the younger ones, even five year olds were highly accurate. Perris *et al.* (1990), among others, demonstrated that even very young children's memory is accurate over a long time period as long as the particular action to be recalled involves a personally meaningful event. Likewise pre-schoolers are very reliable at recounting action-packed events in which they were a participant (Rudy & Goodman, 1991).

Presumably because it is relevant to the investigation of crime, a lot of this research centres on whether children can differentiate between things they and others have actually done and things they and others have imagined doing. The findings in this area are very complex but they do appear to indicate a difference between children's recall of their own real and intended actions and the real and intended actions of others. Under certain circumstances young children (under the age of eight) have more difficulty than older children distinguishing between events that they have only imagined and those that they have actually experienced (e.g. Johnson & Foley, 1984). However, children can distinguish their memories of what other people have done from their memories of merely imagining what other people have done (Lindsay *et al.*, 1995).

Ceci & Bruck (1993) comment that 'in most of the studies that have been reported during the past decade, young children were able to accurately recollect the majority of the information they observed, even though they did not recall as much as older children' (page 433). However, these authors emphasise that young children are more vulnerable to suggestion than older children, so, depending on how it is collected, their evidence is not always reliable. It is to the question of suggestibility that we now turn our attention.

Suggestibility

The degree to which children's testimony is susceptible to suggestion is obviously of vital importance in criminal cases. We have already seen that recall by adult witnesses is vulnerable to the effects of leading questions and other dubious procedures. Given the considerable power imbalance between questioners and child witnesses and the weaker memory trace of young children, it is not surprising that many studies indicate that under certain circumstances children are very suggestible.

Ceci & Bruck (1993) point out that some investigators are polarised on the question of children's suggestibility: some hold that children are particularly vulnerable to suggestions while others contend that they are highly resistant to it. Research findings seem equally divided in support of both camps; we will consider just one example of each.

King & Yuille (1987) staged a live event in which a child was seated in a room when a stranger entered. He checked on some plants and then remarked that it was late. Later the children were asked on which arm the man was wearing his watch; in fact he was not wearing one. Six year olds (the youngest group in this study) were significantly more likely to provide a false response by giving an answer (by showing the appropriate arm or saying left or right) than either nine year olds or 16 year olds.

Some researchers have attempted to investigate whether non-abused children will make false claims of abuse in response to misleading suggestions by adults. Rudy & Goodman (1991) conducted a study in which pairs of children, one aged four and the other aged seven were left with an adult stranger. One child played a game with the adult in which the child was dressed in a clown's outfit, then lifted and photographed while the other child was encouraged to watch carefully. Sometimes the four year old was the observer, at other times it was the seven year old. About ten days later the children were interviewed using both suggestive and non-suggestive questions. Some of the misleading questions concerned actions that were sexually suggestive, such as asking if the adult had removed the child's clothes.

Regardless of the question type, the child who had participated in the game was more accurate than the bystander. Older children were more accurate than younger children except on the misleading abuse-suggestive questions, on which the four year olds were as accurate as the seven year olds. It appears from this study that non-abused children, even very young ones, are unlikely to make false claims of abuse. Some people may be concerned about the ethics of this study but others argue that if we are to address the problem of child witnesses in abuse cases, we need to have relevant evidence. As Ceci & Bruck (1993) comment, there has been nearly a century of research criticising and belittling the accuracy and suggestibility of child witnesses and the balance needs to be redressed.

The actual events about which children are questioned may also affect reliability. Pezdek & Roe (1995) point out that the memory trace in young children is weaker than in adults and therefore more liable to suggestion effects. However, Goodman et al. (1990) contend that the memory trace for very significant, central events in which the child is a participant is likely to be very strong and under these circumstances suggestion effects are diminished or non-existent. The interpretation of these findings has been challenged by Ceci & Bruck (1993) who point to several studies which show that personally experienced actions are not immune to suggestion. For example, Ceci et al. (1993) showed that children can be led to falsely report whether they had been kissed while being bathed.

There are aspects of the social situation when an adult questions a child that are likely to influence the kind of answers a child provides. Children believe that adults are truthful and not deceptive so when asked questions by an adult, children are highly likely to supply the information they think the adult is seeking.

Even when asked a nonsensical question such as 'Is milk bigger than water?' a young child is far more likely to answer yes or no than 'I don't know'. Children believe that adults ask logical questions that must have an answer. This may be because saying you don't know is frowned upon in some classrooms and homes. If, however, it is explained to the child that 'I don't know' is quite acceptable, suggestibility is reduced (Mulder & Vrij, 1996). It is also reduced if the child is told that the adult asking them questions did not see the event. In addition to this, as studies by Piaget revealed, when young children are asked the same question twice, they often change their answers, presumably because they think they must have been wrong before or why were they asked the same question again? Poole & White (1991) found a similar effect for closed-ended questions requiring a yes/no answer. However, for open-ended questions this was not the case, the children saw these as a request for more information and so provided it (Poole & White, 1995). Moreover, repeated questioning *across* sessions rather than *within* sessions can increase recall, just as it does with adults. Several studies have shown that children have recalled about 10 per cent more information on repeated recall than on a single session (e.g. Tucker *et al.*, 1990) and although other studies have shown no such increased recall (e.g. Flin *et al.*, 1992), none have shown a decrease.

Improving accurate recall in children

In order to ensure that child interviews were properly conducted, in 1992 the Home Office published a Memorandum of Good Practice for interviewing children and this was largely well received (Davies *et al.*, 1996). Some of these recommendations and others are briefly considered here.

Establish rapport

Psychologists emphasise the need to build rapport with young children in order that they may feel relaxed and unthreatened. Unfortunately combining this with detached and unbiased questioning is very difficult. One way of establishing rapport is to smile, establish eye contact and make encouraging noises when the child speaks, as would be done in ordinary friendly conversation. However, the reinforcement of certain responses may itself lead to the child offering misleading information that they think the adult wants to hear. The possibility has not been well researched but it appears from what we know that interviewers need to be wary. Nevertheless, Carter *et al.* (1996) found that children who were interviewed in a warm, supportive manner were less vulnerable to misleading questions than those who were challenged and intimidated.

Use free recall

Children are more likely to produce accurate information if they are asked to give an account of what occurred rather than simply being asked a set of specific questions (Poole & White, 1993). Although young children tend to provide a lot less information than adults do in free recall conditions, if given verbal prompts (such as, 'and then what happened?') they can recall a considerable amount. Specific and leading questions should be avoided.

Do not use threats or bribes during questioning

It may seem very obvious that children should not be subjected to threats for non-disclosure, to bribes for disclosures or be encouraged by intimidation to withdraw information they have already supplied, but such interviewing techniques have been reported. Ceci & Bruck (1993) report the following part of an interview by an attorney called Samek with a child who has made allegations against a married couple of baby minders known as Frank and Iliana:

> *Samek: You have been saying a lot of things about Frank and Iliana, haven't you?*
>
> *Child: Yes.*
>
> *Samek: I'm Frank's friend, and I want to help Frank, and I think you're telling lies.*
>
> *Child: No.*
>
> *Samek: I don't think any of the things you are saying about Frank are true. Do you know what a lie is?*
>
> *Child: When you –*
>
> *Samek: No, look at me! You know what a lie is. What's a lie?*
>
> *Child: When you say something that's not true.*
>
> *Samek: OK, that's right. That's right. That's exactly what a lie is. I think you've been lying to me about Frank and Iliana. I don't think Frank and Iliana ever did anything to you. Frank didn't do anything to you, did he?*
>
> *Child: Yes he did.*
>
> *Samek: Frank never put his mouth on your penis, did he?'*

Hollingsworth (1986, p. 76) (page 423)

This child maintained his story in the face of an angry and accusing attorney in a strange and threatening courtroom but we should not be surprised if under these circumstances children are liable to hesitate, give their replies in an unconvincing manner, refuse to answer or change their testimony.

Use close circuit television

Testifying in a court can be a frightening experience for anyone. For a child to have to stand before the person who they have accused of abusing them in a strange and threatening place and be cross-examined must be absolutely terrifying. Many of these children have been abused for months, even years; it seems exceptionally cruel to put them through yet another ordeal. It was with this in mind that part of the 1988 Criminal Justice Act was to permit children in England and Wales to testify by a close-circuit live television link (CCTV) rather than in person. Davies & Noon (1991) were commissioned by the Home Office to examine the effectiveness of such a live link and concluded that its effect was positive. In the USA they are a little more reluctant to use it, believing it to be a constitutional right for a defendant to confront their accuser (Bull, 1998).

In conclusion

As you can see from the small part of the research described here, the issue of the accuracy of children's testimony is very complex. Despite arguments to the contrary, pre-school children do appear to be more suggestible than older children or adults. However, we already know that adults are prone to the effects of leading questions and other biases and the obvious response to this is to devise effective ways of obtaining accurate recall. The same must apply to children. We should be doubly failing our youngsters if we abandoned attempts to investigate allegations made about child abuse just because the only witnesses are very young children. As Bull (1998) comments:

> '*Children can be tricked into providing false information and they can, on occasion, purposely lie. Those who have argued, on the one hand, that children's testimony is less reliable than adults' or, on the other hand, that children should more readily be believed than adults, miss the essential point. It is how the witness's testimony is obtained (Bull, 1995a, 1996; Lamb, Sternberg and Esplin, 1994) and the circumstances surrounding this (including the motivation of the witness) which are very much more important than debates (though academically and theoretically important) as to whether children are more suggestible than adults.*' (page 202)

where to now?

The following is a good source of up-to-date information regarding research on child witnesses:

▶ Bull, R. (1998) Obtaining information from child witnesses. In A. Memon, A. Vrij & A. Bull (eds.), *Psychology and Law: Truthfulness, Accuracy and Credibility.* New York: McGraw-Hill.

research
now

how accurate are child witnesses?

Bidrose, S. & Goodman, G.S. (2000) Testimony and Evidence: A Scientific Case Study of Memory for Child Sexual Abuse. *Applied Cognitive Psychology*, 14, 197–213

Introduction: It is very difficult to ascertain how accurate child witnesses are from laboratory studies because these can never mimic the conditions present during sexual abuse. Sometimes naturally occurring stressful events are used, such as interviewing children after a painful medical procedure (e.g. Merritt *et al.*, 1994). This has some features of sex abuse cases, such as pain and high stress levels, but factors such as secrecy, shame and lack of emotional support cannot and should not be simulated in experimental research.

Aim:

a) To examine the testimony given by a group of children in the course of a sexual abuse investigation.

b) To assess the level of support for allegations made.

c) To assess the extent of abuse about which no allegations were made.

Method: This is a *scientific case study*, a name given by the authors to a case study in which there is objective, detailed evidence with which to compare the witness accounts. This was a 'unique study of the accuracy of children's testimony' because it was based on records made during the abuse itself.

This case occurred in New Zealand; it was initiated when the police received a tip-off that a man was organising a prostitution ring comprising young girls.

Four girls, aged 8, 13, 14 and 15 years, testified about sexual exploitation that involved eight adult men. Each girl gave one police interview and testified at the deposition hearing of the three main perpetrators. The oldest two girls testified in other hearings. In total, four police interviews and five deposition hearing testimonies were coded. The girls' testimony was compared with the several hundred photographs and audiotaped records of the abuse.

Results: Overall, there was supportive evidence for about 80 per cent of the allegations. Specifically, there was evidence for

● 85.6 per cent of alleged sexual acts (such as kissing, fellatio, intercourse)

● 42.9 per cent of coercive acts (such as paying or promising to pay for sex, paying for photographic sessions)

● 82.5 per cent of alleged preparatory acts (such as girls posing for photographs, the arranging of sex sessions with men).

Discussion: The results show that support of some form was found for 78.9 per cent of all allegations made by the girls and 85.6 per cent of sex act allegations.

The level of support is therefore very high and would almost certainly be higher still but for problems in transcribing the tapes. On the audiotapes it wasn't always possible to accurately identify exactly what sexual acts were taking place. There was also evidence that tapes had been reused, so records of acts had been taped over. Considering this, the level of support demonstrates surprisingly high levels of accuracy in the allegations the children made.

There is evidence that the children made more errors of omission than errors of commission. Errors of omission involve acts that were not mentioned by the children but were known to have occurred because of the evidence from photographs and audiotapes. Given how numerous the sex acts were, it's hardly surprising that they were not all mentioned. Errors of commission are those allegations for which there was no evidence; the reason for these, as already discussed, was more likely to be due to missing evidence than fabrication and lying by the girls.

Besides being of interest from the viewpoint of the accuracy of child witnesses, it is worth noting an important point as far as sexual abuse of minors is concerned. Most people who suffer abuse outside the family do not report this to the police or mention it to anyone (e.g. Russell, 1983). In this case, although the girls were totally co-operative once questioned, none of them disclosed the abuse to any adult. Audiotaped conversations showed that the children wanted the abuse to stop but rather than talking to an adult, they tried to persuade John (the organiser) to stop; two ceased visiting him for long periods until tricked and threatened into returning. John used a variety of threats to stop them disclosing – for example, telling them they would be arrested as they had accepted money for sex.

Conclusion: This case demonstrates that children can give accurate, detailed and reliable testimony following sexual abuse.

Methods of improving witness testimony

The extensive investigations into the ways in which witness testimony may be unreliable have opened up many avenues for exploring methods by which psychologists and criminal investigators can attempt to improve its accuracy. We will consider two such methods: the ways in which the identification of individuals can be improved and, in the What's New? section, the use of an innovative interviewing technique known as the Cognitive Interview.

Improving reliability of identification

In considering how we can improve the reliability of identification, we need to bear in mind that when someone is a witness to a crime and is asked later to try and identify the suspect, they need to be able to recognise a strange face which they have seen only fleetingly in conditions that are very different from those of the crime scene. This is made even more difficult if the person to be identified is disguised or presented in a 'still' form as they might be in photographs or in an identity parade. Despite our impressive ability to recognise people we know well, even after many years, we find it extremely difficult to identify a person we have only seen once in very different circumstances. Yet much eyewitness testimony entails trying to identify a person who has been seen only briefly in less than ideal conditions. As Bruce (1998) says: 'Changing the viewpoint, expression, lighting, hairstyle, paraphernalia such as glasses and facial hair, and contextual features such as clothing, all reduce recognition memory performance to a considerable extent. The eyewitness to crime may have to identify someone across variations of any, or all these kinds – not surprising, then, that errors are made.' (page 331)

Improvements on identikits

Identikit pictures pose various problems for a witness. You have probably all seen such pictures and laughed at how artificial they appear. This is because they are based on the construction of a face feature by feature: eyes, nose, mouth and so on. However, evidence indicates that when we judge a face as familiar or unfamiliar, we do not simply judge it on a feature-by-feature basis but on the basis of the overall configuration of the features. It is not surprising therefore that people find it difficult to identify someone from an identikit picture.

There are several ways in which researchers have attempted to improve on this method. One is the use of computers to produce from the witness's description a good pictorial likeness of the suspect, known as an E-FIT. However, the original E-FIT still built up a face on a feature-by-feature basis: as the witness gave a description of, say, the eyes, the computer chose the best set of eyes to fit this description, and so on. The witness did not see the face until it was completed. Researchers from the Face Processing Research Group have recently pioneered a new system of compiling an image of criminal suspects based on the idea that an improved image would be produced by allowing the witnesses to watch the face build up. It is very important that the features are seen as part of the whole face, so a cartoon outline and features are used to replace those elements that have yet to be described. In addition to this, if possible, the evidence from several witnesses is used to create a more accurate image of the suspect's face.

Improving identity parades

Research in which participants see a staged incident and then try to select someone from an identity parade demonstrates that eyewitnesses frequently make mistakes. It is worrying to note that witnesses are more likely to pick someone in clothes similar to those worn by the culprit than select them on the basis of such characteristics as height and facial features (Sanders, 1984). Brigham & Malpass (1985) point out that criminals often change their appearance before an identity parade – with considerable success at evasion, so it would seem.

One problem with identity parades is that people assume that the suspect is present (why otherwise organise the line-up?) and will therefore identify the person who most closely resembles the person they saw, rather than no one. Kohnken *et al.* (1996) therefore recommend that witnesses should be told that the suspect may or may not be present and be urged not to guess.

All members should match the general description of the culprit as described previously by the eyewitness: the target figure should not in any way stand out from the others (Wells *et al.*, 1993). They should all be dressed in similar clothes but *not* similar to those worn by the perpetrator at the scene of the crime (Yarmey *et al.*, 1996). Wearing clothes that are different gives the police the opportunity to conduct a second test in which the witness will be asked to identify the clothes worn by the perpetrator (Vrij, 1998).

Cutler & Penrod (1988) tested a rather different type of identity parade procedure, known as a *sequential line-up*, in which the individuals in the line-up are seen one at a time and the witness has to say 'yes' or 'no' according to whether or not they recognise them. This makes it less likely that they will simply pick the person who, in the whole line-up, most closely resembles the culprit. Cutler & Penrod conducted experiments in which undergraduate participants watched a videotaped re-enactment of an armed robbery and later attempted to identify the robber from an identity parade. They found that participants were significantly more accurate in their identification on the sequential line-up than on the traditional one and were less likely to make a false identification.

Cutler & Penrod's research also demonstrated that further improvement in accuracy of identification would be made if witnesses heard voice samples of the members of the identity parade, if the line-up members were shown from three-quarter poses and if witnesses were allowed to watch the line-up members walking in and out of the observation room (Cutler & Penrod, 1988).

A further improvement would accrue if witnesses were less nervous, since the more relaxed they are, the more accurate they are at picking suspects from identity parades (Wells *et al.*, 1999). Anecdotal evidence indicates that some people find the procedure in an identity parade more stressful than the original incident, especially if the individuals in the line-up are not separated from them at all, even by a sheet of glass, as sometimes happens. People need to be told exactly what to expect, to be familiarised with all aspects of the procedure and would also be more relaxed if one-way mirrors were used.

As shown in the Wells & Bradfield (1998) research reported earlier in Research Now (pages 68–69), witnesses should not be given feedback that

- *Report everything*: Since memories form a network and there are therefore a large number of triggers to recall, the interviewee is asked to recall everything they can, however trivial and incomplete. The partial recall of one witness may intermesh with that of other witnesses and provide the police with important leads.

- *Change the perspective*: In order to try to reduce the effect that personal schemas may have in producing false recall, the witness is asked to try to put themselves in the place of other witnesses and victims and imagine the scenario from their perspective. This is difficult for a young child to do, but most adults are capable of it. However, because this kind of evidence is inferential rather than first hand, it is controversial and may not be accepted in a court of law.

- *Change the order*: Finally, the witness is asked to start at various points during the event, including perhaps the most memorable. This procedure is also based on schema theory, since recalling events in an unusual order may lead witnesses to recall things that do not fit the schema. Geiselman & Callot (1990) found that more information was obtained if witnesses were asked to recall events once forward and once backwards than if they twice recalled events from beginning to end. However, since reverse recall disrupts context reinstatement (thinking yourself back into the situation), it may in fact be counter-productive and produce little if any additional recall (Memon *et al.*, 1997).

The enhanced version of the Cognitive Interview

In order to improve the CI still further by improving the social skills and communication strategies of the interviewers, the following techniques were introduced.

- At the outset, the interviewee is made to feel relaxed, unhurried and, above all, not 'on trial'. The interviewer keeps the number of questions to a minimum, letting the interviewee do most of the talking, only asking additional questions to clarify a point or elaborate on an observation. The interviewee, therefore, takes the more active role, unlike the situation in a typical standard police interview.

- The interviewer helps maximise witness recall by using *focused* memory techniques. Paivio (1971) demonstrated that the use of imagery increases recall because it allows more meaningful elaborations (if, when trying to remember word pairs such as doll and chimney, you picture a doll stuck in a chimney, then you remember it much better than simply remembering the words or separate pictures). Using this principle the interviewee is asked to picture the suspect, to focus on his or her face and describe it; the same goes for other aspects of his or her appearance.

- The questions asked by the interviewer should be guided by the witness, a technique called witness compatible questioning. For example, if the witness is describing what the suspect said, the questioning should not be redirected to what they were wearing.

- Last but not least, the interviewer should create a relaxed atmosphere, be supportive and interested in the interviewee's responses and listen carefully without interrupting.

Geiselman *et al.* (1985) have used the CI in realistic, violent police training films and found that participants gave more accurate accounts and less confabulated information than when the standard police interview was used.

Geiselman *et al.* (1986) also demonstrated that witnesses who had previously been asked suggestive questions were less likely to be misled by them when undergoing a CI than when given a standard one.

Recent research on CI suggests that it can be more effective than a standard interview but not always. If interviewers are well trained in their use then either interview techniques can be used to yield detailed information from witnesses (Memon *et al.*, 1997). On occasion the CI produced more errors but usually only with untrained interviewers. Research is at present being conducted to ascertain where in the interview these errors occur. Geiselman *et al.* (1986) found that the cognitive interview decreases the witness's susceptibility to misleading questions and prevents the original memory trace from being altered. Fisher *et al.* (1990) carried out a field test on the use of the cognitive interview by comparing the performance of police forces before and after training in the cognitive interview technique. The trained detectives collected substantially more information after training, most of which was corroborated, hence accurate.

There are still many unanswered questions in the use of CI: research is required into the range of witnesses, crimes and situations for which the interview is likely to be effective, whether it is appropriate for elderly people and children and whether police officers should be encouraged to use context reinstatement with victims of violent crime. There is no doubt that this is an exciting and innovative development in witness testimony.

where to now?

The following are good sources of further information regarding the cognitive interview:

▶ Memon, A. (1998) Telling it all: the Cognitive Interview. In A. Memon, A. Vrij & R. Bull (eds), *Psychology and Law: Truthfulness, Accuracy and Credibility.* New York: McGraw-Hill – this recent paper covers the theory behind the technique as well as some of the research into its use.

▶ Roy, D.F. (1991) Improving recall by eyewitnesses through the cognitive interview. *The Psychologist*, 4(9), 398–400 – this paper looks at research into the use of CI, both in the laboratory and in the field.

Conclusion

Psychological research on the accuracy of testimony provided by witnesses to crimes has been valuable in providing an insight into the many factors that affect its accuracy and the way they interact. We need to acknowledge the inevitable limitations of using mock witnesses to staged events in laboratory conditions since, as pointed out by Yuille (1993) and others, it might be rather early to start generalising these findings to real-life situations. That notwithstanding, research to date has been instrumental in suggesting ways, such as new interviewing techniques and line-up procedures, that result in a greater amount of more accurate information from witnesses.

what do you know?

1   Define what is meant by estimator variables and system variables when applied to witness testimony.

2   Discuss research into the effect of leading questions on the accuracy of witness testimony.

3   Define what is meant by 'earwitness testimony'. Discuss factors that may affect the accuracy of earwitness testimony.

4   Discuss research into the effects of hypnosis on the accuracy of witness testimony.

5   'Children are such unreliable witnesses that their testimony should not be used in criminal cases.' Discuss this statement in the light of psychological research into the accuracy of child witnesses.

6   Describe what is meant by the 'cognitive interview'. Evaluate its use when interviewing witnesses to crimes.

7   The cognitive interview is one suggested way of improving witness testimony. Discuss two other ways of improving such testimony.

5

Media Influences on Criminal Behaviour

what's
ahead?

On 20 April 1999, Eric Harris and Dylan Kiebold raided the school they attended in Littleton, Colorado, murdered 12 students and a teacher and wounded 23 others before shooting themselves dead. Although the causes of such behaviour are obviously complex and multiple, it was noted that the boys spent a great deal of time playing the video hate game 'Doom' and that for a school project the boys had produced a video in which, dressed in trenchcoats and carrying guns, they killed school athletes. Is it possible, the general public, sociologists, media researchers and psychologists ask, that a continuous diet of violent films, television programmes and games is a major cause of aggression and therefore a significant contributor to crime?

This is far too simplistic a view for some theorists who claim that the media is being used as a convenient scapegoat by parents, teachers and society to deflect the blame away from them. A judge recently threw out a case against 25 media companies after a 14-year-old schoolboy shot dead three girls at a prayer group in 1997. The victims' parents claimed that the 'one hit, one kill' pattern used by the young killer mimicked that of video games. The judge however commented that 'Tragedies such as this simply defy rational explanation, and courts should not pretend otherwise.'

In this chapter we take a critical look at research into the effects of the media on antisocial aggressive behaviour, including some recent work on the effects of violent video games. We consider the conditions under which children may be most susceptible to the influence of media violence and the factors that contribute to its influence.

Finally we take a brief look at research on the effects of pornography, especially violent pornography, and whether this can contribute to certain crimes such as rape.

A woman is reunited with her daughter following the shootings at Columbine High School, Littleton, Colorado, in April 1999

Introduction

There is no doubt that children are exposed to a great deal of media violence. Eron (1995) estimated that by the end of primary school a child is likely to have seen 8,000 murders and more than 100,000 other acts of violence on television and video. Such has been the concern regarding the possible relationship between media violence and violence within society, including the possibility of 'copycat' crimes, that this has been the focus of several public commissions and reports designed to influence social policy (Wood *et al.*, 1991).

The debate about the extent of media influence is not a new one: many years ago Bandura, a major proponent of Social Learning Theory, expressed the view that viewing of violence could encourage imitative aggression in children. His research (for one piece of which see Classic Research), paved the way for many studies investigating the possible link between media violence and violence within society. Such research, however, is beset with methodological problems and various methods have been used in an attempt to obtain some answers. Before looking at the research itself, we will describe and evaluate each of these methods.

Methods used to investigate media influences

There are four main methods by which the link between media violence and aggression has been investigated.

1 Laboratory experiments

These are investigations carried out in a laboratory or similarly controlled environment and usually compare two matched groups on their level of aggression when one has been exposed to some form of media violence (such as film clip or video game) and the other has been exposed to something similar and equally engaging but with no violent content. The participants are then given the opportunity to aggress (or so they believe), by, for example, pressing a button marked 'hurt' to deliver a painful stimulus to another person (the pain is never delivered) and the level of aggression between the two groups is compared. Sometimes, in addition to this, a repeated measures design is used in which levels of aggression are rated before and after viewing violent material.

This method has the important advantage that, being experimental, it can establish cause and effect. However, such studies have been criticised for their lack of ecological validity; there is a world of difference between pressing a button marked 'hurt' or a noisy buzzer and being deliberately cruel to others following exposure to media violence in a natural setting. Doubts have understandably been expressed about whether what is found in the laboratory will occur in real life. Another serious problem with this method is that it only measures very short-term effects.

Ethical concerns have also been voiced. There is, in the eyes of some, an encouragement to be violent by providing such an opportunity. An example of such a study is that of Bandura (1965) – see Classic Research.

2 Field experiments

These are experiments that are carried out in a more natural setting, such as the home of the participant or a boarding school. They have greater ecological validity than laboratory studies but, like the latter, they are looking only at short-term effects. Another problem is that since it is difficult to control extraneous situational variables, such as how much other violence the children witness or who they associate with, there can be less confidence in judging cause and effect. Examples of this type of research include that of Leyens *et al.* (1975) (see page 99) and Parke *et al.* (1977) (see page 99) in which an institutional setting was used.

3 Natural experiments

These are studies carried out in a real-life setting in which the independent variable (the degree of exposure to violent media) exists already and is not therefore controlled and carefully engineered by the investigator.

These studies have a reasonably high level of ecological validity but it is impossible to clearly establish cause and effect since other factors and changes will also have an effect. There are few opportunities to conduct such investigations but recently one has become available: that of the island of St Helena (Charlton *et al.*, 2000) (see page 99).

4 Correlational studies

These studies compare the level of aggression expressed by individuals (by using personality tests, self-ratings or crime statistics) and the amount of media violence experienced to see if there is a positive correlation between the two variables. Some such studies have been conducted over many years, following individuals from childhood through to adulthood, so they have the advantage of looking at very long-term relationships; others measure short-term effects. Their main limitation is that of all correlational studies: they cannot establish cause and effect. When a positive correlation is demonstrated it could be due to the fact that experiencing media violence causes aggression but this is not the only possible explanation. It may be that aggressive children (and adults) seek out violent films and games or that children brought up in a violent household and subculture are exposed to media violence but it is the general upbringing rather than the media influences which cause the high levels of aggression. Examples of such studies are those of Eron *et al.* (1972) (see page 98), Eron & Huesmann (1986) (see page 98) and Phillips (1983, 1986) (see page 98).

Studies investigating the effects of media violence

Early laboratory studies of the effects of viewing violence were conducted by Bandura, the founder of Social Learning Theory. He demonstrated in many laboratory studies that children imitate aggressive models. His famous Bobo doll studies in which young children watched an adult either beat up the large inflatable doll or simply play non-aggressively with other toys, showed that young children imitate aggressive acts and learn from the models new ways of aggressing (Bandura *et al.*, 1961). The study on page 96 in Classic Research demonstrated this, and also showed that if a person is seen to be punished for acting aggressively then children are unlikely to imitate them. This an important point because much media violence is seen to be rewarded, either directly or indirectly. The 'good guys' often use violence to get their own way and are hailed as heroes (or very occasionally heroines) for so doing.

classic
research

how do children respond to TV violence?

Bandura, A. (1965) Influence of Models' Reinforcement Contingencies on the Acquisition of Imitative Responses. *Journal of Personality and Social Psychology*, 1(6), 589–595.

Aims:

1   To observe children's responses to seeing a television presentation of an aggressive model who is seen either to be punished, rewarded or to have no consequences for the behaviour.

2   To see how many of the novel aggressive responses the child will imitate when induced by rewards to do so.

Method: This is an experimental study with a carefully controlled independent variable, that is, whether the model is punished, rewarded or no consequences occur.

The participants were 33 boys and 33 girls aged between 3 years 6 months and almost 6 years. The children were assigned randomly to one of three treatment conditions of 11 boys and 11 girls.

The children viewed the televised film on their own. The film lasted five minutes and involved a character called Rocky being abusive to an adult-sized plastic Bobo doll. The content of the film is described in the paper as follows:

> 'First, the model laid the Bobo doll on its side, sat on it, and punched it on the nose whilst remarking, "Pow, right in the nose, boom, boom." The model then raised the doll and pommeled it on the head with a mallet. Each response was accompanied by the verbalisation, "Sockeroo ... stay down." Following the mallet aggression, the model kicked the doll about the room, and these responses were interspersed with the comment, "Fly away." Finally, the model threw rubber balls at the Bobo doll, each strike punctuated with "Bang." This sequence of physically and verbally aggressive behaviour was repeated twice.'

The ending of the film differed according to the conditions; there were three of these:

a)   Model-rewarded condition: the model was given drinks, called a 'strong champion' and congratulated on the aggressive performance.

b)   Model-punished condition: the model was given a good telling off, called a bully, spanked with a rolled-up newspaper and threatened with a more serious spanking if it happened again.

c)   Non-consequences condition: no extra ending was added to the basic film.

After viewing the film, each child spent 10 minutes in the test room, which was equipped with a Bobo doll, balls, a mallet, dart guns, farm animals and a dolls house. Two observers, who did not know which condition the child had been assigned to, recorded their behaviour and noted the number of imitated behaviours they performed.

After a short break, the children were offered a sticker and juice for each physical or verbal response they reproduced. They were asked to show what Rocky did and what he said in the film.

Results: Children in the no-consequences and the model-rewarded condition imitated significantly more aggressive behaviours than the model-punished group. There was no difference between the no-consequences and the model-rewarded groups.

In the second part of the study, when children were offered rewards to recall the behaviour of the model, there was no difference between the groups. They could all repeat a considerable number of the aggressive actions. The use of positive incentives had completely wiped out any previous performance differences.

Conclusion: Although the administration of punishment reduces whether or not children imitate aggressive behaviours, it does not influence the degree to which they learn them.

Bashing a Bobo doll

Correlational studies

Longitudinal studies

Eron and his colleagues conducted a longitudinal correlational study of a large number of children over more than twenty years. Although the findings may be somewhat dated they are worth considering because the length of the study permits conclusions about long-term effects of television violence. At the beginning of the study, in 1960, Eron *et al.* measured the TV violence level of what the children watched and the aggressiveness of 875 seven and eight year olds and found a positive correlation between the two. Ten years later, with 475 of the original sample remaining, they measured the same two variables and found a negligible correlation (Eron *et al.*, 1972). However, when during the teenage tears the level of violence viewed and the amount of aggressiveness were compared, an even stronger positive correlation was found in the boys, though not in the girls. Furthermore, the more television violence the boys had watched at age eight, the more likely they were to have been convicted of violent crimes at age 30 (Eron & Huesmann, 1986). The methodological problems inherent in such longitudinal studies applied in this case: only 55 per cent of the original sample were available, so they may not have been representative. It is also quite possible that those participants who were predisposed to be aggressive sought out violent television programmes to watch or that a common factor, such as harsh parental punishment, produced children (and, later, adults) who were both aggressive and enjoyed watching others suffer. Nevertheless, while recognising the limitations of the correlational method, the researchers concluded that watching TV violence can cause aggression in later life.

Correlational studies

Huesmann proposes that the cumulative effect of media violence does not only reveal itself in crime statistics but is implicated in general antisocial behaviour such as inconsiderate driving and the use of harsh corporal punishment on children. The pervasive influence of violent television, argues Huesmann, is to make all forms of aggression more acceptable.

Eron (1995) maintains that television violence teaches children attitudes that condone violence and offer examples of specific aggressive behaviours, such as giving someone a good thump, as a way of solving problems. Television violence differs in important ways from that shown in films, fairy stories or at the theatre because these are perceived as fantasy. Not only is a great deal of television violence quite realistic but a child sees a great deal of it – in many homes the television is on most of the time.

Somewhat different correlational research was conducted by Phillips (1983, 1986) who investigated whether there was an association between violent crime and the newspaper and television coverage of 18 heavyweight boxing matches. He found that homicide death rates rose after each of these boxing matches, peaking at about three days afterwards. Phillips even found that murders of white males increased after the defeat of a white boxer and homicides of African-Americans increased following the defeat of an African-American fighter.

Not all correlational studies show a relationship between viewing violence and aggressive behaviour. Over a three-year period, Milavsky *et al.* (1982) found only a small association between viewing violent television and levels of aggression. They concluded that the influence of violent television was extremely weak compared to the family and social environment, a point to which we will return. Hagell & Newbury (1994) compared the television and video watching habits of 78 young offenders with those of a school control group and found that the delinquents reported watching no more violent television and having fewer television sets or video recorders. They were also less able to name favourite television programmes and had more difficulty naming a television character they emulated. They were typically to be found on the streets getting into trouble than indoors watching television. Significantly, though, they tended to come from chaotic, deprived, unhappy homes.

Field studies

A classic field study on media violence was conducted by Leyens *et al.* (1975) in a correctional home for boys. The amount of aggression shown by the boys was measured both before and after a week of watching either violent films (such as *Bonnie and Clyde* and *The Dirty Dozen*) or non-violent ones. Those boys who watched the violent films showed considerably more aggression in the week after watching them than in the week before, whereas those who had seen the non-violent films showed no increase at all.

Parke *et al.* (1977) conducted a similar study, also on juvenile offenders, in three different institutions. These boys were split into two groups matched on the amount of aggression shown in the course of one week. On each of the next five days they were shown either non-violent or violent films, all judged to be equally exciting. Trained observers coded the amount of violence the boys showed during the days of the study and found that the boys watching the violent films were more aggressive than those who had watched neutral films. In addition to this, the boys who had seen the violent films were more likely to give what they believed to be an electric shock to opponents in a game when provoked by them.

Both of these studies used a sample of delinquent boys, so their findings cannot be generalised to most youngsters. They do, however, demonstrate that media violence may increase the antisocial tendencies of youths who are already very aggressive.

A natural experiment: the St Helena study

Recently an opportunity arose to investigate the effects of the introduction of television to a small community. The island of St Helena became the site for a natural experiment when satellite television was first transmitted to it in March 1995. Before and after television was introduced video cameras were installed in two school playgrounds, filming children aged between three and eight during the lunchbreaks and playtimes. Analysis of the videos before the introduction of television showed that the great majority of the children were well adjusted and hard working; in fact the three and four year olds were considered to be among the best behaved in the world.

So did this change after the introduction of television? Not at all. Even though the violent content of the programmes was slightly higher than in the UK (46 per cent as opposed to 41 per cent) and there was no watershed, the amount of hitting, kicking, pushing and pinching was just the same after the introduction of television as it was before. Teachers also rated the children as just as hard-working and co-operative as they had ever been (Charlton *et al.*, 2000).

Conclusions to be drawn

So what we can conclude from all of these findings? Obviously the issue is a complex one and much as the popular press may like to draw simplistic conclusions and even more facile solutions, psychologists and media researchers have a responsibility to weigh up the argument in a rather more considered fashion.

One major problem that besets any attempt to assess the effects of media violence is outlined by Livingstone (2001):

> 'Almost irrespective of the academic legitimacy of claims for media effects, such claims tend to be addressed within a context in which the mass media are constructed as a scapegoat for, or deflection from, broader cultural and political anxieties (concerning say, childhood, sexuality, crime, unemployment or the underclass). The urgency of this moral and political agenda complicates, or even undermines, careful assessment of the academic research literature'. (page 29)

Certainly much of the research indicates that exposure to excessive violence can affect *some* viewers *some* of the time. Huesmann & Malamuth (1986) comment that the great majority of field and laboratory studies indict media violence as a factor in the development of aggressive behaviour. Nevertheless, it is only one factor and even the researcher most convinced of the detrimental effects of media violence would not argue that exposure to it alone would be sufficient to make a person behave aggressively. Cumberbatch (1997) argues that right from the time of 'Penny Dreadfuls' the media has been used as a scapegoat. He considers that the link between media violence and criminal acts is greatly exaggerated and founded more on moral panics fuelled by newspaper hysteria than on factual evidence. He lists some of the criminal acts, including the Hungerford massacre, that were supposedly the result of copycat crimes (as documented in a Panorama programme) and argues that none were supported by convincing evidence.

It is plain common sense to note that ordinary people do not go and murder and maim simply because they watched a gruesome film the night before. Most of us just chat about it to our friends. After a 'Media Watch' we will look at what factors interact with media violence to enhance or inhibit the effects of media violence.

media watch

TV wrestling in the dock over death of girl, 6

The death of six-year-old Tiffany Eunick has shocked America. The little girl's alleged killer is a boy of 13 who is said to have pounded her skull until it was flat, and to have beaten her so badly that her liver was split.

Her attacker's line of defence has caused further alarm. Lionel Tate, one of the youngest defendants to face a murder charge, claims that his actions were inspired by professional wrestling on television.

Tate's assertion puts the flamboyant and aggressive image of wrestlers such as Hulk Hogan and The Rock next to him in the dock of the Florida court where his trial began last week. Central to his defence is his lawyer's claim that the killing was the result of the boy copying moves he had seen in bouts televised by the Worldwide Wrestling Federation (WWF).

According to his lawyer, Jim Lewis, the teenager – who weighs almost 10st but has the mental age of an eight-year-old – was incapable of distinguishing between the mock brutality and phoney personas of the WWF and the real harm he was capable of inflicting. The defence calls Tiffany's death a "horrible accident".

Although at least four other children have died in incidents linked to copycat violence from wrestling shows, the Florida case is the first to put the blame squarely on the effects of television. It comes at a time of growing concern about the impact of screen violence on children and teenagers.

A report released last week by David Satcher, the United States Surgeon General and the country's most senior public health official, stated: "A substantial body of research now indicates that exposure to media violence increases children's physically and verbally aggressive behaviour in the short term."

The allegations are being vigorously countered by the WWF, which is shown in Britain on Sky TV. The federation is suing Mr Lewis for defamation after remarks he made on television chat shows. The WWF, which insists that children can distinguish between screen fiction and reality, has also successfully blocked attempts by the boy's defence team to force star wrestlers including The Rock – otherwise known as Dwayne Johnson – to give evidence during the trial.

The issue of media violence is particularly sensitive in America after a series of violent rampages by children and teenagers, including the

1999 Columbine High School massacre in Denver, in which 12 pupils and a teacher were shot by two pupils who later killed themselves.

An unsuccessful attempt to sue the video-game industry for $33 million (£22 million) was made by the parents of three children killed by another armed pupil in Paducah, Kentucky, in 1997. The killer, Michael Carneal, 13, claimed to have been influenced by violent videos, films and internet sites.

Last week's report by the Surgeon General was originally commissioned by President Clinton in the wake of Columbine. It found that violence in children was usually the result of a combination of factors, of which poverty and abuse were the most significant.

While it concluded that children became more aggressive after watching some television programmes and videos, the report noted that this behaviour did not usually translate into violence against others, except among children who were already disturbed.

A separate study by Stanford University in California, published this month, compared the actions of two primary school classes, one of which had been discouraged from watching television for almost two weeks. The research team found that the group that cut down its viewing by more than a third was almost 50 per cent less likely to engage in aggressive playground behaviour than other pupils.

Sunday Telegraph, 21 January 2001

Discussion points

1 Why might it be unwise to generalise from this particular case to the effects that watching wrestling might have on children in general?

2 What arguments may be advanced in the defence of the media, that it is being being used as a scapegoat and the fundamental causes of violence cannot be laid at its door?

where to now?

The following are good sources of further information on studies into the effects of media violence:

▶ **Newson, E. (1994) Video violence and the protection of children. *Psychology Review*, 1(2), 2–6** – this article discusses a very controversial paper by the author published after the judge's comments at the trial of Jamie Bulger's murderers that 'I suspect that exposure to violent video films may, in part, be an explanation'. Since there was little evidence that the boys had ever watched the film *Child's Play 3*, the debate became very contentious. It is answered in the following article.

Cumberbatch, G. (1997) Media Violence: Sense and Common Sense. *Psychology Review*, **3(4), 2–7** – in this article Cumberbatch reconsiders the link between media violence and behaviour, looking very critically at the research.

www.chelt.ac.uk/ess/st-helena/faq.htm –this website gives the background to the St Helena study and links to other websites that provide a list of relevant research references.

Factors that mediate the effects of media violence

Individual differences

One of the most important individual differences in susceptibility to media violence is the level of aggression already shown by the individual. The relationship between aggression and viewed violence is by no means a one-way street; Bushman (1995) showed that people who are habitually violent seek out media violence and are more affected by it. Bushman conducted a series of experiments in which he compared the responses of aggressive and non-aggressive individuals after watching violent films. He found that, compared to non-aggressive individuals, the aggressive ones felt more angry and were more likely to seize an opportunity to aggress against others.

Other studies indicate that aggressive children not only watch more media violence but are more likely to identify with violent characters and believe that the violence they see on television reflects real life (Huesmann 1988, Eron & Huesmann, 1986).

Family and social influences

We saw in Chapter 2 that children are more likely to be involved in crime if they are raised in families in which aggression is the norm. There are more important models for the child than the media – parents, teachers and peers all provide powerful models of behaviour and children brought up by parents who use reasoning rather than corporal punishment are less prone to behave aggressively after watching violent television (Goldstein, 1975). In general, media effects are insignificant in changing behaviour in families who do not rely on aggressive behaviour to discipline their children or settle arguments amongst themselves (Chaffee & McLeod, 1971). Conversely, the greatest effects are shown by people who, as children, had frequently been frustrated, were habitually victims of violence and who had seen aggression used as the main means of getting one's own way.

The researchers of the St Helena study point out that their

> 'results do not contradict the claims that children **learn** aggressive behaviours from their television viewing. But they suggest that learned

*aggressive behaviours need not necessarily be **practised**. Whether or not they are practised depends upon **the extent to which young viewers are watched over and cared for in the home**, school or community. What is evident on St Helena is that good parenting and schooling, alongside a strong sense of community, have contributed to creating an environment which prevented television from exerting a negative influence upon young children.' (emphasis as original)*

The researchers go on to suggest that perhaps it is not only the media that has become a scapegoat but families and schools as well. Maybe the culprit is 'urban apathy', which, they argue, fosters uncaring attitudes in our young which inevitably have an impact on our crime statistics.

The context and content of the message

Research as far back as Bandura's has demonstrated that the content of the actual media message is an important variable upon its effect on others, as are the circumstances in which the violence is shown. Comstock & Paik (1991) have reviewed data from a very large number of studies using a variety of methodologies and they conclude that media violence has the greatest effect under the following conditions:

- when aggression is shown as an effective means of succeeding

- when any negative, painful effects of the aggression on the victim are not shown and the violence is justified because it is in the support of 'good'

- when the aggressor is an ordinary person in an everyday situation

- when viewers watch in a state of arousal because they are, for example, excited, angry or frustrated.

The amount of exposure people have to media violence can also have an effect on attitudes which in turn influence behaviour. When people are exposed to media violence over a long period of time they become *desensitised* to its effects and are more accepting of it in everyday life. Gerbner *et al.* (1980, 1986) used the term **cultivation** to describe the fact that when we are exposed to the mass media we begin to construct a social reality which is false, even though we perceive it as true to life. For example, if we are constantly shown scenes of late-night muggings, we may be afraid to go out at night for fear of being attacked. If we see the world as a dark and dangerous place we may overestimate the chances of our being victimised, perceive harmless interactions as threatening, and retaliate aggressively rather than risk getting hurt (Gerbner & Gross, 1976).

Research also demonstrates that viewing justified violence increases the likelihood that it will be imitated. In many films and television programmes the 'good guys' often bring the 'bad guys' to justice by beating them to a pulp or killing them. Viewing acceptable violence can make violence more acceptable.

The effects of violent video games

Despite the fact that playing video games has been a popular entertainment for children and adolescents for a number of years, until recently research into its effects was sparse. It is now, however, attracting the attention of a growing body of researchers.

Video games differ in important ways from television. The player or players are actively engaged in the action and can change the course of events. As Bowman & Rotter (1983) point out, video game playing is an active two-way communication medium. Another difference is that unlike television, which is watched by all ages, video games are almost exclusively designed for the young.

In the 1980s few video games had a violent content but this changed dramatically in the 1990s with the introduction of many games featuring destruction and killing. Nowadays the violent games tend to dominate the market. Dietz (1998) sampled 33 popular games and found that nearly 80 per cent of them were violent in nature and, rather worryingly, over a fifth of these portrayed violence towards women. It is hardly surprising then that concern has been expressed that they may encourage aggression. Indeed the adverse effects of such games could be greater than that of television because of the active involvement of the players. Of particular concern is the argument that some video games encourage racism and sexism by providing children with a world populated by the worst of such stereotypes (Provenzo, 1991).

Do video games increase aggression?

The argument as to the effects of playing violent video games on aggression is as contentious as that of the effects of more passive entertainment, with some researchers arguing that it increases aggression while others (e.g. Griffiths) arguing that the case is by no means proven. Emes (1997) has expressed the Freudian view that video game playing is cathartic and as such may be a useful means of coping with pent-up and aggressive energies.

We shall review a small sample of the available research before looking in more detail in the Research Now section at a very recent study designed to test a theory concerned with the way in which video games affect players, both in the short- and long-term. This theory is outlined in the What's New? section (page 108).

A series of correlational studies looked at the relationship between measures of aggression (including self-reports, teacher ratings and peer reports) and video game playing habits. A positive correlation was found in three out of four of these studies (Dominick, 1984; Fling et al., 1992; Lin & Lepper, 1987). However, we need to remember what has been pointed out several times already: that aggressive youngsters may seek out violent games to play. This, coupled with the fact that there was no record made of whether the games played were violent or non-violent, means that we cannot conclude from these studies that playing the games was the cause of the aggression ratings.

Wiegman & van Schie (1998) argue that intense engagement with a violent game can increase the aggressiveness. They reviewed 12 studies, all of which showed that playing violent video games is liable to increase aggression in the players. However, Griffiths (2000) points out that there are at least 11 others that have not yielded the same results.

Several experimental studies have used a design in which children play either a non-violent or violent video game and are then assessed on aggressiveness. Many of these studies demonstrate that levels of aggression are significantly higher after playing the violent games than after playing the non-violent ones. However, there is a very important confounding variable not controlled in these studies. The games played were not matched on difficulty, enjoyment or excitement. As pointed out by Anderson & Dill (2000) and Bushman (1995), violent materials tend to be more exciting than non-violent materials, so the effects could have been the result of higher excitement levels induced by the violent games. Thus the crucial difference between these studies and that of Anderson & Dill in Research Now is that the games used in the recent research have been matched on these key variables. We will now take a look at this research.

Trigger or release?

research
now

do violent video games cause aggressive thoughts and behaviour?

Anderson, C.A. & Dill, K.E. (2000) Video Games and Aggressive Thoughts, Feelings, and Behaviour in the Laboratory and in Life. *Journal of Personality and Social Psychology*, 78(4), 772–790

Aims: The general aim was to investigate video game violence effects and broaden the understanding of media violence in general. Specifically, the aim was to begin laying down empirical evidence to test the GAAM formulation (discussed next in What's New?).

Method: There were two studies which used different methods, a correlation and an experiment, chosen because these were considered to have strengths that complement each other and surmount each other's weaknesses.

Study 1: the correlation
The variables to be correlated were long-term exposure to video game violence and a set of other variables, the most important being aggressive behaviour and delinquency, both aggressive and non-aggressive.

There was a total of 227 participants, 78 males and 149 females, all psychology students.

Participants completed self-report questionnaires to measure

- aggressive behaviour

- delinquency

- irritability and trait aggressiveness

- the amount of time spent playing video games in general

- the amount of time spent playing violent video games.

Study 2: the experiment
A pilot study was conducted to select two video games, one violent, one non-violent. The games selected were Wolfenstein 3D and Myst; this pair were chosen because they produced no difference in physiological measures, difficulty, enjoyment, frustration and action speed (however, Wolfenstein was rated more exciting than Myst). It was important to control for physiological arousal to avoid this becoming an extraneous variable.

Wolfenstein has a blatant violent content, realism and human characters. The human hero can choose from an array of weaponry; the goal is to kill Nazi guards and thereby advance through the levels to the ultimate goal of killing Hitler. Myst is an interactive adventure game designed to be non-violent. It is a fast-paced, thinking game in which players attempt to align geometric figures as they fall down a computer screen.

There was a total of 210 participants, 104 females and 106 males, all psychology undergraduates.

Participants were matched on high or low irritability, then divided by gender and each group was then given either violent or non-violent video games to play. The procedure was that each participant played the game three times, twice in the first session and once in a second session approximately a week later. In the first session, they completed an affective measure (how they felt), a world view measure and a cognitive measure (what they were thinking).

After playing the game for the third time, participants played a game in which they had the opportunity to give an opponent a blast of noise (no noise was actually administered). All games were arranged so that all participants won and lost the same number of contests. This noise level was used as a measure of aggression.

Results:

Study 1: There was a positive correlation between the amount of time spent playing violent video games and both aggressive personality and delinquent behaviour, both aggressive and non-aggressive.

Study 2: The participants who played a violent video game behaved more aggressively towards an opponent than did those who played a non-violent video game.

Conclusion: In the short term playing a violent video game increases aggression, presumably by encouraging aggressive thoughts. The researchers suggest that longer term exposure might alter the person's basic personality structure, making them more likely to have aggressive thoughts and feelings and to behave aggressively. Because of the active nature of these games, this effect is probably stronger than that of watching violent television and films. Consumers and parents of consumers should be aware of these potential risks.

what's new?

G.A.A.M.: General Affective Aggressive Model (Anderson & Dill, 2000)

This new model is designed to describe a multi-stage process by which aggressive personality and certain situational variables lead to aggressive behaviour. It integrates existing theories, such as Bandura's Social Learning Theory, and the data derived from the researchers' own studies (described previously in Research Now). It explains the processes that are involved in both the short-term effects and the long-term effects of video game violence.

Short-term effects

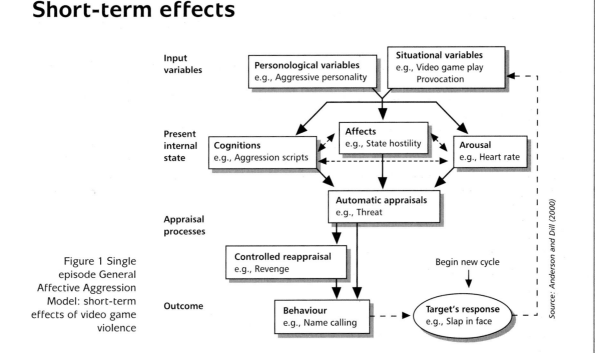

Figure 1 Single episode General Affective Aggression Model: short-term effects of video game violence

Source: Anderson and Dill (2000)

As Figure 1 illustrates, when people with an aggressive personality play a violent video game (especially one in which they experience frustration), this arouses feelings of anger within them, accompanied by biological arousal (such as increased heart rate) and aggressive thoughts, possibly involving revenge. The particular content of the game can influence the aggressive thoughts and behaviours that are shown. For example, being insulted may cause a person to think how to return the insult in a harmful way. More importantly as far as video game playing is concerned, playing a violent game increases the *accessibility* of aggressive thoughts.

Whether an aggressive response is made depends on the person's usual mode of responding. Well-learned behaviours (called, in this model, scripts) come to mind relatively easily and quickly and are expressed fairly automatically. People who score high on aggressive personality have a relatively well-developed and easily accessible array of aggression scripts that are easily activated by relatively minor provocation. What is more, aggressive people have cognitions (thoughts) that encourage violent reactions, such as thinking that there is more violence than there really is, and that the best way to solve problems is to use aggression.

In sum, playing a violent video game primes aggressive thoughts, including aggression scripts. The short-term effects of both an aggressive personality and playing a violent video game have the short-term effect of increasing aggressive responses.

Study 2 in Research Now was designed to test the short-term effects of violent video game playing and, by showing that participants who played a violent video game behaved more aggressively than those who played a non-violent game, it supported the GAAM model.

Long-term effects

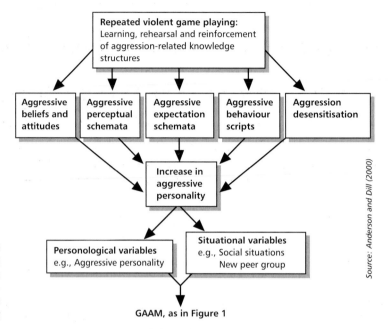

Figure 2 Multiple episode General Affective Aggression Model (GAAM): long-term effects of video game playing

Source: Anderson and Dill (2000)

The long-term effects of playing violent video games are illustrated in Figure 2. This demonstrates that each time people play violent video games, it reinforces the following:

- watchfulness for enemies

- aggressive action against others

- expectations that others will behave aggressively

- positive attitudes towards the use of violence

- beliefs that violent solutions are effective and appropriate.

In addition to this, repeated exposure to scenes of violence desensitises people to its consequences.

Taken together over a long period of time these effects change the individual's personality. Habitual video game players can become more aggressive in outlook and behaviour than they were before the repeated exposure. As the person becomes more aggressive, their whole social environment changes. Their interactions with teachers, parents and non-aggressive peers worsen and they seek out more delinquent peers with whom to associate.

Study 1 in Research Now was designed to test this part of the model and by demonstrating a positive correlation between a person's level of exposure to violent video games and their aggressive behaviour, it was supportive.

where to now?

The following are good sources of further information on the effects of violent video games:

▶ **Griffiths, M. (1998) Violent Video Games: Are they harmful?** *Psychology Review*, 4(4).

Griffiths, M. (1997) Video games and aggression. *The Psychologist*, 10(9).

▶ These two articles cover essentially the same material but the 1997 one is the original and much more detailed. For the purposes of A-level, the *Psychology Review* article is quite sufficient. Griffiths looks critically at empirical research into violent video games.

for and against

the media encouraging antisocial behaviour

+ Correlational longitudinal studies show a consistent positive relationship between the amount of violent television watched and levels of aggression.

+ Laboratory and field experimental studies also show that watching violent television and films or playing violent video games can cause certain people to behave in an aggressive and antisocial manner.

— Correlations do not show that viewing media violence *causes* aggressive behaviour. People who are aggressive may seek out violent programmes to watch, or a third factor, such as a violent family, may be responsible for the connection.

— The media are being used as a convenient scapegoat so that more deep-rooted problems in society can be absolved of blame.

— Psychodynamic theorists argue that viewing aggression may be *cathartic* and therefore reduce violent behaviour, not increase it.

The effects of pornography

Pornography, defined as material intended to arouse sexual excitement, causes as much if not more concern than non-sexual material does, especially with the highly publicised amounts of it to be found on the Internet. Pornography is widely available: 'top shelf' magazines are sold in virtually every newsagent; video rental shops carry sexually explicit material to cater for a range of sexual appetites and, expensive though they are, phone-sex lines are widely used.

Pornography can be non-violent or violent in its content and this is a crucial difference. Violent pornography graphically depicts a violent, degrading form of sexual activity, mostly directed towards women and children who are raped, beaten or even killed. In some of this material, the women are shown as enjoying forcible sex. For our purposes, we will concentrate on research that investigates whether watching such material is liable to increase the likelihood that men will commit sexual crimes; such research is mainly concerned with violent pornography.

Methodological problems

Researching the effects of pornography on behaviour is riddled with methodological problems. Some social psychologists have conducted experimental research based on the same design as that used for laboratory studies of media violence. A typical design would involve male participants being divided into two matched groups and while one watched pornographic material, the other viewed non-sexual footage. The two groups are then compared by, for example, measuring their attitudes to various forms of sexual violence, such as rape. We have already considered the drawbacks of this type of methodology, and they are even more acute when investigating the effects of pornography. Firstly, young college students are not representative and do not necessarily respond to pornography in the same way as other men. Secondly, the situation in which the sexual material is viewed is far removed from that of real life. Being shown a pornographic film in a psychology laboratory is hardly the same as, for example, deciding to sit around with a group of mates and a few beers to enjoy a bit of filmed sex. Last but not least, there is no way that any direct behavioural measures can be taken. All researchers can do is assess attitudes, and attitudes do not predict behaviour (as demonstrated by LaPiere, 1934). Just because an individual may comment that a girl was 'asking for it' does not mean he intends to 'give it to her'.

Other methods carry their own inherent problems. Correlations of real-life events, such as investigating whether rapists and other sexual offenders watched some pornography prior to committing the crime, do not tell us anything about cause and effect. Even if such a relationship exists, it does not reflect the way the majority of people behave, nor does it demonstrate that watching the pornography caused the perpetrator to commit the crime. Most rapists have not viewed pornography prior to the rape; those who have might have raped even if they hadn't seen the film. And clearly, just because a man sees some pornography does not mean he will then commit a sexual offence. Many, many men look at pornographic material but few of them commit sexual offences.

Investigations into the effects of violent pornography

One effect that pornography may have is to make men more likely to believe in so-called 'rape myths', that is, the belief that women really enjoy and want to engage in non-consensual sex. Zillman & Bryant (1984) investigated the longer term effects of watching pornography. Student participants watched 18 or 36 non-violent pornographic films over the course of six weeks while two control groups saw either neutral films or no films at all. Watching pornography reduced the physiological arousal the students had to new pornography and these experimental participants were *less* aggressive than controls when provoked by a same-sex confederate. However, when asked to give their judgements on a rapist, the groups who watched pornography recommended a lighter sentence than the control groups did. This applied to both men and women. The men who had viewed considerable amounts of pornography also expressed more negative attitudes towards women in general.

In a field experiment designed to investigate the effects of violent pornography, Malamuth & Check (1981) showed male students either two films, *Swept Away* and *Get Away*, in which women are seen to enjoy forced sex, or two neutral films. When compared on a 'rape myth acceptance scale', there was a non-significant difference in their attitudes, with the pornography group very slightly more likely to accept them. However, this group did show a slightly greater (though not very large) acceptance of inter-personal violence against women.

Malamuth (1986) suggests that violent pornography is particularly dangerous when viewed by men who already have violent attitudes towards women and who are particularly sexually aroused by viewing this type of material. Demaré *et al.* (1993) in a survey of male college students found that those who reported watching violent pornography admitted to having used force in sex, to having anti-women attitudes and to say that, as long as they were guaranteed to get away with it, they would rape a woman.

In an analysis of 217 studies of media violence, Paik & Comstock (1995) found that violent pornography had a stronger effect on aggression, especially male-to-female aggression, than any other type of violent material.

As with other forms of media violence, it seems to be more dangerous when viewed by already aggressive and disturbed individuals. Some researchers believe that violent pornography is particularly arousing to known rapists and that these effects are particularly pronounced when the victim seems to enjoy the abuse (Abel *et al.*, 1977).

One particular concern with respect to pornography is that it reinforces prejudices against women (Russell, 1984). Even more worrying is the possibility that it leads certain women to believe that they should endure being hurt during sex, that it is 'normal' for men to want to do this and that requests to engage in this sort of sexual activity are reasonable (Wheeler, 1985).

Violent pornography and sexual crime

Perhaps unsurprisingly, the relationship between violent pornography and sexual crime is not straightforward. Certainly no direct causal relationship can be inferred as demonstrated by cross-cultural studies. In Japan where extremely violent pornography is available, rape is rare, whereas in India where pornography is banned and films are not allowed to have any sexual content, there is a high incidence of rape (Pratap, 1990). There is a multitude of other social factors that need to be considered when assessing the conditions under which sexual crimes take place. Nevertheless, it is probable that very violent pornography is extremely dangerous. Feldman (1993) draws our attention to a content analysis by Dietz *et al.* (1986) of detective magazines, referred to by the researchers as 'pornography for the sexual sadist'. As Feldman reports:

> 'A content analysis of contemporary detective magazines revealed covers which juxtapose erotic images with images of violence, bondage and domination. The articles themselves provide lurid descriptions of murder, rape and torture. The magazines publish advertisements for weapons, and for burglary and car-theft tools. With the aid of case histories, the authors illustrate how these magazines might facilitate the development of highly deviant sexual fantasies. It may be that socially isolated individuals with a strong tendency to ruminate about deviant fantasies, and in some cases to act on them, make particular use of the magazines described by Dietz et al. (1986), but there seems no information on this crucial point' (page 217).

interactive
angles

There is a fierce debate about whether pornography should be censored or freely available. Even feminists are divided on the issue. On one side are those who argue that pornography demeans women and reduces them to mere sex objects, whilst on the other side are those who argue that, even though pornography is not desirable, adults should be allowed to make their own decisions about what they read and see, and should not have to be restricted by those who have a political or religious axe to grind. Besides which, the banning of pornography does not prevent other dehumanising portrayals of women as sex objects which abound in the media, especially in advertising. What is your view?

Conclusion

Serious antisocial aggression is determined by multiple factors. Obviously the relationship between media violence and aggression is a complex one and the answer to the question 'Does media violence cause increased aggression and crime?' is 'it depends …'. It depends on a great many things. It depends on the individuals who are watching the programme, the family life they have, the society in which they live. It depends on who they watch it with and what the exact content is. It depends on how much other media violence they are exposed to. Concerns over the amount of violence seen by children does have justification. The American Psychological Association Commission on Violence and Youth reported in 1993 that 'There is absolutely no doubt that higher levels of viewing violence on television are correlated with increased acceptance of aggressive attitudes and increased aggressive behaviour.' However, we still cannot dismiss the idea that a violent society, or norms within subcultures, are responsible both for the enjoyment of violent films and games and for increased antisocial behaviour. Perhaps, as the researchers from the St Helena project comment (Charlton *et al.*, 2000), we need to look more closely at the way in which society is structured and the support systems it provides before we lay the entire blame for antisocial and criminal behaviour at the feet of the media.

what do you know?

1   Evaluate four ways in which the influence of the media on aggressive behaviour has been investigated.

2   Describe and evaluate one study that shows how children may imitate what they see in films.

3   'Blaming the media for criminal and antisocial behaviour is simply a way of shifting the blame from the family and society'. With reference to psychological research, discuss this point of view.

4   What factors may mediate the effects of media violence?

5   Discuss research into the effects of pornography on violent sexual behaviour.

6

Judge and Jury: Psychology in the Courtroom

The use of the jury system has a long history based on the principle that a group of representative people should reach an objective decision about whether or not the law has been broken. As early as the eleventh century in Britain, the neighbours of a person accused of wrongdoing were asked to consider the evidence and come to a verdict. This method of justice has traditionally been held in such high regard that it is used in many democratic countries.

Because the jury lies at the core of our judicial system, factors affecting the decisions they make and the processes by which these decisions are reached are of paramount importance in operating a fair system of justice. In this chapter we will consider how social psychologists conduct research into jury decision making, how juries are selected and the factors other than the evidence that might influence them. We will look at one particular model which suggests the way in which each juror interprets the evidence in a way that helps him or her reach a verdict, and the processes that operate within a jury once they retire to make their verdict. We will also consider whether the size of the jury and the requirement to reach either a unanimous or majority verdict influence these processes. In essence, this chapter's concern is with both the dynamics and effectiveness of the jury system.

Conducting research on trial procedures and court decisions

The study of real jury deliberation is prohibited in the UK and USA, so it is necessary to use less direct methods to study them and this inevitably involves questions of ecological validity. Two main alternatives to studying actual juries have been employed: mock (or simulated) juries and shadow juries.

Mock juries

Mock juries are made up of a group of participants who are asked to consider a case and make judgements about it. The case is often presented as a written, summarised scenario rather than in any other form (such as a film or video clip). An example of the type of trial material presented in such a study is given on pages 132–136. The type of judgements made include degree of responsibility (sometimes of the victims as well as the defendant), guilt or innocence of the accused and the type of sentence that might be deemed appropriate. The problems and limitations with such an approach include the following:

- Often the participants are students and are therefore not representative of the general population.

- The scenarios that give an account of the case are usually brief and even if they represent the presentation of a real-life case, they do not involve any of the complexities of such a trial. Reading a brief summarised report of a criminal case is worlds apart from spending a considerable amount of time listening to evidence from both sides, seeing and hearing the witnesses and defendant, and assessing the summing up of the court prosecutor, the defence lawyer and the judge.

- Any judgements made have no consequences for a real person, whereas in a real-life situation, these can obviously be very serious indeed. This is perhaps the most crucial difference of all between real and artificial jury situations.

On the positive side, the use of mock juries does allow psychologists to investigate effects that are of great significance in ensuring a fair trial but cannot be researched in real court cases. The systematic manipulation of variables whilst others are kept constant means that it is possible to study the effect of such factors as the defendant's appearance, age or race, the amount of damage done and how the order of presentation of evidence affects the final decision reached by jurors.

Shadow juries

The shadow jury method involves selecting a group of people (usually 12) who are eligible for jury service and asking them to sit in the public gallery to hear all the evidence, then retire to somewhere quiet to consider their verdict, whilst all deliberations are recorded. This method avoids some of the most significant problems of mock juries although not the question of consequences. Unlike the mock jury method, it does not allow the researcher to explore the effect of systematic manipulation of variables but does have considerably greater ecological validity. This method is far less frequently used than the simulated jury method, presumably because of the considerable practical problems involved, not least obtaining volunteers to participate in a study that may last for days.

Because of the limitations of both of these methods there are significant problems with drawing conclusions from jury studies, but as long as these limitations are heeded, there is a considerable amount that psychologists and the judicial system can learn from this research.

Factors affecting jury decision making

The selection of jurors

People who are called for jury service are not automatically chosen to serve on the jury; the challenging and vetting of juries is now commonplace, particularly in the USA. Before a trial starts in that country, those called for jury service are subjected to a pre-trial interview known as a *voir dire* during which the judge or opposing lawyers can dismiss a juror if he or she is considered not to be impartial. This process can last literally weeks but typically takes less than an hour. This is not the end of the vetting procedure. After that, the lawyers are permitted to make *peremptory challenges* which involve rejecting a certain number of prospective jurors without giving any reason. The number of these challenges varies according to the type of case and seriousness of the charge.

Occasionally a whole community can be dismissed as being biased, perhaps because of pre-trial publicity, and the trial moved to another location. The effect of this on the trial of those accused of the assault of Rodney King is shown opposite.

The degree to which prospective jurors are challenged in Britain is much smaller than in America. This is reflected in a remark by Goleman (1994) that the difference between jury trials in England and America is that in England the trial begins when the jury is chosen whilst in America it is over once the jury has been selected (quoted in Baron & Byrne, 1997).

Challenges to jurors can have a profound effect on the composition of the final jury and there is genuine concern in the USA about the extent to which the choice of jury should be permitted. It would appear that a whole

The videotaped beating of Rodney King

The first trial of four white Los Angeles police officers accused of the videotaped beating of black motorist Rodney King was moved from urban Los Angeles to neighboring Ventura County as a result of pretrial publicity. The demographics of Ventura County favored the defense – suburban, white, a bedroom community with over 2000 police families, a place to which people move to escape urban problems. It could be expected that jurors would empathize with the defendants – "the thin blue line" regarded by many as protecting the citizens from drugs and gang violence – rather than with Rodney King, a large, black, drunk driver. As one legal specialist put it, "I think the case was lost when the change of venue was granted. I don't think Terry White (the prosecutor) had a chance, and it doesn't do a lot of good to debate whether they should have called Rodney King and all that stuff, because I think from that point on these people approached the case with a mindset" (*National Law Journal*, May 11, 1992, p. 15).

The six-man, six-woman jury, whose verdict of acquittal sparked one of the worst riots in this nation's history, consisted of ten whites, one Hispanic, and one Asian, but no African Americans. The median age of the jurors was 50 years. Five jurors were registered as Republicans and five as Democrats, one did not indicate a party preference, and one was not registered. Three were members of the National Rifle Association, and two others had law enforcement backgrounds. Most of the jurors were married and owned or were purchasing their own homes.

Wrightsman (1994)

industry has developed around it, with advice being offered on how to carry out so-called systematic or 'scientific' jury selection. Understandably, some social scientists object to the use of the term 'scientific' in this context since it is an extremely subjective procedure. The process has been reviewed in detail by Hans & Vidmar (1982) who report some interesting cases in which it has backfired. On the whole though, it is considered to alter the outcome of certain trials in the intended direction and is considered by some to be not so much an exercise in eliminating those who are biased but in 'fixing' the jury to try and guarantee a certain outcome. Adler (1994) argues that peremptory challenges should not be permitted. It is not difficult to appreciate the reason for these concerns when one reads a sample of the recommendations for jury selection put forward by Clarence Darrow, who was a very prominent trial attorney in the USA:

> 'I try to get a jury with little education but with human emotion. The Irish are always the best jurymen for the defense. I don't want a Scotchman, for he has too little human feelings; I don't want a Scandinavian, for he has too strong a respect for the law as law. In general, I don't want a religious person, for he believes in sin and punishment. The defense should avoid rich men who have a high regard for the law, as they make and use it. The smug and ultra-respectable think they are the guardians of society, and they believe the law is for them.' (Quoted in Sutherland & Cressey, 1974, p. 417.)

This kind of selection inevitably results in a very biased jury.

Characteristics of jurors

Jurors will inevitably bring to the courtroom their own preconceptions and theories. People are not raised in a vacuum and the fact that their own personal experiences and other characteristics will impinge on decision making should not necessarily be a cause for concern. However, if jurors have very closed-minded attitudes, in particular if they show open racial prejudice, then this obviously compromises any chance of defendants having a fair trial. Lloyd-Bostock (1988) quotes a case from 1950s America in which a black youth was charged with aiding and abetting the interstate transportation of a stolen car. When jurors were interviewed after the trial, it turned out that several had been racially biased. Two in particular had made comments to the effect that the defendant should be found guilty because 'niggers are just no good' and 'niggers ought to be taught to behave'. To add insult to injury, they were not deterred from making such remarks by the presence of a black female juror. Although this occurred in the 1950s, there is evidence that we cannot afford to be complacent about this type of racism occurring at the present time, especially in cases where a black man is accused of sex crimes against a white woman (Lloyd-Bostock, 1988). For example, Pfeifer & Ogloff (1991), using a mock jury simulation, found that university students rated black defendants more guilty than white ones when accused of the same crime. Stewart (1980) reported that in real trials black defendants were more likely to be sentenced to a term of imprisonment than were white people found guilty of a similar offence.

Even when jurors are not openly or deliberately prejudiced, they may be influenced by their misinterpretation or misunderstanding of the language used by the defendant and/or his or her demeanour.

Size of the jury

People often assume that a jury comprises 12 individuals and although this is true in Britain, it is no longer the case in the USA. Indeed one lawyer, Melvin Tatsumi, attempted to have a jury of just one person because he believed this to be preferable to relying on 'mob mentality'. This request was accepted at first but overturned on appeal. In the now famous constitutional case of *Williams v. Florida* (1970), Williams challenged his conviction on the grounds that there were only six people on the jury. The Supreme Court refused to overturn the verdict, on the basis that a six-person jury could operate as effectively as a 12-person one, and such juries are now permitted in American courts except when the death penalty is a possible sentence. However, most of the evidence presented in favour of smaller juries was scant in the extreme and based on opinions and anecdotes (Zeisel, 1971). The small amount of social psychological research used was completely misinterpreted (Saks, 1974).

Despite the ruling by the Supreme Court, psychological studies show that there are significant differences between the way small and large juries operate and that larger juries tend to be fairer. There are several reasons for this. For a start, larger juries obviously having a greater chance of being representative of the general population. Saks (1977) summarises the other advantages as follows:

1   Larger juries spend more time in deliberation.

2   They spend a greater proportion of their time in discussion (as opposed to vote taking and other activities).

3   Larger juries show more accurate recall of the testimony.

4   The pressure to conform despite being unconvinced is not as extreme in large groups as in small ones. When there is only one person who disagrees with the rest, that person is more likely to feel very uncomfortable about not going along with the majority view. But if they are a member of a larger jury they stand more of a chance of finding an ally than if they were serving on a small jury.

5   Larger juries tend to produce more consistent verdicts.

On the whole then, smaller juries may save money but it very doubtful whether they are as effective as larger ones.

Characteristics of the defendant

Physical attractiveness

Everyone knows that heroes are handsome and villains are ugly, for this is the stereotype we see in films, books, magazines and on television. Indeed, many an actor in 'Wild West' films has been cast as a 'goodie' or an outlaw purely on whether he is handsome or ruggedly scarred. It would appear that this stereotype is not confined to the media but operates in real life, for research indicates that people do believe that villains have a certain type of facial appearance, one that may be described as 'tough' or 'hard'. One of the most distinguishing features of such a stereotype is that criminals are unattractive.

The other side of the coin is that attractive people are rarely considered capable of behaving criminally. Dion, Berschied & Hatfield (1972) coined the now classic expression 'What is beautiful is good' to describe findings which demonstrate that attractive people have a considerable advantage in life. The stereotype they enjoy is to be judged as more intelligent, confident, happy, assertive, serious and truthful than people with average looks.

So do we assume that ugly people are more likely to commit crimes than beautiful ones? In mock jury situations, or in real life, does someone's facial appearance affect the sentence they are given or even whether or not they are judged guilty? Iniquitous though it may be, the answer to both of these questions appears to be 'yes'.

Saladin *et al.* (1988) showed participants eight photos of men and asked them to judge how capable they considered them to be of committing each of two crimes: murder and armed robbery. Overall, the attractive men were considered less likely to have committed either crime than the unattractive ones. This and other studies indicate that, compared to unattractive individuals, attractive people are not only seen as less likely to commit a crime, they are also viewed more sympathetically by jurors and judges and are treated more leniently when deemed guilty. This attractiveness effect is strongest with serious but non-fatal crimes such as burglary, and when females are being judged (Quigley *et al.*, 1995). An exception to this rule occurs if people are considered to be using their attractiveness for illegal material gain, such as in performing confidence tricks or in fraud.

This effect applies not only in the psychology laboratory but also in the actual courtroom. Downs & Lyons (1991) analysed the fines and bail payments of 1,500 defendants accused of minor crimes and asked police officers, who were not told the purpose of their assessments, to rate them on attractiveness. The results showed that, even when the seriousness of the crime was controlled for, attractiveness was negatively correlated with the amount of bail or the fine imposed by the judge. Attractiveness, however, appeared to be irrelevant when imposing fines or setting bail payments for more serious crimes (McKelvie & Coley, 1993). Stewart (1980) sent observers into courtrooms to rate defendants on various traits, including physical attractiveness. The results were similar to those found in simulated jury studies: when seriousness of the crime and race were controlled for, there was a significant negative correlation between attractiveness and length of sentence. In other words, attractive people received shorter sentences than unattractive people accused of a similar crime. In this study only one rating of attractiveness was made. Stewart later extended his research by asking the observers sitting in the courtroom to rate defendants not only on physical attractiveness but also on cleanliness, neatness and quality of dress. Using a seven-point scale, defendants were rated as attractive–unattractive, dirty–clean, sloppy–neat and well dressed–poorly dressed. Over a two-year period, 60 defendants were observed and it was found that those who were perceived as attractive, clean, neat and well-dressed were treated with greater leniency than were those rated lower on these four dimensions. However, although attractiveness affected sentencing, it did not affect whether or not the defendant was convicted or acquitted.

Other factors

Although attractiveness is the main variable that has been shown to influence judges and juries, other features do have an effect. Berry & McArthur (1985) found, in a mock trial study, that defendants with 'baby' faces were more likely than those with mature ones to be found guilty of negligence in not warning customers of the possible dangers of the products they were selling. Those with mature features were more likely to be considered guilty of deliberately deceiving their customers by telling lies about their products.

However, not all studies have found a relationship between defendant features and jury decisions. Bull & McAlpine (1998), in a review of such research, point out that it is quite possible that many studies finding no effect of appearance on judgements may have been rejected for publication. Nevertheless, studies strongly suggest that people do assume that there is a relationship between facial appearance and criminality and they are agreed on which particular face fits a particular crime. This, together with the evidence that, at least in some instances, real-life court decisions are affected by facial appearance, should be a matter of considerable concern.

where to now?

The following is a good source of further information on factors affecting jury decision-making:

▶ **Wrightsman, L., Niezel, M. & Fortune, W. (1994)** *Psychology and the Legal System* **(3rd edition). California: Brooks/Cole** – chapters 13 and 14 consider the dynamics of jury decision making with many examples from case studies of actual trials. It is very detailed but fascinating. The other chapters are equally absorbing and relevant to the study of criminal psychology.

Processes involved in jury decision making

Attribution theory and biases in jurors and witnesses

The physical features of defendants may influence judge and jury, but of far greater importance in our deliberations over criminal behaviour is consideration of *why* someone behaved the way they did. This has a crucial effect on our judgements of guilt or innocence and the degree to which an individual is considered responsible for his or her actions.

It is not only in consideration of crime that we ponder on why someone behaved in a certain way, we do it automatically, with all sorts of everyday behaviours. In order to make sense of our social world, we try to understand the causes of our own and other people's behaviour. Although there are differences between individuals in the extent to which this preoccupies them, all of us need to ask 'why?', especially when important events occur that are both negative and unexpected. For example, when, in November 1994, Susan Smith confessed to deliberately drowning her two young sons, the first thing people asked themselves was what could lead someone to commit such an appalling act – was she evil, was she under some Machiavellian influence or was she crazy?

Attribution theory is concerned with how people explain the reasons for behaviour, specifically, to what they *attribute* the causes of behaviour. Although people use different explanations to account for human behaviour, Heider (1958) (the founding father of attribution theory), found it useful to group such explanations into two categories: **dispositional** (personal) or **situational**. If we consider that a person who was driving too fast has a reckless and irresponsible attitude we are making a dispositional attribution, an attribution based on that individual's personality, whereas if we believe they were hurrying to an urgent appointment, we are making a situational attribution. It is not difficult to appreciate that the way in which jurors attribute causes to people's behaviour is absolutely crucial to the conclusions they draw as to guilt or innocence of the accused and to the mitigating circumstances that might be taken into account.

When considering the way jurors and witnesses make attributions for the causes of criminal behaviour, we need to pay particular attention to the mistaken assumptions they may make. When we make attributions, we are often limited in our ability to process all relevant facts, and indeed, we may only have incomplete information at our disposal. This inevitably means that our attributions are sometimes incorrect. *Attributional biases* are those ways in which short cuts in attribution may lead us to false conclusions. We will now take a look at some of the most relevant of these.

The fundamental attribution error

As a general rule, when people explain the behaviour of others, they tend *to overestimate the role of personal factors and underestimate the impact of the situation.* This is such a pervasive bias that it is known as the fundamental attribution error (Ross, 1977). Many studies have demonstrated that even when the causes of people's behaviour are very obviously situational, people still attribute it to their personality. For example, Jones & Harris (1967) asked students to read out an essay either favouring or opposing Fidel Castro's regime in Cuba. Although it was made quite clear to the audience that the essays had been allocated to the students by their teacher and were not their own work, the narrators were still considered to hold the opinions expressed in the essay they had read.

Many of you will be familiar with the work of Stanley Milgram. He placed people in a situation in which they were required, in the name of research, to give a 'learner' an increasingly severe electric shock (never actually administered) every time he made an error on a simple memory task (Milgram, 1963). The results of this study were profoundly disturbing: a staggering 65 per cent of people were prepared to administer shocks so severe that they could have been lethal, even though the victim could be heard to scream, yell, complain about a serious heart condition and then fall silent. When people hear of such behaviour, their usual conclusion is that any individual capable of performing such acts is a sadist. Psychiatrists, psychologists and members of the general public interviewed by Milgram prior to the study estimated that fewer than one in a thousand people would give the highest level of shock. But the behaviour of the participants during the study showed they certainly were not being deliberately cruel. The great majority of participants were absolutely distraught, continually questioned the procedure and argued to be released from the study. They were not sadistic – they hated every minute of the study but they felt locked into a situation from which they could not escape. It was the situation, not the disposition of these individuals, that was responsible for their potentially cruel behaviour. The assumption that cruel actions are motivated by an 'evil personality' is an example of the fundamental attribution error.

Not only jurors but witnesses also may be liable to be influenced by their biased judgements. In Chapter 4 we looked in detail at the ways in which memory of events can be distorted both at the time of the incident, and afterwards, especially if certain potentially misleading questions are asked or witnesses hear other people's account of what happened. The witnesses' interpretations of why an event occurred – whether, for example, a person who swung a punch at someone was sorely provoked, drunk or just simply an aggressive person – can distort the way memories are encoded and lead to unreliable recall of events.

The just world hypothesis

Lerner (1980) suggested that people have a need to believe in a world that is just and fair, a world in which people get what they deserve. In this way we can protect ourselves from the unpalatable truth that we could fall victim to the cruel twists of fate.

However, this belief is often strongly challenged by the fact that we regularly hear about events that involve the suffering of innocent victims and the unjust treatment of people. Rather than surrender our belief in a just world, we find ways of interpreting the causes of people's behaviour in such a way that it restores our faith in a just world. There are several ways in which this can be done.

- We can blame victims for their own misfortune. For example, we can accuse a victim of burglary as being careless and not securing their property adequately.

- We can vilify the character of victims, so they are perceived as deserving of their fate. For example, we may believe that battered wives provoke their abusive husbands or even have a personality type that is attracted to such behaviour.

- We can help the victims or compensate them in some way.

The tendency to disparage victims can be viewed as yet another example of the fundamental attribution error – too much emphasis is put on the person and not enough on the situation. Although believing in a just world is common, there are marked individual differences in the strength of this belief. A strong believer in a just world is relatively unsympathetic to victims of misfortune and is also unlikely to take account of mitigating circumstances that may lead someone to commit a crime. Such individuals are more likely to be biased in their judgements whether they are witnesses or jurors.

One of the most disturbing aspects of the Just World Hypothesis is the attitude that is sometimes expressed towards rape victims. 'She must have led him on', 'She was asking for it walking home that late at night', 'What does she expect dressed like that?' are the kinds of comments often heard in media reports of rape. Bell *et al.* (1994), using a simulated jury situation, asked male and female college students to consider four different incidents of rape, two of which concerned rape by a stranger and two which involved date rape. Both males and females placed considerably more responsibility for what happened when the victim knew her assailant than when he was a stranger, and males ascribed more blame to the victim in both conditions than did females.

We don't have to denigrate the victim if there is an alternative means of restoring our belief in a just world. The study reported in Research Now demonstrates that when it is possible to compensate the victim, we do not ascribe more blame to one victim than another, but the amount of compensation offered differs according to circumstances. In this study people awarded greater compensation to an older woman than a younger one, indicating that we try to restore our belief in a just world by offering compensation to the victim in proportion to what we believe they deserve.

Pollard (1992) has reviewed many studies looking at judgements about victims and attackers in depicted rapes. He reports that, generally, females make more pro-victim judgements than males do, as do those people with non-traditional sex-role attitudes. The victim's dress and past history also have a consistent effect in that the more scantily or provocatively dressed and the more sex partners the victim has had, the less sympathy they receive. Pollard points out that not all results found in experiments are directly relevant to a trial situation: for example, data on sentencing has no direct application since juries don't recommend sentences. Nevertheless, such studies do shed light on some of the attitudes with which jurors enter the court. In this chapter we are mainly concerned with influences on jurors but it is important to acknowledge the importance of these findings to other legal aspects. As Pollard comments:

> 'Attitudes of individuals to some extent determine the legal processes and have direct bearing on related issues such as whether a victim will report the rape. Given the prevalence of rape and the infrequency of reporting (especially in the case of those rapes that are likely to produce jury trials about consent), jury behaviour is not the only interest. Identification of the social attitudes endemic to the population in which rape flourishes is perhaps a more important goal ... work on the attribution of responsibility paradigm has contributed to this goal.' (page 322)

research
now

how do beliefs in a just world impact on attributions of responsibility and awards of monetary damages?

Foley, L.A. & Pigott, M.A. (2000) Belief in a Just World and Jury Decisions in a Civil Rape Trial. *Journal of Applied Social Psychology,* 30 (5), 935–951

Aim: When an unjust event occurs, there are several ways in which our belief in a just world can be restored. For example, when a person is raped, people often ascribe responsibility to them for what happened, otherwise the event is too unfair to fit comfortably with their view of the world. An alternative way of restoring faith in a just world, if the opportunity arises, is to award the victim some compensation. The more innocent the person is judged to be, the greater the amount of the compensation that will be awarded. If the opportunity exists to offer compensation, then there is no need to ascribe responsibility to someone who is raped.

The general aim of this study is to investigate the impact of people's belief in a just world on attributions of responsibility and awards of monetary damages in a civil rape case.

This was done by testing two hypotheses:

Hypothesis 1. Younger plaintiffs and older plaintiffs will be held equally responsible for rape.

Hypothesis 2. Older women will be awarded more monetary damages than will younger women.

(Additional hypotheses were tested that are not reported here.)

Method:
Design: This is an experiment, using an independent groups design. The independent variable was the age of the rape victim (young or old); the dependent variables were the percentage of responsibility attributed to the plaintiff and the amount of monetary damages awarded to them.

Participants: The participants were in two groups:
a)   47 students of Psychology (undergraduates); 37 females, 10 males, with a mean age of 20.3 years.

b)   59 jury-eligible residents of the same state; 21 males, 38 females, with a mean age of 48.5 years.

Scenario: The participants were given an account of the situation in which the rape occurred. A female nurse, who worked variable shifts, was raped in her apartment by an employee of the apartment owner. Before the rape occurred, the plaintiff complained several times to the apartment owner that someone was entering her apartment. She asked to have the locks changed, but he refused. He said that no one was ever allowed into an apartment without his being present. The rapist, the pool maintenance man, used the master key that hung in the owner's office to enter the apartment. The plaintiff was suing the owner for damages.

Materials: Two different photographs of the rape victim, who was a white woman. The photographs had been generated by a computer so that the features were the same but one victim was young (described as 27 years old) whilst the other was considerably older (described as in her mid-60s).

Results: Hypothesis 1 was found to be accepted: there was no significant difference in the amount of responsibility attributed to women based on their age. Usually, an older, more respectable victim would be considered to be less responsible than a younger one, but in this case the prediction was that the mock jurors would not need to perceive the older victim as less responsible as they could award her more money. This was indeed the case, since the second hypothesis was also accepted: participants awarded significantly higher monetary damages to the older woman than they did to the younger one, despite the two plaintiffs being perceived as equally responsible for the incident.

Conclusion: The awarding of these different amounts of damages appears to support the Just World Hypothesis. Nevertheless, it would be advisable to consider some alternative explanations. It is possible that participants believed the older woman to be more psychologically damaged and/or to have sustained more severe physical injuries from the incident and therefore would need to take more time off work. However, it could also be argued that the younger woman has a greater life expectancy and would therefore be expected to suffer for a longer period of time than the older woman. Future research is needed to determine the rationale behind the decision to award more compensation to the older victim but it does appear to offer support for the Just World Hypothesis in that the older woman was offered more compensation.

One way of restoring our belief in a just world is to offer compensation and the amount of damages will be related to how responsible we feel a person is for their fate. In this case, the older woman was probably considered to be more 'innocent' than the younger one, even though this judgement was not a conscious one. Therefore she was considered worthy of higher compensation in order to restore the world to being a fair place.

Hedonistic relevance

Piaget (1932), writing about the moral development of children, reported that young children tend to judge right or wrong on the basis of how much harm a person has done. Hence, if a child spills a large amount of ink on a new carpet, even though they may be trying to do dad a favour and fill up his inkwell (remember, this is 1932!), then he or she is deemed to be much naughtier and to deserve a harsher punishment than a child who spills ink on a blotter when he or she has been specifically instructed not to go near the inkwell. Older children are more likely to consider the motivation behind the deed and judge the disobedient child as naughtier.

However, there are a considerable number of instances in which adults judge on the basis of consequences, particularly if the consequences are dire. The principle of hedonistic relevance states that the more pain (or pleasure) an action causes, the more likely we are to attribute it to dispositional factors rather than to situational ones. Hence, the more serious the consequences of a behaviour, the more likely we are to hold the perpetrator responsible. (Note that this principle applies equally to behaviours that have very fortunate consequences, but when looking at crime this is not our major focus.)

Just to illustrate the point, imagine the following scenario. A man is driving home along the motorway at about six o'clock after a long day's work. He's been in a meeting all afternoon in a stuffy office and he is a little tired. He has not been drinking. He is not driving particularly fast, is within the legal speed limit and is in the inside lane. For a fraction of a second he 'nods off' and his car veers onto the hard shoulder where the driver, now fully alert and rather shocked, applies the brakes and comes to a halt. A police car is travelling behind and stops. Before reading on, think what, in this situation, you would consider a fair penalty to be. Most people opt for a caution, maybe a fine and points on the licence. Few think a harsher penalty is appropriate.

Now consider an alternative scenario. The circumstances are identical except for the outcome. On this occasion, the driver goes into the car in front, killing the female driver and her four-year-old son. Now what should the penalty be? The majority of people now consider that the driver should receive a much harsher punishment, perhaps of a term of imprisonment. They tend to focus on the ways in which the driver can be blamed – he shouldn't drive when tired. But none of us can pretend that this is as bad as drinking and driving, or that the driver's crime is particularly heinous. The consequences, however, are so very serious that we feel it is unjust not to take account of them.

This principle was demonstrated by Walster (1966), who asked participants to judge the amount of responsibility due to a car owner whose parked car had rolled down a hill because the brake cable on the handbrake was rusted and had broken. The car either injured someone badly or was deflected and caused no harm to any individual. Participants were asked to judge whether the car owner was

a) not responsible at all

b) only slightly responsible

c) somewhat responsible, or

d) very much responsible.

In line with the theory, they attributed more responsibility to the owner when a person was injured than when no one was hurt.

However, this study has been criticised on the basis that the term 'responsible' is too vague and people may interpret it in different ways. One person may view someone as responsible simply because their actions caused the accident; others may deem him or her responsible only if they could have foreseen what might happen; still others may only consider someone responsible if the consequences were both foreseen and intended. Therefore, studies that simply consider how 'responsible' a person was may be too simplistic to be applied to courtroom judgements.

Responsibility in law is based on 'common-sense' notions of when someone can reasonably be held morally responsible for particular outcomes. When judging the degree of responsibility, the legal system takes account of the extent to which the outcomes could have been foreseen, even when the actions leading to them were unintentional. For example, a factory owner may be viewed as negligent and therefore liable to pay compensation if a fire was caused by employees who were permitted to smoke in a paper factory. Psychological studies doubtless help us to understand the processes that operate in jury decision making but we should not lose sight of their limitations.

Failure to use the discounting principle

Sometimes the way in which we make attributions simply depends on the most obvious reason why a person is behaving in a certain way. If, for example, a famous person is advertising a product we usually attribute the cause of their behaviour to the fat fee they will receive rather than their unselfish desire to share with us the advantages of the product. We are operating what is known as the *discounting principle*: we discount all possible causes except the most obvious (Kelley, 1971). Based on this, we may expect that if a defendant confesses while under severe threat during an interrogation, and the jurors are informed of this, they would apply the discounting principle and have doubts about the truth and reliability of such a confession. In other words, they would discount or give less weight to the confession because it was produced by threat of force. Unfortunately, this is not always the case, perhaps because it challenges the belief in a just world. Rather, the fundamental attribution error comes into play and leads people to conclude that 'He confessed, so he must be guilty'. It seems that *what* you say is more important than *why* you say it.

Despite the evidence from social psychology that people do not always make allowances for the circumstances under which evidence is obtained, the Supreme Court in the USA assumes that jurors can be trusted to use potentially inaccurate confessions cautiously and therefore even confessions gathered under duress should be admissible (Wrightsman *et al.*, 1994). The courts erroneously assume that jurors will be able to disregard testimony if they are furnished with information that calls into question the reason why it was made.

The story model for juror decision making

Pennington & Hastie (1993) have formulated a theory to account for the way in which jurors make decisions in criminal trials. They call this theory the Story Model for juror decision making and have investigated it by asking people to make decisions on simulated trials. Before we consider the model, read the account below of one such trial that has been used in much of their research. Think about what verdict you would have reached and the reasons why you made that particular decision. You have to decide between

- First degree murder

- Second degree murder

- Manslaughter

- Not guilty on the grounds of self-defence.

Use the following as guidance:

- *First degree murder*: the unlawful and intentional killing of someone with malice aforethought, characterised by deliberation or premeditation.

- *Second degree murder*: the unlawful killing of someone by intent but without deliberation or premeditation.

- *Manslaughter*: the unlawful killing of another without malice aforethought or intent, for example, as the result of negligence, provocation or diminished responsibility.

- *Not guilty by reason of self-defence* (justifiable homicide): killing without evil or criminal intent, for which there can be no blame, such as self-defence to protect oneself.

Abbreviated Version of Stimulus Trial, *Commonwealth of Massachusetts v. Johnson*

Indictment

The defendant Frank Johnson is charged with killing Alan Caldwell with deliberate premeditation and malice aforethought.

The Defendant's Plea

The defendant, Frank Johnson, pleads NOT GUILTY.

Officer Richard Harris

On May 21st at about 11:00 P.M. I was on my usual foot patrol when I heard shouts from the direction of Gleason's Bar and Grill and hurried in that direction. From across the street I saw Caldwell (the victim) hit the defendant Johnson in the face. Johnson staggered back against the wall, then came forward and raised a

---

knife above his head with his right hand. I yelled, "Frank, don't do it." But he plunged the knife downward into Caldwell's chest. Caldwell had fallen to the ground by the time I reached the scene. I apprehended Johnson, phoned for a police cruiser and an ambulance.

Cross-examination. I had a clear view of the fight from across the street approximately 75 feet away. I did not see anything in Caldwell's hand although I could not see Caldwell's right hand which was down by the side away from me. Johnson did not resist arrest, but he did say, "Caldwell pulled a razor on me so I stuck him." (This last statement was declared inadmissible by the trial judge.) The knife Harris retrieved from the ground near Caldwell is introduced as evidence. It measures eleven inches from end to end.

State Pathologist, Dr. Robert Katz

I found the following items on the body of Alan Caldwell: a ring, a watch, and small change in the right front pocket, and a straight razor in the left rear pocket. Caldwell was killed by a stab wound to the heart between the third and fourth ribs. I was unable to determine the angle at which the knife entered Caldwell's chest. His blood alcohol level was .032. This is enough alcohol that Caldwell may have been drunk. Caldwell had numerous surgical scars on his body. There were other scars of undetermined origin. The straight razor is introduced as evidence.

Patrick Gleason

I am the owner of Gleason's Bar and Grill. That night I had occasion to run to the window because there were some shouts outside. Actually, I expected it because I had watched Caldwell and Johnson leave the bar together a few minutes before. Through the window I saw Johnson raise his hand up and stab Caldwell. I didn't see anything in Caldwell's hand. Caldwell and Johnson didn't come to the bar together. First, Johnson and his friend Dennis Clemens arrived at about 9:00 P.M. and later Caldwell arrived. Then later, Caldwell and Johnson were talking at the bar and then they walked outside together. On the way out Caldwell put his watch in his pocket. Earlier in the day Johnson and Caldwell had both been in the bar. At that time they were arguing. Caldwell pulled out a razor and threatened to kill Johnson. A couple of patrons said something to Johnson and he left. That was earlier in the afternoon – before this fight in the evening.

Cross-examination. There was a neon light in the window which partially obstructed my view and I could only see Johnson and Caldwell at an angle. Frank Johnson has a reputation for peacefulness and has never caused trouble in the bar. (The judge does not allow Gleason to testify about Alan Caldwell's reputation.)

Dennis Clemens

I stopped at Frank Johnson's home on the evening of May 21st and asked Johnson to join me for a drink at Gleason's, which is where we usually go. Before we went in the bar, we looked around. We didn't see anything. At about 9:30 P.M. Caldwell entered, and after a while motioned Johnson to come and talk. In a few minutes, Johnson and Caldwell left the bar. I could not hear what they said, but went near the front door which was open. I heard a few shouts, saw Caldwell punch Johnson to the ground, and begin to attack him with a razor. Johnson tried to hold Caldwell off but Caldwell attacked, there was a scuffle, Caldwell staggered back, and after about twenty seconds fell to the ground. I didn't go outside to stop the fight because it happened so quickly.

Cross-examination. Johnson and I did not go to Gleason's looking for Caldwell, and Johnson was reluctant to go into Gleason's until we had assured ourselves that Caldwell was not there. I saw the razor clearly in Caldwell's right hand. I didn't see the knife in Johnson's hand because of the angle of the two men.

Janet Stewart

I am a waitress at Gleason's Grill, and on the night of the fight I noticed both Caldwell and Johnson in the grill before the fight. There was shouting outside. When I ran outside I saw Caldwell on the ground. I also noticed Caldwell's car, which I recognized, was parked illegally in front of the grill and would have obstructed a view of the fight from across the street.

Frank Johnson

I was in Gleason's Grill on the afternoon of May 21st. A woman asked me to give her a ride somewhere the next day. Alan Caldwell immediately came over screaming at me and threatening me; he pulled a razor and threatened to kill me. I was quite upset and frightened and I went home and spent the day with my wife and six children until 9:00 P.M. when Dennis Clemens came by and suggested we go out for a drink. When we got to Gleason's Grill, I was afraid to go in but was finally convinced when we could find no evidence that Caldwell was in the grill. Later Caldwell entered and sat at the bar. Twenty minutes later Caldwell motioned me over in a friendly way and suggested we go outside. Caldwell was calm and friendly and I thought he wanted to talk. Once outside though, Caldwell became angry, threatened to kill me, and then hit me in the face with his right fist. The blow knocked me back against the wall and stunned me but I noticed that Caldwell had pulled his razor again. I unthinkingly reached for my fishing knife, pulled it out and held it in front of me to keep Caldwell away. But Caldwell rushed in with his razor and lunged on the fishing knife. The next thing I remember is Officer Harris arriving at the scene. I almost always carry my fishing knife because I am an avid fisherman and my wife does not like the knife to be lying around where the smaller children may pick it up. I couldn't get away from the fight because I was knocked down and cornered against the wall. I reached for the knife instinctively and tried to protect myself. I didn't mean to kill Caldwell.

Cross-examination. I don't think I had my knife with me in the afternoon but I don't really know because I carry it with me a lot.

Judge's Instructions

Now I want to define the elements of the charges against the defendant. These definitions are essential to determining which verdict you should return. The Commonwealth has charged the defendant with murder in the first degree. You actually have four verdict alternatives: murder in the first degree, murder in the second degree, manslaughter, and not guilty by reason of self defense. Murder in the first degree is a killing committed with deliberately premeditated malice aforethought. Both first and second degree murder require malice aforethought. This includes feelings of hatred or ill will, but is more than that. It means any intentional infliction of an injury where there is a likelihood of causing death. Malice may be inferred from the intentional use of a deadly weapon without just provocation or legal excuse. If you find a killing with malice, then you must return a verdict of at least murder in the second degree. To return a verdict of first degree murder, you must find that the killing was performed with deliberately premeditated malice aforethought. Deliberate premeditation is a sequence of thought processes. You must be convinced that a plan to murder was formed. It is the sequence of thought, not the time taken that determines premeditation; it may take place over weeks, days, hours, or only seconds. First the deliberation and premeditation, then the resolution to kill, then the killing in pursuance of the resolution.

The third verdict alternative is manslaughter. Manslaughter is a killing without malice, a killing resulting from a sudden passion or heat of blood produced by a reasonable provocation or sudden combat. Reasonable provocation requires more than just words or insults or a general dislike or general feeling of anger. Your final verdict alternative is self defense. If you find that the killing was in self defense then the defendant is not guilty of a crime and should be found "not guilty". The right to self defense arises from a threat to one's life but does not come into existence at all until the defendant has exhausted all reasonable means to escape from the confrontation and once the threat is over, the right evaporates. The method one uses to defend oneself can only be reasonable, but this judgment is made with some consideration for the frailties of human impulses in a stress situation. If the defendant does not have a reasonable fear of great bodily harm or has not exhausted all reasonable means of escape or has used more than reasonable force to protect himself, then self defense does not apply and the defendant is guilty of at least manslaughter. Since the defendant has raised the issue of self defense, the burden is on the Commonwealth to prove it was not a situation of self defense. Finally, remember it is your duty to find the defendant guilty of the more serious charge of which he is in fact guilty beyond a reasonable doubt. If the Commonwealth has failed to prove the elements of the charged offenses, it is your duty to find the defendant not guilty.

Pennington & Hastie (1993)

Jurors don't have an easy task. They are faced with a lot of evidence, often presented over several days. This evidence usually appears in a question and answer format which makes it very disconnected. Different witnesses present various pieces of information in no particular order and these witnesses are not allowed to speculate on the reason why people behaved the way they did or on their emotional reactions. The only opportunity the juror has of listening to a coherent tale of events is if the attorney presents it in this way in the opening or closing remarks, but this is not always done.

So how does a juror cope with all this disjointed information in a way that allows him or her to come to a conclusion about guilt or innocence? According to the Story Model, jurors go through three stages in their decision making.

Stage 1: constructing a story

During the first stage, jurors impose a *narrative story organisation* on trial information. This story is constructed from three types of information:

- information acquired during the trial

- knowledge about events that are similar (for example, knowledge about a similar crime in the juror's community)

- expectations about what makes a complete story.

Jurors consider the actual evidence and use this, together with their knowledge of the world, to come to certain conclusions about what is most likely to have happened. This leads to one or more interpretations of the evidence. One of these interpretations, or stories, will be accepted by the juror as the best explanation of the evidence.

A typical sequence of reasoning (suggested by Pennington & Hastie) may go as follows.

- A person who is big and known to be a troublemaker causes people to be afraid.

- Caldwell was big.

- Caldwell *was known to be a troublemaker*.

- Johnson was afraid.

The first proposition represents world knowledge about how people respond when faced with a large aggressive individual. The second one is undisputed evidence. The third proposition is based on a previous inference drawn from what people have said about Caldwell. So far, the jurors are probably all in agreement. The fourth statement is a *conclusion* that might be reached by some jurors (although certainly not all). This is based on the individual's own personal experiences and how they may feel in that situation. This is a reasonable inference and will be tested by the juror in various ways. As an example, we will follow the reasoning of a male juror. First of all, he may consider how he would have felt in a similar situation. He may comment in the way that one mock juror in Pennington & Hastie's study did, that 'If someone like Caldwell came up to me in a bar and threatened me, I would be afraid.' He will also test this version against alternative inferences, for example, that Johnson was angry: 'I don't think Johnson was angry. If he had been angry, he would have gone right back to the bar. He didn't go right back.' This alternative is therefore rejected: 'No, Johnson was afraid of Caldwell and he took his knife with him because he was afraid.'

Different jurors construct different stories. Because all jurors hear the same evidence, variations in story construction are, according to this model, due to differences in experience and beliefs about the social world, that is, differences in world knowledge. For example, another juror might decide that being confronted by a bully is an insult to manly pride and that therefore anger is a more likely response. Their interpretation, based on their own personal experiences, may lead them to a completely different conclusion.

The story that will be accepted by the juror as the best explanation of the evidence is the one that provides the greatest *coverage* of the evidence and is the most *coherent* to that particular juror. The story's coverage is the extent to which the story accounts for the evidence presented at the trial. The greater the story's coverage, the more confident the juror will be. The coherence depends on how consistent, plausible and complete the story is. If there are no contradictions within the story then it is consistent; if it corresponds to world knowledge, then it is plausible; if it has few or no gaps, then it is complete. If it is inconsistent, implausible or incomplete, then it is likely to be rejected.

Having constructed a story, the juror then goes on to the next two stages.

Stage 2: learning verdict definitions

When making a decision about a particular case, rather than simply deciding on guilt or innocence, jurors sometimes have to decide which particular crime, if any, a defendant is guilty of. In the Johnson case, this could be first degree murder, second degree murder, manslaughter or not guilty by reason of self-defence. The jurors have to learn and understand the different verdict categories that might apply in the case they are judging, and for each of these verdict categories, they have to learn what criteria apply. Most of the information for this stage is given to them at the end of the trial in the judge's instructions on the law. These instructions are usually abstract and couched in unfamiliar language. For example, the 'features list' for first degree murder (quoted by Pennington & Hastie) is

IDENTITY:	Right person
MENTAL STATE:	Intent to kill Purpose formed
CIRCUMSTANCES:	Insufficient provocation Interval between resolution and killing
ACTIONS:	Unlawful killing Killing in pursuance of resolution

If the juror has no previous knowledge of the legal categories, then learning this abstract information is extremely difficult. When prior knowledge is available, it is usually through the media, particularly television dramas (episodes of Perry Mason perhaps!) and is likely to be inaccurate and misleading. The juror's task does not get any easier.

Stage 3: Making a decision

Finally, the juror has to match the story he or she decided on in the first stage with the verdict category. For example, the juror may have to think carefully about whether 'pinned against a wall' constitutes a good match for 'unable to escape', for a verdict of not guilty by reason of self-defence.

This stage also involves a decision about what constitutes 'reasonable doubt'. If the match between the story and the verdict categories is not sufficiently convincing, then the jury must reach a verdict of innocence.

The difficult nature of such decision making by a jury is demonstrated by the results of one of the many studies conducted by Pennington & Hastie. Of 16 mock jurors, five found Johnson guilty of first-degree murder; four judged him guilty of second-degree murder; four decided he was guilty of manslaughter and three deemed him not guilty by reason of self-defence (Pennington & Hastie, 1986). So whatever verdict you reached, you are not alone.

Conclusions

In summary, the Story Model proposes that jurors go through three stages in their decision making.

1   They decide on a story that, in their opinion, provides the best account for the events that occurred. This story will depend on the evidence, on world knowledge and on the personal experiences of the juror.

2   In the second stage the jurors are required to learn the verdict categories that could apply in that particular case.

3   Finally they have to find the best fit between the verdict category and the story and come to a conclusion about the guilt or innocence of the defendant.

Pennington & Hastie have tested their model by conducting many studies in which mock jurors are requested to carry out their deliberations out loud. As a result, they have presented substantial empirical evidence in support of the model. Their current research focuses on aspects of the model not yet investigated, such as when exactly the story is created and whether jurors construct several stories and then choose between them, or if they construct just one. This model fits neatly with information processing theories currently popular in cognitive psychology and offers very promising opportunities for understanding the way in which jurors decide on a verdict.

where to now?

The following is a good source of further information on the processes involved in jury decision-making:

▶   **Hastie, R. (ed.)** *Inside the Juror: the psychology of juror decision making*. **Cambridge: Cambridge University Press** – the Story Model is one paper in this very interesting book which covers many of the influences on how juries reach their verdicts.

The interpersonal influences on jury decision making

Once the evidence has been heard, the jury is ushered into a room and given brief instructions by the judge about how to proceed. The judge informs them of relevant legal concepts, tells them about verdict options (whether a majority verdict or unanimous one is required and what that majority must be), instructs the jury members to disregard extralegal factors (such as inadmissible evidence) and advises them on how to conduct their deliberation. What we will now consider are the processes underlying how the final verdict is reached.

Leadership

Before any deliberation takes place, the jury selects a foreman who is responsible for calling for votes, liaising between the judge and jury and announcing the verdict to the court. The foreman is not necessarily a leader in the sense of controlling proceedings or being more influential than others, but more often than not it is the foreman who takes on that role.

Several factors influence who becomes the foreman. Strodtbeck & Hook (1961) conducted a series of impressively realistic simulated jury studies in order to examine in detail the procedures involved. With the co-operation of the court, Strodtbeck and colleagues chose people from a remaining jury pool, used *voir dire* to eliminate the biased ones, played them a recording of the trial and then asked them to retire and reach a verdict. This research, and evidence both from real-life and other mock jury studies, showed that certain people are more likely than others to be chosen as the foreman. In the main, people who have previously served on a jury, those of high socio-economic status and those who spoke first were most likely to be selected. Men rather than women are also preferred as a foreman. Kerr *et al.* (1982) found that in 179 real-life trials in which half the jurors were women, in only 10 per cent of cases was a woman selected as the foreman. Factors other than the individuals involved can also be influential. Strodtbeck *et al.* found that people who sit at the 'head' of a rectangular table are more likely than those sitting at the side to be chosen. This may not, of course, be independent of individual factors, since a confident middle-class man who has served on a jury before may seat himself in such a position. In summary, then, as Ainsworth & Pease (1987) comment '... the person most likely to be chosen as foreman is an upper-class male who sits at the end of the table and opens the discussion. These findings are important as the person elected foreman may have more influence in the group than any other member' (page 71).

Group polarisation and majority influence

The opinions of the majority are hugely influential in the final decisions made within a group and juries are no exception to this rule. Hastie *et al.* (1983) found that if the first decision favoured acquittal, then in 86 per cent of cases a not guilty verdict was returned. If at the outset the majority favoured a guilty verdict, then in 90 per cent of cases, that was the final outcome.

The study of group processes reveals that when a majority of group members favour one side, discussion usually results in the group moving to an even stronger position, a phenomenon known as **group polarisation**. Myers & Kaplin (1976) demonstrated the power of group polarisation on mock juries who were asked to assess the guilt of people accused of traffic offences. The weight of the evidence was varied to make it likely that some juries would have a majority in favour of acquittal while others would favour a guilty verdict. In both groups, discussion increased the strength of feeling in the original direction.

Social psychologists explain group polarisation in terms of the need to make sense of the social world. Many people hold the view that if most people think something is correct then it probably is. Interviews with jurors and studies of mock juries show that the majority has a powerful influence over the minority. The extent of this influence is surprisingly strong, as shown by Asch (1955) whose studies are described in Classic Research. If people are prepared to deny the clear evidence of their own eyes on a simple task, as 75 per cent of the participants in this study did at least once, consider how much more powerful the influence of the majority may be when considering whether they are right or wrong in a far more ambiguous situation. The experience of being in a small minority, especially a minority of one, can create considerable anxiety, which is reduced by conforming to the majority decision.

Studies of conformity such as that by Asch give us valuable insight into the conditions under which a majority may influence a small minority. But jurors do not simply sit round a table and express a single decision, they are involved in a deliberation process during which each member gives his or her own opinion and seeks to influence others. It's time therefore to move to a consideration of how the majority has influence and why this influence is so strong.

The strength of majority influence

Smith & Mackie (1995) suggest that there are several factors which operate in favour of the majority position.

- Firstly, when the majority is offering a certain opinion *the arguments are more numerous* and almost certainly more varied. The minority of the jurors who disagree with the majority are likely to be presented with a set of persuasive arguments that they had not previously considered and this is likely to move them towards the majority view (Hinsz & Davis, 1984).

- Secondly, when information and opinions are shared by several members of a group, they tend to be *discussed for longer* than views held by one person. Stasser & Stewart (1992) devised a situation in which the majority of members of a group shared certain information but other information was only given to a single individual. Even though the group were specifically instructed to discuss all the information, they focused almost entirely on that which was shared, to the almost total exclusion of the non-shared information. This is another reason for majority influence: their opinions receive considerably more discussion.

- Thirdly, majority arguments *are usually more compelling* than minority ones. When several people make the same arguments, it has more impact than one offered by a single individual. People generally believe that if several individuals have come to the same conclusion, then it is more likely to be the correct one. Therefore the arguments that are advanced by the majority of jurors tend to be very persuasive and move the group further towards the extreme of their original opinion.

- Fourthly, majority views tend to be *expressed more convincingly* than minority views. With the benefit of knowing that most people are on their side, members of a majority use a forthright and argumentative style that is compelling (Kerr *et al.*, 1987). Perhaps it is for this reason that members of a majority are viewed as being more confident, logical and intelligent than those of a minority (McLachlan, 1986), resulting in the likelihood that they will convert them. Once again, the end result is group polarisation.

In summary, the majority view is more likely than the minority one to be accepted because this view is expressed more often, is discussed more and in greater depth, seems more compelling and is expressed more persuasively than the opinions of the minority. This quantitative and qualitative advantage leads to group polarisation.

classic
research

what is the effect of a majority influence on a minority?

Asch, S.E. (1955) Opinions and Social Pressure. *Scientific American*, 193 (5), 31–35

Aim: To investigate the effect of a majority influence on a minority of one, using a simple perception task.

Method: This is a laboratory study using a total of 123 participants from three different institutions.

On each series of trials a group of 7–9 young male students were seated at a table to take part in a perception task. Only one of them was a true participant and he was seated in the penultimate or last seat; the remainder were confederates.

The experimenter told them that they would be comparing the lengths of lines and then showed two large white cards. On one there was a single vertical line, called the standard. On the other there were three vertical lines of varying length, one the same length as the standard, the other two substantially different in length from it. The students were asked to choose the one that was the same length as the standard. The students gave their answers in turn, starting at number one and proceeding around the table.

Before the study started, the confederates were requested to give the same incorrect answer on certain crucial trials. On the first two trials they gave the correct answer, and on some of the remaining ones, so as to reduce the possibility of the naive participant suspecting the collusion. There were 18 trials in each series; on 12 of these the majority responded incorrectly. In only a few cases did the participant actually show suspicion: when this happened the experiment was stopped and the results were not counted.

Variations on the basic study:
a) The number of people seated around the table was varied from two (one confederate plus the true participant) to sixteen (fifteen confederates).

b) A single dissenter (placed in a position before the participant) stated the correct answer. The participant was no longer on his own in his judgement.

c) A single dissenter answered differently from the other confederates but incorrectly (he chose the other incorrect card).

Results:
The basic study: An incorrect answer (one that agreed with the majority) was given in 36.8 per cent of the trials.

There were considerable individual differences in the amount of conformity. About 25 per cent of participants never agreed with the incorrect judgements of the majority. In contrast, some individuals went with the majority nearly all the time. Those who were independent did not, as a rule, succumb to the majority even over a large number of trials.

Interviews at the end of the study established different reasons for independence and yielding.

Reasons for independence: Some firmly believed in their own judgements; they were responsive to the majority but were able to recover from doubt and re-establish their equilibrium.

Others believed that the majority was correct but nevertheless felt obliged to 'call the play as they saw it'.

Reasons for yielding: Some believed that they were wrong and the majority was correct.

Others said they did not want 'to spoil your results'. These participants believed that the majority were sheep going along with the first respondent or that the majority were victims of an optical illusion, but these suspicions were not sufficient to make them give an answer they believed to be correct.

Some believed themselves to be deficient and defective and felt they must hide this from the others.

Interestingly, all the yielding participants underestimated the frequency with which they conformed.

The size of the majority: When the true participant was only one of two, he invariably remained independent and did not conform. Conformity rose to 13.6 per cent of trials when there were two confederates and to 31.8 per cent when there were three. After that, the conformity rate remained steady regardless of the size of the majority.

The effect of breaking unanimity: The presence of a supporting dissenter had a striking effect. It reduced the amount of yielding to less than a quarter of what it had been. The fellow dissenter was warmly regarded and felt to inspire confidence. Even when the other dissenter chose a different incorrect response, yielding was reduced, although not as much as with an agreeing dissenter.

Conclusion: The fact that conformity is so strong that people will deny the evidence of their own eyes is a matter of concern. This raises questions about education methods and the values that guide our conduct. Nevertheless, the capacity to be independent should not be underestimated; those who participated agreed without exception that independence was preferable to conformity. Their actions, however, did not match their beliefs.

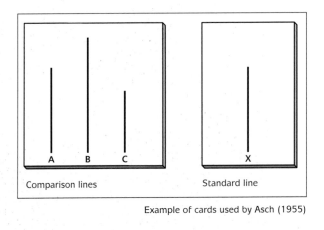

Example of cards used by Asch (1955)

Minority influence

In the classic and brilliant film, *Twelve Angry Men*, a lone juror, played by Henry Fonda, persuades a sceptical jury to change their original view and acquit a young man of a murder charge. For anyone interested in psychology the film makes compulsive viewing. You see the questioning of what appeared originally to be very convincing witness testimony, you experience the raw prejudice of certain jury members and gain insight (as they do) into the causes of their bigoted views.

Real life is seldom as dramatic as the cinematic world and, as we have already seen, minorities in situations such as a jury room rarely win the day. Nevertheless, they do occasionally convert the majority and the way in which this is done has been studied in detail by Moscovici (1976, 1980, 1985). He maintains that the success of minorities is dependent on the *behavioural style* of the individuals involved. If the minority is *consistent* and *flexible* and their arguments are *relevant*, then they may eventually win over the opinions of the majority. The first of these factors, the consistency with which the group defends and advocates its position, is the most crucial. This consistency must be maintained between the minority group and over time. If the minority members agree amongst themselves and continue to do so, they may persuade the majority to question its own assumptions and seriously consider those of the minority. To be successful, those people in the minority must not appear to be rigid and dogmatic but flexible in their

A scene from the film
Twelve Angry Men

approach and willing to discuss the reasons why they disagree with the majority.

Just as we looked at why majorities are influential, it is appropriate to consider why some minorities are successful in converting others to their point of view. Nemeth (1977) suggests that when majorities are faced with a consistent minority sticking to their guns, they are puzzled and try to work out why they are so convinced they are right and so determined to express publicly these unpopular views. The majority is therefore prepared to scrutinise these minority views and, on occasions, be convinced by them. Even when minorities fail to sway people initially, they may start a questioning process which disconcerts the majority and may eventually lead to change.

The character played by Henry Fonda behaved with such consistency and confidence that he swayed the jury. However, in real jury rooms, establishing a minority consensus and maintaining it with consistency and confidence are so difficult that minorities rarely win over majorities.

A unanimous or a majority verdict?

One of the reasons why a minority is rarely influential may be the fact that not all jury decisions have to be unanimous. In Britain a jury does not have to be in total agreement; a majority of 10 to 2 is sufficient to secure a conviction. In the USA the rules vary from state to state, with respect to both the size and unanimity of juries. Nowadays few states allow a less-than-unanimous verdict in criminal trials, although many do so for civil cases.

There are important implications for the interaction of group size and majority verdicts. As mentioned earlier in the chapter, in the ruling *Florida v. Williams* (1972) the US Supreme Court ruled that a 5 to 1 majority was the equivalent of a 10 to 2, citing Asch's work in support of this contention. Even a cursory reflection on this research shows what a gross misinterpretation this is. As Asch's work demonstrated, the presence of one ally (a fellow dissenter) reduced conformity drastically, so a minority of two, even when opposed to 10 people, is much stronger than a minority of one and less likely to be persuaded.

The effect of using a majority versus a unanimous verdict system was investigated in mock trials by Nemeth (1977). He asked student jurors to make decisions about the guilt or innocence of a person charged with murder and organised the juries so that they included some members initially in favour of acquittal and some who were initially predisposed towards conviction. Some juries were required to reach a unanimous verdict while others were allowed to reach a verdict based only on a two-thirds majority. Some significant differences emerged between the two groups. Compared to the majority-verdict groups, those who had to reach a unanimous decision debated for longer, were more likely to take account of minority views and were more confident in their final decision. More significantly, they were also more likely to change from their original judgement. Hastie *et al.* (1983) conducted a similar study using 69 mock juries and requiring either a 12 to 0, a 10 to 2 or an 8 to 4 verdict. Compared to the juries requiring a unanimous verdict, those requiring a majority one spent less time discussing and more time voting and they did not continue any deliberation after the required majority had been reached. As in the previous study, these jurors were less confident and less satisfied with the decisions they had made. Perhaps even more disturbing is the observation by Hastie *et al.* that when a unanimous verdict was not required the jurors who were in the majority used coercive, forceful and bullying tactics to try to persuade those who disagreed with them.

The general opinion of social psychologists is that a majority verdict reduces the effectiveness of juries. There may, however, be some occasions on which it is useful. If, for example, a single bigoted juror insists on sticking to an opinion despite it not being based on any evidence ('I don't care what anyone says, you can tell by looking at that lad that he did it') then at least they can be ignored. Nevertheless, the overall verdict is that expressed by Brehm & Kassim (1996) when they state that 'it is clear that this procedure weakens jurors who are in the voting minority, breeds close-mindedness, inhibits discussion and leaves many jurors uncertain about decisions' (page 487).

where to now?

The following social psychology textbooks contain a section on jury decision making and are good sources of further information on the interpersonal influences involved:

▶ **Brehm S.S. & Kassim, S.M. (1996)** *Social Psychology*, **3rd edition. Boston and Toronto: Houghton Mifflin Company** – see Chapter 12.

▶ **Forsythe, D. (1987)** *Social Psychology.* **California: Brooks/Cole** – see Chapter 10. Although this book is a little dated now, it is brilliantly written and still has many relevant points to make.

▶ **Brigham, J.C. (1991)** *Social Psychology*, **2nd edition. London: Harper Collins** – see Chapter 13.

▶ **Hewstone, M., Strobe, W., Stephenson, G. (eds) (1996)** *Introduction to Social Psychology*, **2nd edition. Oxford: Blackwell** – see Chapter 18.

The effectiveness of juries

In 1979 Baldwin & McConville canvassed the opinions of judges, the police and lawyers for both the defence and prosecution on the verdicts given in 370 jury trials in the UK. The findings were quite disturbing – in 36 per cent of those cases that were acquitted, and in 3.2 per cent of cases involving conviction, the judges had serious doubt about the verdict. In the cases that were acquitted, the police had doubts in 40 per cent of them, the prosecuting lawyer in 26 per cent and even the defence solicitor was doubtful in 10 per cent of cases.

In the United States, Kalven & Zeisel (1966) published an influential work, *The American Jury*, in which they estimated that judge and jury disagreed on 22 per cent of all verdicts. They proposed that jurors, being more inexperienced than judges, were likely to give the benefit of the doubt and incline more towards leniency than did the latter. There seem to be no clear-cut reasons why jury decisions should be so very different from those of members of the judiciary. As long as observation of real-life juries continues to be forbidden, we are unlikely to be any more enlightened on the issue.

The effectiveness of juries can also be compromised by pre-trial publicity, by misunderstanding of the law and, as already mentioned, by group pressures or individual biases. By definition, jurors are ordinary citizens from all walks of life, so it is hardly surprising that there are occasions when they fail to understand the evidence presented. This has caused particular concern in cases of fraud and in some complex medical cases in which the jury finds it so difficult to comprehend the evidence that they tend to rely unduly on the judge's summing up rather than on expert testimony.

In an attempt to increase the objectivity and effectiveness of juries, Wrightsman *et al.* (1994) have put forward a set of recommendations based on empirical evidence and case studies of actual trials:

1   Jury exemptions should be restricted so that juries are more representative of the whole population.

2   The number of peremptory challenges that can be made should be limited, and during *voir dire* the questions should be framed so that they increase the likelihood of an honest response from jurors and reduce the attorneys' ingratiation techniques. Judges, rather than attorneys, should do most of the questioning.

3   To prevent the influence of inadmissible evidence, the trial should be videotaped and edited to remove objectionable material (the researchers acknowledge that this may be impracticable).

4   During deliberation the jury should have access to a transcript or videotape of the trial to which they can refer when questions arise.

5   Jurors should be permitted to take notes during the trial or refer questions to the witnesses.

6   Instructions should be clearly worded, given in written as well as oral form and delivered at the beginning and at the conclusion of the trial. In complex trials in which several verdicts must be given, the questions that the jurors must answer should be put into a logical sequence.

Conclusion

Research into the workings of juries and their effectiveness is difficult to conduct as the observation of real juries during their deliberations is not permitted. Social scientists must therefore rely on the use of mock juries or shadow juries. These methods can never provide a completely valid picture of how juries come to their final verdict but they can and do provide valuable insights into the decision making process. They have been used effectively by Pennington & Hastie in devising a model, known as the Story Model, of how jurors reach decisions.

what do you know?

1   Describe the ways in which psychologists conduct research on trial procedures and court decisions. Evaluate these methods in terms of their advantages and limitations.

2   Using psychological evidence, discuss two characteristics of defendants that may influence jurors in their decision making.

3   Discuss two attributional biases that may affect witnesses in criminal trials.

4   Discuss research into the effect that the size of a jury has on the decision making process.

5   With respect to juries, discuss research into (a) the way in which the majority may influence the minority and (b) the way in which a small minority may influence the majority.

6   Consider the evidence that has been presented on the effectiveness of juries and discuss recommendations of ways in which their effectiveness could be improved.

7

The Treatment of Offenders and Prevention of Crime

what's ahead?

The criminal justice system has many punishments at its disposal. It can sentence offenders to a period of imprisonment or it can use more lenient deterrents such as a suspended sentence, a period of probation, community service or a fine. Imprisonment is a very serious penalty, which is costly for the state and extremely disruptive not only to the lives of the offenders themselves but also to the lives of their families. It is used because, besides protecting the public, it is considered to be the ultimate deterrent. But is it? In this chapter we will consider the effects of both custodial sentences and some non-custodial sentences and assess their relative effectiveness.

Once offenders are imprisoned some of them will be part of a treatment programme aimed at improving their immediate behaviour and reducing the chances of them reoffending. Behaviour modification, social skills training and anger management are the ones we will describe and assess.

Outside the prison, there are many people and agencies working to reduce or prevent crime. The crime rate in New York in the 1980s was escalating at such a rate that the extreme policy of 'zero tolerance' was adopted. Did this policy of clamping down on every petty crime pay off and, if so, were there any significant side effects? Would it be appropriate to adopt such a policy elsewhere, including Britain? We will consider these questions and then assess the effects that the architecture of buildings can have on the crime rate. Could the design of housing estates and high-rise apartments really increase or decrease the opportunity for crime and if so, how? Let's see.

The effect of custodial and non-custodial sentencing

Non-custodial punishments

Fines

The levy of a financial penalty, known as a fine, is the most frequently used punishment, with a million being levied in 1995 (Home Office, *Criminal Statistics*). There are several advantages of using fines rather than other punishments, as suggested by Caldwell (1965):

- they are relatively economical to administer
- they are a source of income for the state; some of this can be used to compensate victims
- they do not prevent the offender from earning a living or caring for dependants
- they do not stigmatise the offender or disrupt family life
- the offender is not exposed to the possible criminalising influence of prisons
- they are an effective deterrent both to the offender and to the rest of the population
- they are flexible – they can be adjusted to suit the offender's ability to pay.

There are a few disadvantages that include:

- the opportunity for others to take on the punishment – fines can be paid by family or friends, so they may not act as a deterrent
- if fines are used to punish regular offenders such as drug addicts or prostitutes, they have no reforming effect
- often the amount levied is not enough to deter people from criminal acts that involve a financial gain, such as drug dealing.

Fines have been found to be more effective than either probation or imprisonment for first offenders and even for a considerable number of recidivists (Feldman, 1993). However, there is always the possibility that if they were used more widely as an alternative to prison, then the crime rate would increase because offenders would remain in the community, free to reoffend.

Probation

Probation is the main type of community penalty and involves the suspension of a sentence while the offender is still under the control of the courts and is supervised by a probation officer. Probation is intended to serve the dual purpose of keeping offenders under surveillance and providing them with help, although the exact aims and objectives have always remained ambiguous and vague. The probation service has traditionally been viewed as the 'decent, caring, face of the criminal justice system' whose significance, Mair (1997) argues, is underestimated by researchers and the general public, yet it serves a vital role. It deals with far more offenders than the prison system does (almost twice as many in 1995) and is far less expensive than a custodial sentence. Besides its relatively low cost, probation has the advantages of not exposing the offender to the criminalising influences of prison or removing his or her ability to earn a living and care for the family.

One of the most significant factors in the development of the probation service was the massive rise in crime from the 1950s onwards and the consequent rise in the prison population which led to serious overcrowding. By the mid-1970s the idea of keeping offenders out of prison was seen as a major objective of the work of the probation service.

In 1996 the Home Office laid out a three-year plan listing its main responsibilities, some of which were:

- to implement community sentences passed by the courts

- to design, provide and promote effective programmes for supervising offenders safely in the community

- to help communities prevent crime and reduce its effects on victims.

The original idea behind the probation service was that each individual probation officer should be responsible for a certain number of offenders to whom they would offer supervision and help, often in the form of a specific treatment programme. This ethos changed somewhat in the late 1970s when the emphasis shifted to the probation service becoming involved in community-based crime prevention initiatives. The probation service was now seen as a service that should be working in high-crime communities, offering social intervention in such areas as housing and employment.

The effectiveness of any punishment is very difficult to assess and is usually done with reference to reconviction rates. Lloyd *et al.* (1994) compared these for prison, straight probation orders and community service orders. They concluded that there was little to choose between these sentencing options in terms of their impact on reoffending. Mair (1997), commenting on this research, notes that 'it may be worth emphasizing that one conclusion which is certainly not sustainable is that prison is more effective than community penalties in terms of reconviction rates' (page 1220).

Imprisonment

Goals of imprisonment

There are four main functions that prisons serve:

1　incapacitation

2　rehabilitation

3　punishment

4　deterrence.

The *incapacitation* of certain prisoners, especially those guilty of serious violent offences, is obviously essential in order to protect other members of the public. There are groups of criminals, however, from whom the public does not need protection, for example, those who get into debt or do not buy a television licence. Heavy reliance on imprisonment as a punishment is very expensive and liable to lead to problems of overcrowding. It also removes or seriously reduces the opportunity for criminals to find worthwhile employment both for the duration of the sentence and thereafter. Since only 8–10 per cent of criminals commit around 50 per cent of all crimes (Peterson *et al.*, 1981), it makes sense to operate a system of selective incarceration, concentrating mainly on high-rate and dangerous offenders. However, it is not always easy to predict who these will be and the selection of such people for incarceration raises problems of justice and fairness in sentencing.

The *rehabilitation* of prisoners entails the use of education, training and treatment to restore them to a useful life in the 'outside world'. The extent to which this is a desirable or practical aim is controversial. In the next section of this chapter, we will take a look at three methods of treatment and consider the extent to which they are effective. It's worth noting that a minority think that prison should not be concerned with attempting to change prisoners and should concentrate mainly on incapacitation and deterrence (Clarke, 1985).

The functions of *punishment* and *deterrence* are inextricably linked. Punishment has always been assumed to be an effective deterrent in all walks of life, no less so in prison than elsewhere. The fear and threat of punishment can act as a deterrent to offending in the first place; an example with which most of us are familiar is the sign in shops warning that 'shoplifters are always prosecuted'. Punishment is also believed to deter criminals from reoffending and to deter the public in general from embarking on a life of crime. However, the very high recidivism rates among ex-prisoners appear to suggest that they are 'schools for crime' rather than effective deterrents, but it seems reasonable to suppose that the threat of punishment does prevent a significant number of people from breaking the law in the first place.

Detention centre inmates

The psychological effects of imprisonment

Bartol (1995) comments that 'clinical case studies on the effects of prison life have often concluded that, for many individuals, imprisonment can be brutal, demeaning, and generally devastating' (page 393).

It is, however, very difficult to generalise about the effects that imprisonment may have on psychological functioning. Firstly, there are considerable individual differences in the way people adjust. Secondly, few controlled longitudinal studies have been conducted. Thirdly, different prisons have very different regimes so there is bound to be a wide variation in effects. Fourthly, both the different length of sentence and the reason for incarceration are likely to have an effect on individual reactions.

A common initial reaction to imprisonment is, perhaps unsurprisingly, one of depression but many offenders soon adjust (Toch *et al.*, 1989). Bukshel & Kilmann (1980) report that symptoms of stress such as sleeplessness, restlessness and anxiety tend to occur at the beginning of the sentence when initial adjustments are being made and towards the end when inmates are perhaps becoming concerned about how they will cope with life outside the institution.

Some researchers report very serious effects on the mental health of prisoners, mainly those convicted of serious violent crimes. For example, Heather (1977) reported psychotic symptoms in a fifth of prisoners sentenced to life. It is not easy to ascertain whether some of these symptoms are related more to the crime than to imprisonment itself. Kruppa (1991) argues that perpetrators of serious crime may experience post-traumatic stress disorder, showing symptoms like flashbacks to the crime and severe depression.

Suicide in jail is unfortunately not uncommon and is an increasing problem; the rate doubled between 1972 and 1987 in England and Wales (Dooley, 1990). Most at risk are young single men during the first 24 hours of confinement. Self-mutilation is another serious problem; Newton (1980) reports that 86 per cent of a group of female delinquents in a training school cut themselves, apparently as a way of becoming part of the inmate culture.

Zamble & Porporino (1988) concluded from their study of Canadian prisoners that very few suffered permanent harm but there was little if any positive behavioural change. Many of the prisoners had led problematic and unstable lives prior to conviction and having to adjust to loss of freedom and other aspects of prison life was yet another hurdle with which they had to cope. Once free, they simply returned to their old ways of surviving.

One aspect of prison life which some inmates have to endure and which can cause particular problems is crowding. It can result in physical illness, socially disruptive behaviour and emotional distress, especially in women's prisons (Bukshel & Kilmann, 1980). Psychological studies in everyday situations have shown that in crowded conditions it is lack of privacy and control that are liable to produce dissatisfaction, not necessarily the amount of space available. If you can put a curtain around your bed to shield yourself from the gaze of others then the psychological effects of being 'cooped up' are not so bad. The same applies in prison. When inmates are provided with the means of obtaining some privacy and a place to put personal possessions, then some of the negative effects of crowding are diminished. This, of course, does not ameliorate all of the unpleasant effects of crowding, which include lack of control over social interaction and too much stimulation in terms of activity, noise, smelliness and violations of personal space.

Effectiveness of prisons

Some research evidence indicates that for many offenders a period of probation is likely to be as effective in preventing reoffending as a custodial sentence. Glaser (1983) reviewed the evidence and concluded that supervision in the community is better for new offenders since prison often encourages and reinforces criminal behaviour. This is particularly true for 'low risk' offenders, especially those who are not only in the early stages of offending but have good job prospects and/or are in stable relationships. On the other hand, a term of imprisonment was more effective in reducing recidivism in habitual offenders.

With respect to the length of the sentence, evidence indicates that longer prison terms are no more effective in reducing reconviction rates than shorter ones. However, this may again depend on the type of prisoner. Walker & Farrington (1981) found that the length of sentence made little difference to rates of reoffending among habitual offenders, more than 85 per cent of whom go on to commit further crimes. Many researchers argue that a minimum amount of intervention has the greatest effect, especially for first offenders. For example, Klein *et al.* (1977) found that cautions were a more effective deterrent than arrests, which were in turn more effective than taking the accused to court.

Davies & Raymond (2000), both members of the judiciary, are highly critical of imprisonment as a means of fulfilling most of the four goals discussed earlier. They do not believe that longer jail sentences deter others and that they are often imposed as a result of public demand and political expediency rather than as a means of reducing crime. Nor, they argue, does the prospect of imprisonment act as a serious deterrent to a large number of people. For example, it is unlikely to deter those who commit crimes whilst under the influence of alcohol or drugs, or who steal to obtain money to support an addiction or who commit 'crimes of passion' when they have lost emotional control. Most studies indicate that when offenders do make rational choices, they weigh up the risk of being caught rather than the sentence they may receive (Indemaur, 1996). Davies & Raymond argue that the evidence that imprisonment achieves any goal except punishment is so unconvincing that it should only be used as a last resort not, as it is in many countries, as an increasingly popular means of coping with crime.

media watch

Horrors grow in Britain's violent jails

The teenager looked the prison governor in the eye. Jailed for a series of petty crimes, he was due to be released the following day. But he was not a reformed character. Nor was he scared of the governor.

'I get out tomorrow,' the youth calmly informed Danny McAllister, who took charge of the Brinsford Young Offenders' Institution, regarded as the most violent jail in Britain, last April. 'Before I go,' the inmate added, 'I'm going to smash up my cell. And there's nothing you can do.'

McAllister told the story last week to illustrate his extreme frustration. 'This young man went off and did just what he said he would. And he was right; there was nothing I could do.'

Last week McAllister was praised for his attempts to turn Brinsford around in an otherwise damning report from Chief Inspector of Prisons Sir David Ramsbotham. But he admits he is swimming against a tide of drug-fuelled violence and the total breakdown of respect for authority.

'We are not dealing with a cross-section of society here,' Ramsbotham said. 'This is a distillation of young men in crisis who have been failed by family, schools and the community. It is very strong stuff.'

The Observer, 4 March 2001

Discussion points

1 In what way might the youngsters have been 'failed by family, schools and the community'?

2 What problems result from using imprisonment rather than other means to deal with the problems of youth crime?

for and against

the use of custodial sentencing

+ It protects society from criminals since the opportunities to reoffend are extremely limited while in jail.

+ It acts as a deterrent to others who may be contemplating breaking the law.

+ In the better prisons, it provides opportunities for rehabilitation.

− It may simply act as a training ground for young offenders to learn more about how to commit serious crimes.

− It may have serious deleterious effects on the mental health of those who are imprisoned.

− Some members of the judiciary argue that jail sentences are often imposed to appease public opinion and that they do not act as a deterrent.

where to now?

The following is a good source of further information regarding the effects of imprisonment:

▶ **Davies, G.L. & Raymond, K.M. (2000) Do Current Sentencing Practices Work?** *Criminal Law Journal* 24, 236–247. Davies is a Judge of Appeal and Raymond an Associate to him, so this article offers a view from 'the bench' of the effects of imprisonment. Both authors are Australian and offer thought-provoking, modern views on the situation from the perspective of a country not often featured in Psychology books.

Some therapies used for treatment of offenders

Behaviour modification

The principles of learning have not only been used in the laboratory but have also been applied in many real-life settings, such as the classroom, mental hospital and prison. The use of operant conditioning in such real-world settings is called behaviour modification, also known as behaviour therapy.

Many behaviour modification programmes rely on a technique called the *token economy*, in which desirable behaviour, such as co-operation and compliance, is reinforced by the use of tokens. These tokens have no intrinsic value but can be exchanged for primary reinforcers. When used in prisons, most of the programmes also involve the use of negative reinforcement and punishment in order to reduce undesirable behaviour such as non-compliance and aggression. Typical negative reinforcers would be removal of privileges, such as watching television or going into the exercise yard, while a typical punishment would be isolation.

Token economy programmes tend to have a direct, short-term effect on specific behaviours. For example, Hobbs & Holt (1976) recorded the effects of introducing a token economy to young delinquents across three small institutional units while the fourth unit acted as a control. Tokens were given for behaviours such as obeying rules, doing chores properly, co-operative social interactions and appropriate behaviour when queuing for meals. Extra positive reinforcers such as soft drinks, sweets, leisure activities, cigarettes and passes home were also used. The programme showed a significant increase in the targeted behaviours compared to the group not involved in the programme. Other studies show that token reinforcement also works with adult prisoners (Ayllon & Millan, 1979). However, Ross & Mackay (1976) reported a deterioration in behaviour when such a programme was used with delinquent girls, but such results are unusual.

Although these programmes are popular, especially in the US, not many of them have been evaluated in terms of the conduct of the offenders after release. Moyes *et al.* (1985) reported limited success with hospitalised behaviourally disordered males and females with a criminal history. After a year they had had fewer contacts with the police than a control group of similar patients, but after two years there was no difference. One long-term follow-up failed to find any benefit at all of the token economy programme (Rice *et al.*, 1990).

The advantages of behaviour modification are that:

- It is successful in changing specific behaviours under controlled conditions.

- It requires little training and can be done by paraprofessionals.

- It is economical.

- It quickly controls unmanageable behaviour.

- It can be easily evaluated and researched.

However there are several problems and limitations with its use:

- It requires a high degree of commitment from everyone who is evenly remotely involved in the programme.

- Although relatively simple to operate in controlled conditions, it is extremely difficult in an actual prison. There are many other sources of reinforcement and punishment, such as approval of other prisoners or threats by them.

- Its effects have not convincingly been shown to generalise from institutions to life in the real world.

Perhaps the most important concern with behaviour modification is its potential for violation of civil rights. Many programmes rely heavily on negative reinforcement (such as the removal of privileges until the offender complies) rather than positive ones, with little or no emphasis on new skills. There are ethical objections to prisoners having to 'earn' basic rights, such as recreation time, by behaving compliantly.

Opinion on the use of behaviour modification is sharply divided. Some researchers argue that offenders need to feel responsible for their treatment, not have it imposed on them. Others maintain that such programmes make the whole prison environment more bearable and humane for all concerned; after all, the behaviours that are targeted for reduction are those that hurt others and make life unpleasant in the institution.

Social skills training

Social skills are those skills such as making eye contact, standing a certain distance from someone and turn-taking during conversation which make social interactions run smoothly. We learn them as children and take them for granted as adults. If we do not have these skills or if we use them clumsily, we make others and ourselves feel extremely uncomfortable, as anyone who has tried to have a conversation with an individual who makes no eye contact or stands too close is all too well aware. Many offenders are believed to be lacking in these skills and social skills training is a technique aimed at improving the competence of offenders in dealing with social interactions. The programmes are based on the assumptions that being deficient in these skills is associated with offending and that acquiring such skills will reduce rates of reoffending. Neither of these assumptions has gone unchallenged.

Social skills training (SST) is one of a number of cognitive-behavioural programmes which are all based on the principle that attitudes and thoughts (cognitions) affect behaviour. There is a variety of SST programmes, all of which have certain common elements. Clients are first taught the skills by a combination of modelling, instruction, role play and rehearsal. They then attempt to re-enact these skills themselves in various arranged situations and receive feedback on their performance, the emphasis being on the use of social reinforcement such as praise. They are also given homework assignments which aim to help them practise and consolidate the skills they have learned in various situations, including real-life ones for those who are not incarcerated.

Some programmes start by teaching certain non-verbal skills, known as micro-skills, such as eye contact, gesture and posture and then move on to all-round skills such as how to maintain a good conversation, how to interact with members of the opposite sex or how to negotiate (e.g. Hollin *et al.*, 1986). The type of situation that might be practised is how to enter a room full of strangers, how to return faulty goods to a shop, how to politely decline getting involved in a drinking binge when you've already had enough, and how to say what you want to say without being embarrassed and 'tongue-tied'.

Results of SST

Feedback from social skills training programmes is mixed. Goldstein (1986) reviewed 30 studies of SST used with aggressive or delinquent teenagers and found that various skills such as the use of appropriate eye contact and how to negotiate with a probation officer had been learned. However, Goldstein *et al.* (1989) found that only 15–20 per cent of trainees could use the skills they had learned during training in a more real-life situation. These researchers did, however, manage to increase this to 50 per cent by providing additional teaching.

Some other programmes report improved self-esteem and a feeling of greater control over life (a shift to a more internal locus of control) (Spence & Marziller, 1981). However, in this programme, individuals in a control group who received no training but spent an equal amount of time discussing their problems showed an equivalent improvement in self-esteem, so perhaps attention alone is the key to improvement. With respect to locus of control, Hollin *et al.* (1986) found no change in individuals to whom they gave SST.

Rates of recidivism (reconviction) are a more long-term measure of effectiveness of SST. When the offending records of individuals in the Spence & Marziller programme were examined six months later, the SST group did have a lower level of conviction, but when asked about offending this group reported having committed more offences. There is evidence that both the appearance of a suspect and their general demeanour (bearing and expression), including the amount of respect shown, can affect whether an adolescent is detained by the police for questioning (Piliavin & Briar, 1964). In this case, it may be that the lads trained in SST were better at talking to the police and therefore less likely to be arrested.

There have been very few studies that have investigated the effects of SST on recidivism. Hollin (1990) has made two important points in this respect. Firstly, there simply is no research to show whether or not lack of social skills is associated with offending and secondly, in some SST programmes, there has been no evidence that the participants who received it were actually lacking in the skills in the first place.

It seems reasonable to conclude that short-term changes in social behaviour can be achieved with SST, but it has yet to be shown that they are either long-lasting or that they can be generalised to real-life situations. As Blackburn (1993) suggests, it may be a useful programme for offenders who have very serious social difficulties, but 'the available evidence does not warrant the routine use of SST in correctional settings' (page 357). Hollin (1990) also comments that SST alone is unlikely to be a cure for crime but it can be a powerful means of personal change.

Anger management

Anger management programmes are based on the idea that anger is a primary cause of violent criminal acts and once offenders can learn to control this anger, bad behaviour in prisons will decrease, as will rates of recidivism. Anger management is a cognitive-behavioural approach, which originated in North America in the mid-1970s. Its aim was to teach individuals how to apply self-control in order to reduce interpersonal anger (Towl, 1993, 1995), with the long-term goal of reducing disruptive behaviour (Law, 1997).

There is a variety of such programmes which are run in many prisons as well as in other settings. One anger management programme used in Britain is outlined below in What's New.

what's new?

the National Anger Management Package

Keen (2000) provides an example of the preparation and delivery of an anger management course within a young offender institution, conducted with young male offenders aged between 17 and 21 years. The programme, first devised in 1992 and updated in 1995, was developed by the Prison Service in England and Wales and is known as the National Anger Management Package (Prison Service, 1995).

The aims of the course are as follows:

- to increase course members' awareness of the process by which they become angry
- to raise course members' awareness of the need to monitor their behaviour
- to educate course members in the benefits of controlling their anger
- to improve techniques of anger management
- to allow course members to practise anger management during role plays.

The course involves eight two-hour sessions, the first seven over a 2–3 week period, with the last session a month afterwards. The details of the course are as follows (for more details see Towl & Crighton, 1996).

Keen's experiences of using the course are generally positive, though there are various predictable problems with young incarcerated males, such as failure to bring the anger diary to sessions, grins and sniggers at the mention of 'bodily arousal' and a certain degree of egocentrism which can make relationships and progress in the group a little difficult at times. Overall, though, the feedback from the individuals completing the course indicates that they have increased their awareness of their anger management difficulties and have increased their capacity to exercise self-control.

Results of anger management programmes

With the increasing use of anger control programmes in prisons, it is crucial to determine its effectiveness. Studies of effectiveness are few, and the results range from very limited to substantial. On the negative side, Law (1997) reported that only one individual who completed an eight-session course showed any improvement. In contrast, Hunter (1993) reported considerable improvements in certain specific areas, such as a reduction in impulsiveness, depression and interpersonal problems. The effectiveness of programmes in producing these short-term benefits is shown in Research Now.

research now

do anger management courses work?

Ireland, J. (2000) Do Anger Management Courses Work? *Forensic Updates*, 63, 12–16.

Aim: To assess the effectiveness of a brief group-based anger-management programme with a sample of male young offenders.

Method: A quasi-experimental design was used in which there were two comparisons made:

- pre- and post-programme scores for a 'treatment' (experimental) group
- two scores taken at the same interval for the 'awaiting treatment' (control) group.

The design: This is a quasi-experimental design because the two groups are not equivalent. In real-world research it is not possible to randomly assign individuals to each group. It would have been possible to carry out research using the experimental group only, comparing pre- and post-programme scores but the control group gives the design extra experimental rigour.

The participants: The experimental group consisted of 50 prisoners who had completed the anger management course. The control group consisted of 37 prisoners who had been assessed as suitable for the course but had not yet completed it. The two groups did not differ significantly in terms of age, offence and level of angry behaviours reported prior to completing the course.

The programme: The anger management used in this study was an adapted version of the national package which was developed in the UK by Clark (1988). It includes 12 one-hour sessions run over a three-day period.

Measures used to assess prisoners on suitability for the course: There were two measures:

1   A cognitive-behavioural interview. This consisted of various questions concerned with how often they lost their temper, what provoked this temper loss and what happened when it occurred.

2   Wing Behavioural Checklist (WBC) – a checklist completed by prison officers concerning 29 different angry behaviours with scores of 0, 1 or 2 for how often any particular prisoner had shown them in the previous week.

3   A third measure, the Anger Management Assessment questionnaire (AMA), which was a self-report questionnaire completed by the prisoners, consisted of 53 items which could indicate an anger problem.

All prisoners in the study had been deemed suitable for the course on the basis of these measures.

Pre- and post-test measures: Pre-test scores were obtained for both groups of participants two weeks before the start of the course and eight weeks later (after course completion for the experimental group and while the control group remained on the waiting list).

Results:
Wing-based measures: There was a significant reduction in wing-based angry behaviours in the experimental group but no difference in the control group.

AMA: The experimental group scored significantly lower on self-reported angry behaviours after completion of the course. There was no difference for the control group.

Overall, 92 per cent of the prisoners in the experimental group showed improvement on at least one measure; 48 per cent showed improvement on both the AMA and WBC; 8 per cent showed a deterioration on both measures after completing the course.

Conclusion: Short-term measures indicate that this programme was a success and significantly reduced the disruptive behaviour of these offenders in the prison. Future research could usefully be directed at assessing the characteristics of the 8 per cent who showed no improvement. There is also a need for future research aimed at long-term evaluation of such interventions.

Evaluation of anger management programmes

The effectiveness of anger management programmes to reduce recidivism in violent offenders is called into question by several researchers. Although it may seem common sense to propose that anger is a serious problem among those convicted of violent crimes such as assault, researchers disagree about whether there is a link between anger and violent crime. For example, while Zamble & Quinsey (1997) argue in favour of such a relationship and propose that uncontrolled anger is a risk factor in predicting violence and recidivism, others dispute it (e.g. Muirhead, 1997).

Prominent amongst those who do not believe that anger is a primary cause of violent criminal acts are Loza & Loza-Fanous (1999). They argue that many of the research findings linking anger with violence and rape were based on laboratory studies using students (e.g. Zillman, 1993) or offenders' own explanations of their violent acts (Zamble & Quinsey, 1997). In fact they maintain that

> '*Unfortunately, most of the opinions supporting a link between anger and violent behaviour, rape, or recidivism are based on speculations with very little empirical support such as results of valid and reliable psychometrics.*' (page 492)

They studied 271 Canadian male offenders, comparing a group of violent offenders with non-violent ones and a group of rapists with non-rapists. Violent offenders were those who had committed crimes such as murder, assault and robbery with violence. The non-violent offenders had a history of moderate or minor offences such as fraud or property offences. Using several psychometric measures of anger, they found no difference between violent offenders and non-violent offenders and between rapists and non-rapists on anger measures. Loza & Loza-Fanous argue that not only are anger treatment programmes ineffective with violent offenders, they have the potential to be harmful by encouraging the offender to attribute his violent actions to anger for which he cannot be blamed, rather than taking full responsibility for his actions.

Anger management programmes have, as we have seen, proved to be useful in controlling aggressive antisocial behaviour in prisons, but there needs to more research into the relationship between anger and crime before an assessment of its use and effectiveness in reducing rates of recidivism amongst violent criminals can be made.

for and against

anger management as an effective treatment for criminal behaviour

+ Some research shows that these programmes are an effective means of reducing antisocial behaviour in prisons.

+ The programmes may provide criminals with greater insight into the causes of their behaviour and offer alternative ways of responding to provocation.

— Some researchers argue that there is no link between anger and violent crime, which is often done in a cold, calculated manner.

— There is a lack of research into whether or not these programmes have any long-term benefits in preventing recidivism.

where to now?

The following is a useful source of further information regarding anger management courses:

▶ **Loza, W. & Loza-Fanous, A. (1999) The Fallacy of Reducing Rape and Violent Recidivism by Treating Anger,** *International Journal of Offender Therapy and Comparative Criminology,* **43(4), 492–502** – this gives an interesting evaluation of anger management courses which is complementary to the Research Now article, allowing you to appreciate two very different angles on the use of such courses.

Zero tolerance

One method by which crime has been tackled is the use of a policy known as zero tolerance. Zero tolerance policing has its roots in an approach nicknamed 'broken windows', developed by Kelling & Wilson in 1982. They argued that if one broken window was not repaired in a building, then others would be broken and the building vandalised, followed by other buildings, then the street and the neighbourhood. The area would soon go into rapid decay and act as a breeding ground for serious crime such as drug dealing and prostitution. This would lead to a downward spiral in which respectable law-abiding citizens would leave the area and crime rates would escalate. An unrepaired window is a sign that no one cares and therefore more damage will occur.

The original idea behind broken windows was that there should be more police 'on the beat', who negotiated acceptable public behaviour and worked with the neighbourhood to maintain a decent standard of behaviour. However, since this thesis was first proposed, zero tolerance policing has become a much more punitive policy, based on cracking down on minor offences such as offensive language, loitering and begging, in the belief that this will help reduce more serious crimes as well.

The term 'zero tolerance' eventually was applied to other areas of public policy, some of which were concerned not so much with policing as with changing attitudes. One such policy was a campaign against domestic violence, sexual assault and child abuse in various countries including Britain.

We will take a look at two programmes based on zero tolerance: the first one is a campaign in New York to reduce the very high crime rates by a severe clampdown on all crime; the second is a community-based project designed to prevent violence against women.

Zero tolerance in New York

The argument in favour

By the late 1980s and early 1990s, New York had the unenviable reputation of being one of the most crime-ridden cities in the world. William Bratton, who eventually became Police Commissioner of the City of New York, describes his experience in arriving in New York in 1990:

> 'I remember driving from LaGuardia Airport down the highway into Manhattan. Graffiti, burned out cars and trash seemed to be everywhere. It looked like something out of a futuristic movie. Then as you entered Manhattan, you met the unofficial greeter for the City of New York, the Squeegee pest. Welcome to New York City. This guy had a dirty rag or squeegee and would wash your window with some dirty liquid and ask for or demand money. Proceeding down Fifth Avenue, the mile of designer stores and famous buildings, unlicensed street peddlers and beggars everywhere. Then down into the subway where every day over 200,000 fare evaders jumped over or under turnstyles while shakedown artists vandalised turnstyles and demanded that paying passengers hand over their tokens to them. Beggars were on every train. Every platform seemed to have a cardboard city where the homeless had taken up residence. This was a city that had stopped caring about itself ... The City had lost control.' (pages 33–34)

Once Bratton had taken up his position in 1994, the problems were tackled on many fronts. Seven thousand extra police officers had been employed since 1990 and a programme of clear-cut goals and priorities was begun. In addition to serious crime, particular attention was to be paid to actions that interfere with quality of life (such as public drinking), graffiti and other minor street crime. Crime hotspots were to be identified to which patrol officers, detectives and narcotics officers were assigned. Twice-weekly meetings were held at which the Department's top executives were called to account for the previous month's crime statistics and asked about plans for the following month.

In three years the city's crime rate dropped by 37 per cent and the homicide rate by over 50 per cent. In answer to critics who suggested that crime rates were somehow massaged, Bratton responded by pointing particularly to the figures for homicide which is a crime that cannot easily be covered up or over-reported. He believes that this approach, involving as it does decentralisation and co-ordination, is a successful way of policing, as borne out not only by the crime statistics but also by the fact that New Yorkers now feel safer and the city is slowly revitalising itself. Long-term problems still exist but the foundations for dealing with them have been firmly laid.

Problems in New York City

The argument against: short-term fix, long-term liability?

Pollard (1998), the Chief Constable of Thames Valley Police, urges caution in the use of the policy of zero tolerance. He argues that the crime reduction in New York is not necessarily a direct result of this policy, since crime has fallen elsewhere in America, including cities such as San Diego in which the approach is very different. The success in New York, he maintains, may be due in no small part to an extra 7,000 police officers (a huge increase), greater accountability and an enormous pressure to reduce crime such that the rates would have fallen regardless of the particular policy adopted.

Pollard describes zero tolerance as being aggressive, uncompromising law enforcement based on ruthlessness in cracking down on low-level crime and disorderliness, including acts which are not, strictly speaking, criminal, such as drinking but not being drunk, and vagrancy that involves lying on the edge of a pavement but not blocking pedestrian access. More worryingly, it may involve the harassment of the mentally disturbed who are doing nothing other than causing discomfort in others by their strange behaviour. It is interesting to note that whilst Pollard describes zero tolerance as based on heavyhanded aggressive tactics Dennis (1998) describes it as 'humane, good-natured control'.

While not disagreeing at all with the philosophy behind the 'broken windows' approach, Pollard argues that this theory was based on a solution to crime that includes a wide variety of tactics, with the police working in close co-operation with other social agencies, rather than a quick, uncompromising response to petty crime and disorder. Without this the policy creates an atmosphere of distrust between the police and public which destroys any opportunity for future effective policing. 'Going in heavy' provides a short-term fix at the expense of a long-term solution and can become positively counter-productive. As Pollard says, once this policy has been operational for some time,

> 'It may then be too late. Firstly, the police will have lost touch with the community. Confidence will have drained away. Tensions will have risen. It will then need only a spark to ignite serious disorder, as happened in Los Angeles following the Rodney King case. We know about these in England too. They happened in our own inner cities in the 1980s, and we have learned hard lessons of our own.' (pages 55–56)

Pollard points out that decay and disorderliness in a neighbourhood have many causes and these need to be tackled in a co-ordinated way, not just by papering over the cracks. This can only be done if the police work in close co-operation with many other agencies, such as with the refuse collection service so that the area is tidy, with the education and youth departments, with social services and the probation department, to name but a few. In this way it is not just the physical environment that is attended to but other problems as well such as the lack of amenities for the young, design of buildings that encourage crime (such as those described in the next section) and the failure of public services. Such a policy tackles the root causes of crime and disorder rather than offering a superficial solution.

It is very difficult to make objective judgements on the success of any policy because each era and area is different. Comparisons between America and Britain are especially difficult not least because of the gun culture in the States which does not exist in Britain. With respect to New York, this is a unique city – Pollard himself acknowledges that Bratton was faced with a crisis that required drastic action and that he should be congratulated on his success. He does, however, urge great caution in assuming that a policy of zero tolerance would necessarily be the best policy elsewhere.

Zero tolerance applied to violence against women

The first UK project based on zero tolerance was launched by Edinburgh City Council in November 1992 and run by the Zero Tolerance Charitable Trust (ZTCT). This ongoing campaign aims to highlight the prevalence and nature of male violence towards women and to challenge some of the attitudes that made it appear acceptable.

The need to change attitudes was revealed in research undertaken by the Trust. They interviewed over 2,000 young people aged between 14 and 21 years in Glasgow, Fife and Manchester. The results were quite shocking. Half of the boys and a third of the girls thought there were some circumstances in which it was acceptable to hit a woman or force her to have sex. Over a third of boys (36 per cent) thought they might use violence in future relationships and both boys and girls thought that forced sex was more acceptable than hitting. Over half of the young people interviewed knew someone who had been hit by a male partner and exactly half knew someone who had been sexually abused (Burton et al., 1998). Group discussions revealed that although hitting women was considered 'unmanly' and 'cowardly', it was seen as okay to hit your wife if she nagged; one young man commented that 'Some women just need a slap to the jaw and put into the bedroom to calm down.' It is interesting to note that the young people who took part in these focus group discussions welcomed the opportunity to express their opinions and discuss issues in depth, rather than simply being told that certain types of behaviour are wrong.

The Trust tackles the problem of male violence to women on many fronts. It lobbies the Government, commissions research and develops educational intervention and training programmes. It has initiated a three-year advertising campaign to raise awareness and change attitudes, including a series of television advertisements, which began in December 2000. It also provides quality practical support for abused women and children.

One such programme targeted at school children and started in January 2001 is known as *Respect*. It involves the development of primary and secondary curriculum materials, support materials for teachers and youth workers and a publicity campaign involving school posters and bus side advertising. The idea is to prevent violence before it happens. It encourages boys and girls to develop healthy relationships based on equality and mutual respect, and emphasises that violence against women is unacceptable in any context and should not be tolerated.

At present it is too early to evaluate the effect of *Respect*, but it appears to be a very necessary and positive step on the road both to educating youngsters and to encouraging a healthier, more positive and happy attitude not only to women but to relationships in general.

where to now?

The following are good sources of further information on zero tolerance:

▶ **Dennis, N. (ed.) (1998)** *Zero Tolerance. Policing a Free Society* **(2nd edition), IEA Health and Welfare Unit. Lancing: Hartington Fine Arts Ltd** – a series of papers written by various members of the criminal justice system and academic departments on both sides of the Atlantic, though mainly in Britain. It contains classic papers by Dennis and Bratton and a useful editorial discussing the principal issues surrounding zero tolerance.

▶ **www.cabinet-office.gov.uk/womens-unit/fear** – a Home Office site that looks at zero tolerance projects concerned with violence towards women across the country.

▶ **www.zerotolerance.org.uk/splash.htm** – the website address of the Zero Tolerance Charitable Trust and provides details of their various projects.

The Zero Tolerance Charitable Trust is at 25 Rutland Street, Edinburgh, EH1 2AE and will provide full reports of its work.

Environmental crime prevention

The work of Jane Jacobs

In 1961 Jane Jacobs, an architectural journalist, published a book which changed the focus of criminology from a view that placed the blame on the disposition of the criminal to one that looked at the development of many urban areas as a possible cause of many of the problems involved in crime. In a swingeing attack, Jacobs blamed urban planners for 'making cities unsafe places, where vandals, robbers and other street criminals could ply their unnatural trades without fear of apprehension' (Gilling, 1997). She argued that the more modern parts of many US cities, with their separate zones and physical barriers, encouraged a fortress mentality rather than community spirit. This was in contrast to the older urban quarters in which crime rates remained relatively low because, although they may be 'slum' areas, the narrow streets with lots of doorways in which to stop and talk meant that there was plenty of social interaction; streets and parks were widely and more frequently occupied as places of both work and leisure. She recommended that, in order to reduce crime,

- buildings should be orientated towards the street so that natural surveillance occurred

- there should be a clear demarcation between public and private areas so that the public ones could be protected by paid employees and the private ones valued by their owners

- semi-public outdoor space (such as lawns and play areas) should be located near areas that were easily overlooked so that they were less likely to be vandalised.

Jacobs was at pains to point out that she was not offering a universal panacea to urban crime since, in her opinion, it was essential to address the social ills that lay behind delinquency and crime; however, she did maintain that the design of cities was no small contributor to these problems. Her suggestions for crime prevention were not well received by the criminal justice system. This may have been partly due to prejudice. Her ideas were revolutionary and the solutions she offered were more dependent on architects and planners than on the criminal justice system. They were also being proposed by a female 'outsider' to this justice system.

There were, however, some legitimate objections to this work, the main one being that Jacobs may have had a rather romantic notion of pre-modern urban districts as friendly, community-spirited, crime-free areas. There is evidence that rather than reduce crime, increased street activity may well result in more opportunities for it. Furthermore, her ideas were inspirational rather than based on scientific evidence.

Nevertheless, despite its limitations, Jacobs' work offered a very different and previously neglected focus on the causes and prevention of urban crimes.

The work of Oscar Newman

Rather better received was the work of Oscar Newman who developed Jacobs' ideas into his **defensible space theory** (Newman, 1972). Newman pointed out that many new high-rise developments went into rapid decay with high rates of residential dissatisfaction. He suggested that this was caused by the design of the housing projects because they offered little opportunity for residents to defend any secondary territory within or around buildings. Newman coined the term *defensible space* to describe the bounded or semi-private areas surrounding living quarters that residents can territorialise so that they appear to belong to someone. Newman pointed out that the design of many urban residential areas, especially those around high-rise apartment buildings, meant that there was a lack of defensible space which tended to encourage vandalism and crime because the residents had such limited opportunity for surveillance or social control and no real sense of ownership or community. Lack of surveillance was caused by several factors.

- Buildings housed large numbers of people with many entrances, all of which gave access to the whole building. With such frequent pedestrian traffic, residents could not be distinguished from outsiders who could, once in the building, move freely within it using the undefended staircases.

- The areas between the buildings were desolate open spaces with no territorial markings.

- The height of the buildings meant that there were 'corridors' of space between them that could not be overlooked from the windows.

Newman argued that if defensible spaces are created through design, then residents are more likely to feel ownership of them, informally keep surveillance over them and have a sense of social cohesion amongst themselves.

Elevator waiting area in the high-rise buildings of a housing project in Philadelphia

He advanced several recommendations to increase defensible space and thereby reduce crime. These were

- the use of boundary markers (real or symbolic barriers, such as pathways, small walls or fences) to reduce the likelihood of intrusion so that residents had control over the outside areas adjacent to their homes and over hallways and staircases

- planning which enabled surveillance of these semi-public areas, for example by the strategic placement of windows

- a design which encouraged positive social attitudes and a sense of community such that residents felt that the area was theirs and worth looking after; such housing should not be stigmatised and should not be designed to set it off from other types of housing such that it was easily identified as housing for the poor

- projects should be sited in low-crime areas.

Entry buffer area at an apartment block in Philadelphia

Support for Newman's theory was drawn from a study in which he looked at crime rates in 100 estates in New York and found that the greater the amount of defensible space, the lower the incidence of crime. Further support was offered by a comparison he made between two adjacent housing estates in New York City, that of Van Dyke and Brownsville. Although Brownsville was eight years older than Van Dyke, it had a far lower crime rate. The design of this development meant that it had a considerable amount of defensible space. It consisted of six X-shaped buildings with some three-storey wings and entrances which, being used by a relatively small number of families, were easy to keep an eye on. Anyone approaching an entrance could be seen from any one of a large number of windows. Within the buildings the hallways and stairwells were easily monitored; children played on them and residents often left their doors ajar. This greater defensibility meant that there were strong bonds between the neighbours and a positive attitude towards the location and the police, as well as lower maintenance and crime rates. Van Dyke, in contrast, consisted of mostly large 14-storey buildings separated by open spaces that provided little or no defensible space. A similar project, that of Pruitt-Igoe in St Louis, which was designed to reduce crime and vandalism by incorporating open areas between buildings and vandal-proof fixtures, had become such a ruined wasteland that it had to be demolished.

Central grounds of Van Dyke Houses

Entrance to Van Dyke Houses – no defensible space, high crime rates and a 'run down' appearance

Brownsville Houses from the street – a considerable amount of defensible space and low crime rates

Further support for Newman's theory comes from a project in Ohio (reported in Bell *et al.*, 1996) in which a neighbourhood called Five Oaks was split from one large residential area into several small ones by the blocking of certain streets and alleys and the use of speed bumps. Once these 'mini-neighbourhoods' were established, crime rates decreased by 26 per cent. However, the use of barriers to separate areas into smaller units and restrict access has been heavily criticised by some groups who see this as a means of restricting the access of poorer people to higher-income areas.

Criticism of Newman's ideas

Newman's work has provided a commonsense and practical approach to crime prevention but it is not without its critics. The relationship between crime rates and defensible space is only correlational and therefore does not demonstrate cause and effect. Furthermore, as

Repetto (1976) pointed out, we should be cautious about any theory heavily dependent on a single case study (the comparison between Brownsville and Van Dyke), especially since there were many other housing projects that could have been studied but were not. Other factors may also have been neglected in the analysis of crime rates. Mawby (1977), in a study based in Sheffield, found that while business premises based in the lower floors of residential high-rise buildings did indeed suffer from higher crime rates, this was because of greater reporting of crime rather than design features.

Taylor *et al.* (1980) suggest that Newman's model is inadequate because it does not take sufficient account of other social factors – such as the number of families on welfare – which could have contributed to the different crime rates. They contend that sociocultural variables and social conditions, as well as design, determine the level of crime in any neighbourhood. Merry (1981) suggests that defensible space is necessary for crime prevention but it is not enough on its own. Even when the architecture of a site lends itself to defensible spaces these may not be defended if there is a heterogeneous ethnic mix of residents which results in them not intervening in each other's affairs.

Several studies indicate that there are certain social factors which may, at least in some cases, have a greater impact on crime than defensible space does. Wilson (1980) found that rates of vandalism are most closely correlated with the number of children living in an area: the more children, the more vandalism.

Newman himself now acknowledges that social variables, such as the percentage of families on welfare benefits, the percentage of single-parent families, the income level and the ratio of teenagers to adults, are more closely related to crime rates than are the design features of the immediate environment. However, even though defensible space may not be the best explanation for crime, it offers a very practical way of improving things.

In Britain

Like America, Britain has had considerable problems with housing projects that were at one time considered to be 'Utopian' (Coleman, 1990). Jephcott & Robinson (1971) conducted a large-scale study of high-rise developments in Britain, interviewing nearly 1,000 residents of 168 multistorey blocks. There tended be an equal number of likes and dislikes, with likes being the interiors of the flats and features independent of design such as a good bus service and local amenities. The dislikes, on the other hand, were very much rooted in the design features inherent in high-rise blocks: the lifts, the loneliness and isolation, the entrances, vandalism, noise, poor maintenance and problems of refuse disposal.

Alice Coleman, a defender of Newman's theory, has extended the work on defensible space and points to various design features (namely number of storeys, number of dwellings per entrance, number of dwellings per block, overhead walkways and spatial organisation) which she believes encourage all manner of antisocial behaviour. She maintains that some design features promote child crime by undermining the normal child-rearing practices that operate when residences are separate and do not incorporate shared space (Coleman, 1990). She compared housing estates with blocks of flats (apartments) in terms of litter, graffiti, vandal damage, children in care, urine pollution and faecal pollution. The 3,893 houses surveyed showed far less sign of social breakdown than purpose-built flats. Litter was less common, graffiti extremely rare and excrement virtually unheard of. Like those before her, Coleman acknowledges that design is not the only factor in the promotion or prevention of social breakdown but thinks that criminology would do well not to ignore its probably considerable influence.

where to now?

The following are good sources of further information regarding environmental crime prevention:

▶ **Gilling, D. (1997)** *Crime Prevention, theory, policy and politics*. **London: UCL Press Limited** – provides an up-to-date account of crime prevention. Chapter 3 is concerned with environmental crime prevention.

▶ **Bell, P.A.** *et al.* **(1996)** *Environmental Psychology* **(4th edition). Harcourt Brace** – this contains a section on environmental problems and possible solutions. Chapter 10 in particular discusses revitalisation of residential areas.

▶ **Newman, O. (1972)** *Defensible Space*. **New York: Macmillan** – this is a classic text well worth looking at not only for the text but also for the photographs which illustrate the theory wonderfully well. Even a cursory flick through the illustrations brings the whole theory to life.

Conclusion

Neither the treatment of offenders nor the prevention of crime is easy to achieve. There is little evidence that imprisonment is more effective than non-custodial punishments in reducing rates of recidivism, but valid evaluation of effectiveness is very difficult to achieve. Programmes designed to treat offenders in prisons, such as behaviour modification, social skills training and anger management programmes are equally difficult to assess in terms of effectiveness and have met with variable success. This is hardly surprising given the wide range of prison management systems, types of programme and personnel responsible for the implementation of them, not to mention the enormous variety of offenders and offences.

There have been many attempts to tackle crime by changing the type of environment that is believed to harbour it. The policy of zero tolerance adopted in New York was considered by many to be a successful and a necessary, if somewhat drastic, answer to a crisis, but one that would not necessarily generalise to other environments and cultures. Oscar Newman's defensible space theory gave a completely new perspective on some of the causes of and cures for crime, placing the emphasis on the design of buildings as one factor worthy of consideration. His ideas and those of his successors have made a valuable contribution to crime prevention. While acknowledging that this is by no means the only factor we need to consider when reflecting on the causes of crime, it is one that might well make a significant contribution to social breakdown or social cohesion.

what do you know?

1 Evaluate the use of two non-custodial means of punishment for criminal behaviour.

2 Outline and discuss the psychological effects of imprisonment.

3 Describe what is meant by behaviour modification. Evaluate its use within prisons.

4 Describe a research study that evaluates the use of Anger Management courses in a prison setting.

5 Describe and discuss two projects based on zero tolerance.

6 Outline and evaluate Oscar Newman's theory of defensible space.

glossary

Affectionless psychopathy A condition proposed by Bowlby in which an individual feels no guilt for crimes or concern for the victims. This condition is believed to be caused by a prolonged separation from the mother (or main caregiver) in the first three years of life.

Anger management A programme designed to teach individuals how to apply self-control in order to reduce anger against others.

Attachment An enduring emotional bond between two people; often used with particular reference to the bond between an infant and their main caregiver.

Attribution theory A theory that seeks to explain the causes of behaviour in terms of either dispositional (personality) factors or situational factors.

Attributional bias In **attribution theory**, common faults in attributing causes to behaviour such that mistakes are made and the causes of behaviour are misunderstood. An example is self-serving bias in which we attribute our own good and worthy behaviours to personality factors (I gave my mum a bunch of flowers because I am kind) and any bad or unworthy behaviours to situational factors (I shouted at mum because I've got a headache).

Autonomic nervous system (ANS) Part of the peripheral nervous system that controls activities that are not normally under conscious control, such as processes of bodily maintenance like heart rate.

Behaviour modification A technique based on the use of **operant conditioning** to change behaviour. The **token economy** is a form of behaviour modification sometimes used in prisons.

Biological theories Theories that focus on the functioning of genes, the brain, the nervous system and hormones as the causes of behaviour.

Bottom-up approach In the context of **offender profiling**, an approach that starts from the available evidence from the crimes committed by a particular offender (the 'bottom') and attempts to look for connections and links between them that will give a clue to the characteristics of the criminal.

British Crime Survey A regular, large, face-to-face survey of adults living in private households in England and Wales. Its main purpose is to monitor trends in crime but it also covers a range of other topics such as attitudes to crime.

CID Criminal Investigation Department, a branch of the British police force.

Cognitive interview A procedure in which the witness is asked to imagine themselves back in the situation and in the same mood as when the incident occurred and is asked to recall all they can.

Cognitive-behavioural programmes Programmes designed to modify behaviour by changing attitudes and thoughts.

Contextual reinstatement In the context of criminal psychology, a way of improving memory for an event by returning to the place where it happened or asking the witness to imagine themselves back in that place and in the same emotional state.

Copycat crimes A slang term for crimes that appear to mimic another crime. Typically this refers to well-publicised crimes that are then imitated by another individual.

Correlational study A study that measures whether there is a relationship between two variables. For example, a study that investigates whether rates of crime are associated with social class or with family size.

Cross-cultural study A study conducted across two or more cultures in order to make comparisons between them.

Custodial punishment A punishment that involves confinement, such as imprisonment.

Defence mechanisms Strategies that are used by the **ego** in an attempt to balance the desires of the **id** with the demands of the **superego**. Their purpose is to prevent the conscious mind being overwhelmed by anxiety.

Differential association theory A theory of crime postulated by Sutherland, stating that criminal behaviour is learned through social groups. The more associations a person has with attitudes favourable to criminal activity in proportion to attitudes unfavourable to criminal activity, the more likely they are to commit crimes.

Discounting principle In **attribution theory**, the tendency to discount all but the most obvious cause as a reason for behaviour. If, for example, there were black ice on the road, the cause of a car accident would be attributed to the ice rather than to carelessness.

Earwitness testimony Testimony produced by a witness based on what they have heard. This may, for example, involve identifying a particular voice.

Ecological validity The extent to which a finding or theory applies to everyday life.

Ectomorphs People of light and delicate build, thought to correspond to characteristics of alertness and inhibition.

Ego In psychoanalysis, the part of the mind that represents reason, good sense and realistic self-control. It strives to keep a balance between the **id** and **superego**.

Encoding specificity hypothesis An hypothesis advanced by Tulving & Thompson (1973), which states that people have better and more accurate recall for events when they are asked to recall them in the same state and/or place in which they occurred, rather than in a different place or state.

Endomorphs People with a rounded body build, thought to have a personality type which is placid, pleasure seeking and lacking anxiety.

Estimator variables In witness testimony, those variables that affect the accuracy of witness testimony but over which the police (and justice system in general) have no control. These may include variables such as the witness's eyesight, the weather and the amount of time the witness viewed the scene.

External locus of control See **locus of control**.

Extravert (also spelt extrovert) According to Hans Eysenck, a person who is outgoing, impulsive, sociable and willing to take risks.

Face overshadowing effect The tendency for witnesses who have seen someone's face to find it more difficult to identify them by voice than if the face had not been seen.

FBI Federal Bureau of Investigation; a branch of the American police force.

Field experiment An experiment that is conducted in a natural setting. As it is an experiment, the researcher manipulates the independent variable but has limited control over other variables. The participants may not know they are taking part in a study.

Flashbulb memory The type of memory allegedly associated with an emotionally arousing event. The name derives from the analogy that it is as if a flashbulb picture had been taken of the event causing an indelible impression in the mind.

Fundamental attribution error In **attribution theory**, the tendency to overemphasise the importance of dispositional factors and underestimate the influence of situational factors as a cause of someone's behaviour. For example, if someone we do not know well speaks rather sharply to us, we are more likely to believe that they are a grumpy, bad-tempered individual than that they are very tired.

Group polarisation The exaggeration through group discussion of the initial attitudes of the group.

Hedonistic relevance In **attribution theory**, it applies to the fact that when the consequences of an event are serious, we are more likely to make a dispositional attribution than a situational one. It is an **attributional bias**.

Id In psychoanalysis the part of the mind that contains instinctual, sexual and aggressive urges.

Identikit picture A device for building up a composite portrait from a large number of different features, such as a selection of eyes, noses, chins and so on. It is used as a means of assisting a witness to provide a likeness of someone sought by the police.

Identity parade A number of individuals (usually presented in a line – a 'line-up') from whom a witness selects the one they identify as the person sought by the police.

Internal locus of control See **locus of control**.

Introversion According to Hans Eysenck, a person who is inward looking, reflective, controlled and unwilling to take risks.

Just world hypothesis The assumption that the world is a fair and just place in which people get what they deserve, such that the deserving get rewarded and the undeserving get punished. In relation to criminal psychology, it is used to account for the fact that victims (especially rape victims) are often blamed for their fate.

Leading questions Questions that are liable to encourage a certain answer, for example, 'Did you see the stop sign?' which implies that a stop sign was present at the scene.

Learning theory There are many theories that seek to explain learning. Within the context of this book, learning theory refers to attempts to explain learning in terms of classical and **operant conditioning**. Classical conditioning is learning by association; operant conditioning is learning by the consequences of behaviour.

Line-up See **identity parade**

Locus of control A dimension of personality that involves the extent to which people see the results of their actions as either under their own control (referred to as having an *internal* locus of control) or as being due to circumstances outside of them (referred to as having an *external* locus of control).

Longitudinal study A study conducted by investigating the same group of individuals over a long period of time, typically over several years.

Mesomorphs People of muscular body type, thought to correspond to a characteristically aggressive and extroverted personality type.

Mock juries These consist of a group of participants who are asked to behave as if they were members of a jury and make appropriate decisions about guilt/innocence and sentencing.

Natural law approach An argument that the law should closely reflect moral values.

Negative reinforcer Used in **operant conditioning** programmes, it involves the removal of an unpleasant stimulus after a response as a way of increasing the strength of the response. An example is locking someone in their cell and only releasing them when they behave appropriately.

Non-custodial punishment A punishment that does not involve confinement (such as imprisonment), for example, a fine.

Observational learning Learning that takes place as a result of an individual observing the behaviour of another (usually referred to as a model) rather than through direct experience. This is a form of vicarious learning.

Oedipus complex In psychoanalysis, a conflict in which a child desires the parent of the other sex and views the same-sex parent as a rival. This is the crucial issue in the phallic stage of development.

Offender profiling A technique used to provide a description of an offender based on an analysis of the crime scene and the activities involved in the crime itself. It was originally coined by the FBI.

Operant conditioning Learning that takes place as a result of the consequences of the behaviour. If behaviour is reinforced (if it results in pleasant consequences), the behaviour is likely to be repeated; if it is punished (if it results in unpleasant consequences) then the response is weakened and less likely to occur.

Photospreads An array of photographs offered to a witness from which they are asked to identify the person they saw.

Physiognomy The belief that a person's personality can be judged by their physical appearance.

Positive reinforcer Used in **operant conditioning** programmes, it involves offering something pleasant after a response as a way of increasing the strength of a response.

Post-event information Information given after an event has taken place (and which may influence a witness's memory for events beforehand).

Psychoanalytic theories Theories based on Freud's assertion that personality is shaped by, and behaviour is motivated by, powerful inner forces that come from the unconscious part of the mind.

Psychodynamic approach An approach originating in Freud's theory of psycho-analysis, which emphasises the importance of energy dynamics within the individual such as inner forces, conflicts, or the movement of instinctual energy.

Psychometric tests Tests and measures of psychological factors, including person-ality and intelligence.

Psychoticism A severe mental disorder characterised by a lack of contact with reality.

Quasi-experiment An umbrella term for any experiment in which the researcher does not have full control over the independent variable.

Recidivism Relapsing into crime (usually refers to habitual relapse).

Reticular activating system (RAS) An area of the brain extending from the central core of the medulla (the upper brain stem) to all parts of the cerebral cortex and involved with arousal.

Schema In the context of social psychology, a schema is a way of organising infor-mation about past events, which in turn results in inferences that have an influence on our expectations of future events.

Shadow juries A method by which a group of participants eligible for jury service are asked to sit in the courtroom so they hear all the evidence, and then to retire to reach a verdict, much as a real jury would.

Simulated juries See **mock juries**.

Social construct A judgement that is based on social or cultural influences rather than an objective truth. In the context of criminal psychology, crime can be regarded as a social construct since there is no universal definition of what constitutes a crime. Any definition depends to some extent on the society/culture.

Social learning theory A version of **learning theory** that emphasises the influence of observation and the imitating of behaviour that is observed in others.

Social skills training A programme designed to teach people how to improve skills such as making eye contact, holding reasoned discussions and dealing with confrontation without using aggression.

Superego In psychoanalysis the part of the mind that represents conscience, morality and social standards.

System variables In witness testimony, those variables that affect the accuracy of witness testimony and over which the police (and justice system in general) have some influence. These may include the interviewing techniques and the way an identity parade is conducted.

Token economy A behaviour modification technique in which secondary reinforcers called tokens, which can be collected and exchanged for primary reinforcers (for example, desirable substances such as confectionery), are used to encourage certain behaviour.

Top-down approach In the context of **offender profiling**, an approach that starts from a classification of serious crimes (the 'top') and appraises which category a particular crime fits into, based on the evidence at the crime scene.

Victimless crimes A crime in which there is no obvious harm done to others, and therefore no victim. This includes taking drugs, certain sex acts, some types of gambling and prostitution.

Voir dire A pre-trial interview of potential jurors during which the judge or opposing lawyers (those for the prosecution and the defence) can apply for the dismissal of anyone they consider not to be impartial.

Weapon focus effect The tendency for witnesses to a crime involving a weapon to remember details of the weapon, but to be less accurate on other details such as the perpetrator's face (as compared to witnessing events not involving a weapon).

Yerkes-Dodson law This law states that performance will first improve as a person's arousal level increases but then reach a point at which further arousal (possibly in the form of stress) will result in a decrease in performance. In terms of witnessing a crime, if the situation causes great stress, the ability of witnesses to recall events accurately will be adversely affected.

Zero tolerance An umbrella term for any regime in which certain behaviours, however mildly exhibited, are not tolerated. In terms of crime control, it usually refers to the apprehension of people performing any crime however small, such as begging or throwing litter.

references

Abel, G., Barlow, G., Blanchard, D.H., & Guild, D. (1977) The components of rapists' sexual arousal. *Archives of General Psychiatry*, 34, 895–903.

Abbott, C. (1999) Investigating the face shadowing effect in earwitness testimony. Unpublished student project. Department of Psychology, Royal Holloway, University of London

Adler, S.J. (1994) *The Jury*. New York: Times Books

Agnew, R. (1990) The origins of delinquent events: an examination of offender accounts. *Journal of Research in Crime and Delinquency*, 27, 267–294

Ainsworth, P.B. & Pease, K. (1987) *Police Work*. London & New York: Methuen

Akers, R. (1990) Rational choice, deterrence and social learning theories in criminology: the path not taken. *Journal of Criminal Law and Criminology*, 81, 653–676

Akers, R. (1977) *Deviant Behaviour: A Social Learning Approach*, 2nd edition. Belmont, California: Wadsworth

American Medical Association (1986) Council Report: Scientific status of refreshing recollection by the use of hypnosis. *International Journal of Clinical and Experimental Hypnosis*, 34, 1–12

Anderson, C.A. & Dill, K.E. (2000) Video Games and Aggressive Thoughts, Feelings, and Behaviour in the Laboratory and in Life. *Journal of Personality and Social Psychology*, 78(4), 772–790

Asch, S.E. (1955) Opinions and Social Pressure. *Scientific American*, 193 (5), 31–35

Aultman, M.G. (1980) Group involvement in delinquent acts: A study of offence types and male–female participation. *Criminal Justice and Behavior*, 7, 185–192

Ayllon, T. & Millan, M.A. (1979) *Correctional Rehabilitation and Management: A Psychological Approach*. New York: Wiley

Baker, A. & Duncan, S. (1985) Child Sexual Abuse: A Study of Prevalence in Great Britain. *Child Abuse and Neglect*, 9, 457–467

Balay, J. & Shevrin, H. (1988) The subliminal psychodynamic activation method: A critical review. *American Psychologist*, 43, 161–174

Baldwin, J. & McConville, M. (1979) *Jury Trials*. London: Oxford University Press

Bandura, A., Ross, D. & Ross, S.A. (1961) Transmission of Aggression through Imitation of Aggressive Models. *Journal of Abnormal and Social Psychology*, 63(3), 575–582

Bandura, A. & Walters, R.H. (1963) *Social learning and personality development*. New York: Holt, Rinehart & Winston

Bandura, A. (1965) Influence of Models' Reinforcement Contingencies on the Acquisition of Imitative Responses. *Journal of Personality and Social Psychology*, 1(6), 589–595

Baron, R.A. & Byrne, D. (1997) *Social Psychology*, 8th edition. Boston: Allyn and Bacon

Bartol, C.R. & Holanchock, H.A. (1979) A test of Eysenck's theory of criminality on American prisoner population. *Criminal Justice and Behavior*, 6, 245–249

Bartol, C.R. (1995) *Criminal Behaviour: A Psychosocial Approach*, 4th edition. London: Prentice-Hall International (UK) Ltd

Bell, P.A., Greene, T.C., Fisher, J.D., Baum, A. (1996) *Environmental Psychology*, 4th edition. Fort Worth, Texas: Harcourt College Publishers

Bell, S.T., Kuriloff, P.J. & Lottes, I. (1994) Understanding attributions of blame in stranger rape and date rape situations: An examination of gender, race, identification, and students' social perceptions of rape victims. *Journal of Applied Social Psychology*, 24, 1719–1734

Belsky, J., Robins, J. & Gamble, W. (1984) The determinants of parental competence: toward a contextual theory. In M. Lewis (ed.) *Beyond the dyad*. New York: Plenum Press

Benyan, J. (1994) *Law and Order Review 1993: an Audit of Crime, Policing and Criminal Justice Issues*. Centre for the Study of Public Order, University of Leicester

Berry, D. & McArthur, L. (1985) Some components and consequences of a babyface. *Journal of Personality and Social Psychology*, 48, 312–323

Bidrose, S. & Goodman, G.S. (2000) Testimony and Evidence: A Scientific Case Study of Memory for Child Sexual Abuse. *Applied Cognitive Psychology*, 14, 197–213

Blackburn, R. (1993) *The Psychology of Criminal Conduct: Theory, Research and Practice*. England: Wiley

Blumstein, A. (1995) Violence by young people: Why the deadly nexus? *National Institute of Justice Journal* (August), 2–9

Boon, J. & Davies, G. (1992) Fact and fiction in offender profiling. *Issues in Legal and Criminological Psychology*, 32, 3–9

Bowlby, J. (1946) *Forty-four Juvenile Thieves*. London: Bailliere, Tindall & Cox

Bowlby, J. (1979) A reprint of Bowlby (1977) 'The making and breaking of affectional bonds'. *British Journal of Psychiatry*, 130, 201–210 and 421–431. Reprint: New York: Methuen Inc.; London: Tavistock

Bowman, R.P. & Rotter, J.C. (1983) Computer games: Friend or foe? *Elementary School Guidance and Counselling*, 18, 25–34

Box, S. (1983) *Deviance, Reality and Society*, 2nd edition, London: Holt, Rinehart & Winston

Box, S. (1987) *Recession, Crime and Punishment*. Basingstoke: Macmillan

Bratton, W.J. (1998) Crime is down in New York City: Blame the Police. In N. Dennis (ed.) *Zero Tolerance. Policing a Free Society*. IEA Health and Welfare Unit

Brehm, S.S. & Kassim, S.M. (1996) *Social Psychology*, 3rd edition. Boston and Toronto: Houghton Mifflin Company

Brigham, J.C. (1991) *Social Psychology*, 2nd edition. London: Harper Collins

Brigham, J.C. & Malpass, R.S. (1985) The role of experience and contact in the recognition of own- and other-race persons. *Journal of Social Issues*, 41, 139–155

Britton, P. (1992): Home Office/ACPO Review of offender profiling: unpublished. Reported in Copson (1996)

Brown, S.E. (1984) Social class, child maltreatment, and delinquent behavior. *Criminology*, 22, 259–278

Brown, R. & Kulik, J (1977) 'Flashbulb memories'. Cognition, 5, 73–99

Bruce, V. (1998) Identifying people caught on video. *The Psychologist*, 11(7), 331–337

Bucke, T. (1997) *Ethnicity and contacts with the police: Latest findings from the British Crime Survey*. Home Office Research and Statistics Directorate, no. 59

Buikhuisen, W. & Hoekstra, H.A. (1974) Factors related to recidivism. *British Journal of Criminology*, 14, 63–69

Bukshel, L.H. & Kilmann, P.R. (1980) Psychological effects of imprisonment on confined individuals. *Psychological Bulletin*, 88, 469–493

Bull, R. (1998) Obtaining information from child witnesses. In A. Memon, A. Vrij & A. Bull (eds), *Psychology and Law: Truthfulness, Accuracy and Credibility*. New York: McGraw-Hill

Bull, R. (1995) Interviewing people with communication difficulties. In R. Bull & D. Carson (eds), *Handbook of Psychology in Legal Contexts*. Chichester: Wiley

Bull, R. & McAlpine, S. (1998) Facial Appearance and Criminality. In A. Memon, A. Vrij & R. Bull (eds), *Psychology and Law: Truthfulness, Accuracy and Credibility*. New York: McGraw-Hill

Burton, S., Kitzinger, J., with Kelly, L. & Regan, L. (1998) *Young people's attitudes towards violence, sex and relationships*. Zero Tolerance Charitable Trust, Edinburgh

Bushman, B.J. (1995) Moderating role of trait aggressiveness in the effects of violent media on aggression. *Journal of Personality and Social Psychology*, 69, 950–960

Caldwell, R.G. (1965) *Criminology*, 2nd edition. New York: Ronald Press

Campbell, C. (1976) Portrait of a mass killer. *Psychology Today*, 9, 110–119

Canter, D. (1989) Offender Profiles. *Psychologist*, 2 (1), 12–16

Canter, D. (1994) *Criminal Shadows*. London: Harper

Carlen, P. (1988) *Women, Crime and Poverty*. Milton Keynes: Open University Press

Carter, C., Bottoms, B. & Levine, M. (1996) Linguistic and socioemotional influences on the accuracy of children's reports. *Law and Human Behaviour*, 20, 359–374

Ceci, S. & Bruck, M. (1993) Suggestibility of the child witness: a historical review and synthesis. *Psychological Bulletin*, 113, 403–439

Ceci, S.J., Leichtman, M. & Nightingale, N. (1993) Age differences in suggestibility. In D. Cicchetti & S. Toth (eds), *Child abuse, child development, and social policy*, pp. 117–137. Norwood, NJ: Ablex

Chaffee, S.H. & McLeod J.M. (1971) Adolescents, parents and television violence. Paper presented at the meeting of the American Psychological Association, Washington, D.C.

Charlton, T., Gunter, B. & Hannan, A. (eds) (2000) *Broadcast Television Effects in a Remote Community*. Mahway, N.J: Lawrence Erlbaum Associates

Clark, D.A. (1988) Wakefield Prison Anger Management Course Tutors Manual. Unpublished. HMP Wakefield.

Clarke R. & Mayhew, P. (eds) (1980) *Designing out crime*. London: HMSO

Clarke, R. (1985) Jack Tizard Memorial Lecture. Delinquency, environment and intervention. *Journal of Child Psychology and Psychiatry*, 26, 505–523

Cohen, A. (1955) *Delinquent Boys*. New York: Free Press

Coleman, A. (1990) *Utopia on trial*, 2nd edition. London: Hilary Shipman

Comstock, G. & Paik, H. (1991) *Television and the American Child*. New York: Academic Press

Cook, S.A. (1998) Earwitness testimony: Length effects, familiarity effects and the role of context with special reference to faces. Unpublished PhD thesis, University of London

Cook, S. & Wilding, J. (1997) Earwitness testimony 2: Voices, faces and context. *Applied Cognitive Psychology*, 11, 527–541

Coolican, H. (ed.) (1996) *Applied Psychology*. London: Hodder & Stoughton

Copson, G. (1995) Coals to Newcastle? Part 1: a study of offender profiling. Police Research Group, Special Interest series, 7, London: Home Office Police Department

Copson, G. (1996) At last some facts about offender profiling in Britain. *Forensic Update*, 46, 4–10

Cortes, J.B. & Gatti, F.M. (1972) *Delinquency and Crime: A biopsychosocial approach*. New York: Seminal Press

Crawford, C. (2000) Gender, race, and habitual offending sentences in Florida. *Criminology*, 38(1), 263–280

Crawford, C., Chiricos, T. & Kleck, G. (1998) Race, racial threat, and sentencing of habitual offenders. *Criminology*, 36, 481–511

Crombag, H.F.M., Wagenaar, W.A. & VanKoppen, P.J. (1996) Crashing memories and the problem of source monitoring. *Applied Cognitive Psychology*, 10, 93–104

Cumberbatch, G. (1997) Media Violence: Sense and Common Sense. *Psychology Review*, 3(4), 2–7

Cutler, B.L. & Penrod, S.D. (1988) Improving the Reliability of Eyewitness Identification: Lineup Construction and Presentation. *Journal of Applied Psychology*, 73(2), 281–290

Davies, G. & Noon, E. (1991) An evaluation of the live link for child witnesses. London: Home Office

Davies, G. (1997) in J.L. Jackson & D.B. Bekerian (eds), *Offender Profiling. Theory, Research and Practice*. Chichester: Wiley

Davies, G.L. & Raymond, K.M. (2000) Do Current Sentencing Practices Work? *Criminal Law Journal*, 24, 236–247

Davies, G., Wilson, C., Mitchell, R. & Milson, M. (1996) *Videotaping children's evidence: an evaluation*. London: Home Office

Deffenbacher, K.A. (1983) The influence of arousal on reliability of testimony. In S.M.A. Lloyd-Bostock & B.R. Clifford (eds), *Evaluating witness evidence*, pp. 235–243. Chichester: Wiley

Dekke, D.J., Beal, C.R., Elliot, R. & Honeycutt, D. (1996) Children as witnesses: A comparison of lineup versus showup identification methods. *Applied Cognitive Psychology*, 10, 1–12

Demare, D., Lips, H.M. & Briere, J. (1993) Sexually violent pornography, anti-women attitudes and sexual aggression: A structural equation model. *Journal of Research in Personality*, 27, 285–300

Dennis, N. (ed.) (1998) *Zero Tolerance. Policing a Free Society*. IEA Health and Welfare Unit. Lancing: Hartington Fine Arts Ltd

Dent, H. & Flin, R. (eds) (1992) *Children as witnesses*. New York: Wiley

Devlin, Lord P. (1976) *Report to the Secretary of State for the Home Department of the Departmental Committee on Evidence of Identification in Criminal Cases*. London: HMSO

Devlin, P. (1965) *The Enforcement of Morals*. Oxford: Oxford University Press

Diamond, B.L. (1980) Inherent problems in the use of pretrial hypnosis on a prospective witness. *California Law Review*, 68, 313–349

Dietz, P., Hazelwood, R. & Harry, B. (1986) Detective magazines: pornography for the sexual sadist. *Journal of Forensic Sciences*, 31, 197–211

Dietz, T.L. (1998) An examination of violence and gender role portrayals in video games: Implications for gender socialisation and aggressive behaviour. *Sex Roles*, 38, 425–442

Dion, K.K., Bershied, E. & Hatfield (Walster), E. (1972) What is beautiful is good. *Journal of Personality and Social Psychology*, 24, 285–290

Dishion, T.J., Patterson, G.R., Stoolmiller, M. & Skinner, M.L. (1991) Family, school, and behavioral antecedents to early adolescents' involvement with antisocial peers. *Developmental Psychology*, 27, 172–180

Ditton, J. (1977) *Part-time Crime*. London: Macmillan

Dobash, R.E. & Dobash, R.P. (1979) *Violence against Wives*. London: Tavistock

Dobash, R.E. & Dobash, R.D. (1992) *Women, Violence and Social Change*. London: Routledge

Dodd, V. (2000) Racism 'rife in justice system'. *The Guardian*, 20 March

Dominick, J.R. (1984) Videogames, TV violence and aggression in teenagers. *Journal of communication*, 34, 134–144

Dooley, E. (1990) Prison suicide in England and Wales. 1972–1987. *British Journal of Psychiatry*, 156, 40–45

Douglas, J.E. (1981) Evaluation of the (FBI) psychological profiling programme: unpublished. Reported in Pinizzotto (1984) and Copson (1996)

Downs, A.C. & Lyons, P.M. (1991) Natural observations of the links between attractiveness and initial legal judgements. *Personality and Social Psychology Bulletin*, 17, 541–547

Dwyer, D. (2000) *Interpersonal Relationships*. Routledge: London

Dwyman, J. & Bowers, K. (1983) The use of hypnosis to enhance recall. *Science*, 222, 184–185

Ehrlich, I. (1974) Participation in illegal activities. In G. Becker and W. Landes (eds), *Essays in the Economics of Crime and Punishment*. New York: Columbia University Press

Elliot, C. & Quinn, F. (1996) *English Legal System*. London & New York: Longman

Emes, C.E. (1997) Is Mr Pacman eating our children? A review of the effect of video games on children. *Canadian Journal of Psychiatry*, 42, 409–414

Eron, L. (1995) Media violence: How it affects kids and what can be done about it. Invited address presented at the annual meeting of the American Psychological Association. New York

Eron, L.D. & Huesmann, L.R. (1986) The role of television in the development of antisocial and prosocial behaviour. In D. Olweus, J. Block, & M. Radke-Yarrow (eds), *Development of Antisocial and Prosocial Behaviour, Theories and Issues*. New York: Academic Press

Eron, L.D., Huesmann, L.R., Leftowitz, M.M. & Walder, L.O. (1972) Does television violence cause aggression? *American Psychologist*, 27, 253–263

Eysenck, H.J. & Gudjonsson, G.H. (1989) *The causes and cures of criminality*. New York: Plenum

Eysenck, H.J. (1977) *Crime and Personality*, 2nd edition. London: Routledge & Kegan Paul

Farrington, D.P. (1996) The Development of Offending and Antisocial Behaviour from Childhood to Adulthood. In P. Cordella & L. Siegel (eds), *Readings in Contemporary Criminological Theory*. Boston: Northeast University Press

Farrington, D.P., Biron, L. & Le Blanc, M. (1982) Personality and delinquency in London and Montreal. In J. Gunn & D.P. Farrington (eds), *Abnormal Offenders, Delinquency and the Criminal Justice System*. Chichester: Wiley

Feldman, D. (1964) Psychoanalysis and crime. In B. Rosenberg, I. Gerver & F.W. Howton (eds), *Mass Society in Crisis*. New York: Macmillan

Feldman, P. (1993) *The Psychology of Crime*. Cambridge: Cambridge University Press

Fisher, R.P., Geiselman, R.E. & Raymond, D.S. (1987) Critical analysis of police interviewing techniques. *Journal of Police Science and Administration*, 15, 177–185

Flin, R., Boon, J., Knox, A. & Bull, R. (1992) Children's memories following a five-month delay. *British Journal of Psychology*, 83, 323–336

Fling, S., Smith, L., Rodriguez, T., Thornton, D., Atkins, E. & Nixon, K. (1992) Videogames, aggression and self-esteem: a survey. *Social Behaviour and Personality*, 20, 39–46

Foley, L.A. & Pigott, M.A. (2000) Belief in a Just World and Jury Decisions in a Civil Rape Trial. *Journal of Applied Social Psychology*, 30(5), 935–951

Forsythe, D. (1987) *Social Psychology*. California: Brooks/Cole

Freud, S. (1925) Some psychical consequences of the anatomical distinction between the sexes. *The Standard Edition of the Complete Psychological Works of Sigmund Freud*, vol. 19. London: Hogarth Press

Freud, S. (1966) New Introductory lectures on psychoanalysis. In J. Strachey (ed. and trans.), *The Standard Edition of the Complete Psychological Works of Sigmund Freud*, vols 15–16. London: Hogarth Press (original work published 1933)

Gale, A. & Edwards, J.A. (1983) EEG and human behaviour. In A. Gale & J.A. Edwards (eds), *Physiological Correlates of Human Behaviour*, vol. 2. New York: Academic Press

Geiselman, R.E & Callot, R. (1990) Reverse versus forward recall of script based texts. *Applied Cognitive Psychology*, 4, 141–144

Geiselman, R.E, Fisher, R.P., MacKinnon, D.P. & Holland, H.L. (1985) Eyewitness memory enhancement in the police interview: *Journal of Applied Psychology*, 70, 401–412

Geiselman, R.E, Fisher, R.P., Cohen, G., Holland, H.L. & Surtes, L. (1986) Eyewitness responses to leading and misleading questions under the cognitive interview. *Journal of Police Science and Administration*, 14, 31–39

Gerbner, G. & Gross, L. (1976) The scary world of T.V.'s heavy viewers. *Psychology Today*, 9, 41–45

Gerbner, G., Gross, L., Morgan, M. & Signoriella, N. (1980) The "mainstreaming" of American violence: Profile No. 11. *Journal of Communications*, 30(3), 10–29

Gerbner, G., Gross, L., Morgan, M. & Signoriella, N. (1986) Living with television: The dynamics of the cultivation process. In J. Bryant & D. Zilmann (eds), *Perspectives on media effects*. Hillsdale, NJ: Erlbaum

Gibson, H.B. (1982) The use of hypnosis in police investigations. *Bulletin of the British Psychological Society*, 35, 138–142

Gibson, H.B. (1989) The Home Office attitude to forensic hypnosis: A victory for scientific evidence or medical conservatism? *British Journal of Experimental and Clinical Hypnosis*, 6, 25–27

Gilling, D. (1997) *Crime Prevention. Theory, policy and politics*. London: UCL Press

Glaser, D. (1983) Supervising offenders outside of prison. In J.Q. Wilson (ed.), *Crime and Public Policy*, pp. 207–227. San Francisco: ICS Press

Glueck, S. & Glueck, E.T. (1956) *Physique and Delinquency*. New York: Harper & Row

Gold, M. (1978) Scholastic experiences, self-esteem, and delinquent behaviour: A theory for alternative schools. *Crime and Delinquency*, 24, 290–308

Goldstein, J.H. (1986) *Aggression and crimes of violence*, 2nd edition. Oxford: Oxford University Press

Goldstein, J. (1975) *Aggression and crimes of violence*. New York: Oxford University Press

Goleman, D. (1994) Study finds jurors often hear evidence with a closed mind. *The New York Times* 29 November, pp. C1, C12

Goodman, A., Johnson, P. & Webb, S. (1997) *Inequality in the UK*. Oxford: Oxford University Press

Goodman, G.S. & Bottoms, B.L. (1993) *Child victims, child witnesses: Understanding and improving testimony*. New York: Guilford Press

Goodman, G.S., Rudy, L., Bottoms B. & Aman, C. (1990) Children's concerns and memory: issues of ecological validity in the study of children's eyewitness testimony. In R. Fivush & J. Hudson (eds), *Knowing and Remembering in Young Children*, pp. 249–284. New York: Cambridge University Press

Goring, C. (1913/1972) *The English convict: A statistical study*. Montclair, NJ: Patterson Smith

Gottfredson, M. & Hirschi, T. (1990) *A General Theory of Crime*. Stanford, CA: Stanford University Press

Gove, W.R. & Crutchfield, R.D. (1982) The family and delinquency. *The Sociological Quarterly*, 23, 301–319

Griffiths, M.D. (2000) Video game violence and aggression. *British Journal of Social Psychology*, 39, 147–149

Hagan, J. (1994) *Crime and Disrepute*. Thousand Oaks, CA: Pine Forge Press

Hagan, J. & Gillis, A. (1979) The sexual stratification of social control. *British Journal of Sociology*, 30, 25–38

Hagell, A. & Newbury, T. (1994) *Young Offenders and the Media*. London: Policy Studies Institute

Hans, V. & Vidmar, N. (1982) Jury selection. In N.I. Kerr & R.M. Bray (eds), *The Psychology of the Courtroom*, pp. 39–82. New York: Academic Press

Hargreaves, D.H. (1980) Classrooms, schools, and juvenile delinquency. *Educational Analysis*, 2, 75–87

Harrower, J. (1998) *Applying Psychology to Crime*. London: Hodder & Stoughton

Hart, H.L.A. (1963) *Law, Liberty and Morality*. Oxford: Oxford University Press

Harvey, L., Burnham, R., Kendall, K. & Pease, K. (1992) Gender differences in criminal justice: An international comparison. *British Journal of Criminology*, 32, 208–217

Hastie, R., Penrod, S.D. & Pennington, N. (1983) *Inside the Jury*. Cambridge, MA: Harvard University Press

Heather, N. (1977) Personal illness in lifers and the effects of long-term indeterminate sentences. *British Journal of Criminology*, 17, 378–386

Hedderman, C. (1987) Children's evidence: the need for corroboration. Research and Planning Unit. Paper 41. London: Home Office

Heidensohn, F. (1996) *Women and Crime*, 2nd edition. Basingstoke: Macmillan

Heidensohn, F. (1991) Women and crime in Europe. In F. Heidensohn & M. Farrell (eds), *Crime in Europe*. London: Routledge

Heider, F. (1958) *The psychology of interpersonal relations*. New York: Wiley

Hewstone, M., Strobe, W., Stephenson, G. (eds) (1996) *Introduction to Social Psychology*, 2nd edition. Oxford: Blackwell

Hinsz, V.B. & Davis, J.H. (1984) Persuasive argument theory, group polarization, and choice shifts. *Personality and Social Psychology Bulletin*, 10, 260–268

Hirschi, T. & Hindelang, M. (1977) Intelligence and delinquency: A revisionist review. *American Sociological Review*, 42, 571–586

Hirschi, T. (1969) *Causes of Delinquency*. Berkeley, CA: University of California Press

Hobbs, T.R. & Holt, M.M. (1976) The effects of token reinforcement on the behavior of delinquents in cottage settings. *Journal of Applied Behavior Analysis*, 9, 189–198

Hoffman, M.L. (1977) Moral internalisation: Current theory and research. In L. Berkowitz (ed.), *Advances in Experimental Social Psychology*, vol. 10. New York: Academic Press

Hollin, C.R. (1989) *Psychology and Crime: An Introduction to Criminological Psychology*. London and New York: Routledge

Hollin, C.R. (1990) *Cognitive-Behavioral Interventions with Young Offenders*. New York: Pergamon

Hollin, C.R., Huff, G.J., Clarkson, F. & Edmondson, A.C. (1986) Social skills training with young offenders in a borstal: an evaluative study. *Journal of Community Psychology*, 14, 289–299

Hollingsworth, J. (1986) *Unspeakable acts*. Chicago: Congdon & Weed

Holmes, R. (1989) *Profiling Violent Crimes*. Newbury Park: Sage

Holmes, R.M. & Holmes, S.T. (1996) *Profiling violent crimes: An Investigative Tool*, 2nd edition. California: Sage Publications

Home Office (1992) *Gender and the Criminal Justice System*. London: HMSO

Hough, M. (1995) Anxiety about crime: findings from the 1994 British Crime Survey. *Home Office Research Study No. 147*. London: Home Office

Hough, M. & Roberts, J. (1998) Attitudes to punishment: findings from the British Crime Survey. *Home Office Research Study No. 179*. London: Home Office

Huesmann, L.R. & Malamuth, N.M. (1986) Media Violence and Antisocial Behaviour: An Overview. *Journal of Social Issues*, 42, no. 3, 1–6

Hunter, D. (1993) Anger management in the prison. An evaluation. *Research on Offender Programming Issues*, 5, 1, 3–15

Indemaur, D. (1996) Offender and Sentencing. *Australian Psychologist*, 31 (1), 15

International Society of Hypnosis (1979) *Handbook*. Philadelphia: ISH

Ireland, J. (2000) Do Anger Management Courses Work? *Forensic Updates*, 63, 12–16

Jackson, J.L., van Koppen, P.J. & Herbrink, J.C.M. (1993) Does the service meet the needs? *Report NSCR 93-05*. Netherlands Institute for the Study of Criminality and Law Enforcement

Jackson, J.L. & Bekerian, D.B. (1997) *Offender Profiling. Theory, Research and Practice*. Chicester: Wiley

Jacobs, D. (1981) Inequality and Economic Crime. *Sociology and Social Research*, 66, 12–28

Jacobs, J. (1961) *The death and life of great American cities*. London: Cape

Jarvis, M., Russell, R., Flanagan, C. & Dolan, L. (2000) *Angles on Psychology*. Cheltenham: Stanley Thornes

Jephcott, P. & Robinson, H. (1971) *Homes in High Flats*. Edinburgh: Oliver & Boyd

Johnson, M. & Foley, M. (1984) Differentiating fact from fantasy: the reliability of children's memory. *Journal of Social Issues*, 40, 33–50

Jones, E.E. & Harris, V.A. (1967) The attribution of attitudes. *Journal of Experimental Social Psychology*, 3, 1–24

Jones, S. (1998) *Criminology*. London: Butterworth

Kalat, J.W. (1993) *Introduction to Psychology*, 3rd edition. Belmont, Ca.: Wadsworth

Kalven, H. & Zeisel, H. (1966) *The American Jury*. Boston: Little, Brown

Katz, R. C. & Marquette, J. (1999) Psychosocial characteristics of young violent offenders: a comparative study. *Criminal Behaviour and Mental Health*, 6, 339–348

Keen, J. (2000) A practitioner's perspective. Anger management work with male young offenders. *Forensic Update*, Issue 60, January

Kelley, H.H. (1971) Attribution in social interaction. In E.E. Jones, D. Kanouse, H.H. Kelley, *Attributions: Perceiving the causes of behaviour*, pp. 1–26. Morristown, NJ: General Learning Press

Kerr, N.L., Harmon, D.L. & Graves, J.K. (1982) Independence of multiple verdicts by jurors and juries. *Journal of Applied Social Psychology*, 12, 12–29

Kershaw, C., Budd, T., Kinshott, G., Mattinson, J., Mayhew, P. & Myhill, A. (2000) The 2000 British Crime Survey, England and Wales. *Home Office Statistical Bulletin 18/00*. London: Home Office

King, M. & Yuille, J. (1987) Suggestibility and the child witness. In S.J. Ceci, M. Toglia & D. Ross (eds), *Children's eyewitness memory*, pp. 24–35. New York: Springer-Verlag

Klein, N.C., Alexander, J.F. & Parsons, B.V. (1977) Impact of family systems intervention on recidivism and sibling delinquency: A model of primary prevention and program evaluation. *Journal of Consulting and Clinical Psychology*, 45, 469–474

Kline, P. (1987) Psychoanalysis and crime. In B.J. McGuirk, D.M. Thorton and M. Williams (eds), *Applying Psychology to Imprisonment: Theory and Practice*. London: HMSO

Kohnken, G., Malpass, R.S. & Wogalter, M.S. (1996) Forensic applications of lineup research. In S.L. Sporer, R.S. Malpass & G. Kohnken (eds), *Psychological Issues in Eyewitness Identification*, pp. 205–232. Mahway, NJ: Lawrence Erlbaum Associates

Kolvin, I., Miler, F.J.W., Fleeting, M. & Kolvin, P.A. (1988) Social and parenting factors affecting criminal offence rates: Findings from the Newcastle Thousand Family Study (1947–1980) *British Journal of Psychiatry*, 152, 80–90

Kramer, T.H., Buckhout, R. & Eugenio, P. (1990) Weapon focus, arousal and eyewitness memory. Attention must be paid. *Law and Human Beaviour*, 14, 167–184

Kruppa, I. (1991) Perpetrators suffer trauma too. *The Psychologist*, 4, 401–403

Lamb, M., Sternberg, K. & Esplin, P. (1994) Factors influencing the reliability and validity of statements made by young victims of sexual maltreatment. *Journal of Applied Developmental Psychology*, 15, 255–280

LaPiere, R. (1934) Attitudes versus action. *Social Forces*, 13, 230–237

Law, K. (1997) Further evaluation of anger-management courses at HMP Wakefield: An examination of behavioural change. *Inside Psychology: The Journal of Prison Service Psychology*, 3, 1, 91–95

Lerner, M.J. (1980) *The Belief in a Just World: a fundamental delusion*. New York: Plenum

Levi, M. & Pithouse, A. (1992) The Victims of Fraud, in D. Downes (ed.) *Unravelling Criminal Justice*. Basingstoke: Macmillan

Lewis, D. & Pincus, J. (1989) Epilepsy and violence: evidence for the neuropsychiatric–aggressive syndrome. *Journal of Neuropsychiatry and Clinical Neurosciences*, 1, 413–418

Leyens, J.P., Camino, Parke, R.D. & Berkowitz, L. (1975) Effects of movie violence on aggression in a field setting as a function of group dynamics and cohesiveness. *Journal of Personality and Social Psychology*, 32, 346–360

Lilly, L.R., Cullen, F.T. & Ball, R.A. (1995) *Criminological Theory: Context and Consequences*. Newbury Park, California: Sage

Lin, S. & Lepper, M.R. (1987) Correlates of children's usage of video games and computers. *Journal of Applied Social Psychology*, 17, 72–93

Lindsay, S., Gonzales, V. & Eso, K. (1995) Aware and unaware uses of memories of post event suggestions. In M. Zaragoza, J. Graham, G. Hall, R. Hirschman and Y. Ben-Porath (eds), *Memory and Testimony in the Child Witness*. Thousand Oaks, CA: Sage

Livingstone, S. (2001) Media effects research. *Psychology Review*, 7(3), 29–31

Lloyd, C., Mair, G. & Hough, M. (1994), Explaining Reconviction Rates: A Critical Analysis. *Home Office Research Study No. 136*. London: HMSO

Lloyd-Bostock, S. (1983) Attributions of cause and responsibility as social phenomena. In J.M.F. Jaspers, F.D. Fincham & M. Hewstone (eds), *Attribution theory and research: Conceptual, developmental and social dimensions*. London: Academic Press

Lloyd-Bostock, S. (1988) *Law in Practice*. London: Routledge

Loeber, R. & Stouthamer-Loeber, M. (1986) Family factors as correlates and predictors of juvenile conduct problems and delinquency. In N. Morris & M. Tonry (eds), *Crime and Justice: An Annual Review of Research*, vol. 7. Chicago: University of Chicago Press.

Loftus, E.F. & Zanni, G. (1975) Eyewitness testimony: The influence of wording of a question. *Bulletin of the Psychonomic Society*, 5, 86–88

Loftus, E.F. (1986) Experimental psychologist as advocate or impartial educator. *Law and Human Behaviour*, 10, 63–78

Loftus, E., Loftus, G. & Messo, J. (1987) Some facts about 'weapon focus'. *Law and Human Behaviour*, 11, 55–62

Loftus, E.F. & Palmer, J.C. (1974) Reconstruction of automobile destruction: An example of the interaction between language and memory. *Journal of Verbal Learning and Verbal Behaviour*, 13, 585–89

Logan, C.H. (1972), Evaluation of research in crime and delinquency: A reappraisal. *Journal of Criminal Law, Criminology and Police Science*, 63, 378–387

Lombroso, C. (1876) *L'Uomo delinquente*. Milan, Italy: Torin

Lombroso-Ferrero, C. & Ferrero, G. (1895) *The Female Offender*. London: Unwin

Lombroso-Ferrero, G. (1972) *Criminal Man*. Montclair, NJ: Patterson Smith

Loza, W. & Loza-Fanous, A. (1999) The Fallacy of Reducing Rape and Violent Recidivism by Treating Anger. *International Journal of Offender Therapy and Comparative Criminology*, 43(4), 492–502

Luus, C. & Wells, G.L. (1994) The malleability of eyewitness confidence: Co-witness and perseverance effects. *Journal of Applied Psychology*, 79, 714–724

MacLeod, C. & Shepherd, J.W. (1986) Sex differences in eyewitness reports of criminal assaults. *Medicine Science and Law*, 26, 311–318

Maguire, M., Morgan, R. & Reiner, R. (eds) (1994) *The Oxford Handbook of Criminology*. Oxford: Oxford University Press

Maguire, M., Morgan, R. & Reiner, R. (eds) (1997) *The Oxford Handbook of Criminology*, 2nd edition. Oxford: Oxford University Press

Mair, G. (1997) A brief history of the probation service. In M. Maguire, R. Morgan & R. Reiner (eds), *The Oxford Handbook of Criminology*, 2nd edition, pp. 1198–1231

Malamuth, N.M. & Check, J.V.P. (1981) The effects of mass media exposure on acceptance of violence against women: A field experiment. *Journal of Research in Personality*, 15, 436–446

Malamuth, N.M. (1986) Predictors of naturalistic sexual aggression. *Journal of Personality and Social Psychology*, 50, 953–962

Mars, G. (1982) *Cheats at Work*. London: Allen & Unwin

Marshall, R.J. (1983) A psychoanalytic perspective on the diagnosis and development of juvenile delinquency. In W.S. Laufer & J.M. Day (eds), *Personality Theory, Moral Development and Criminal Behavior*. Lexington: Heath

Mattinson, J. & Mirrlees-Black, C. (2000) Attitudes to Crime and Criminal Justice: Findings from the 1998 British Crime Survey. *Home Office Research Study No. 200*. London: Home Office

Mawby, R. (1977) Defensible space: a theoretical and empirical appraisal. *Urban Studies*, 14, 169–79

McCord, W., McCord, J. & Zola, I.K. (1959) *Origins of crime: A new evaluation of the Cambridge-Somerville Youth Study*. New York: Columbia University Press

McGurk, B.J. & McDougall, C. (1981) A new approach to Eysenck's theory of criminality. *Personality and Individual Differences*, 2, 338–340

McKelvie, S.J. & Coley, J. (1993) Effects of crime seriousness and offender facial attractiveness on recommended treatment. *Social Behaviour and Personality*, 21, 265–277

McLaughlan, A. (1986) The effects of two forms of decision reappraisal on the perception of pertinent arguments. *British Journal of Social Psychology*, 25, 129–138

Memon, A. & Yarmey, A.D. (1999) Earwitness recall and identification: Comparison of the cognitive interview and the structured interview. *Perceptual and Motor Skills*, 88, 797–807

Memon, A. (1998) Telling it all: the Cognitive Interview. In A. Memon, A. Vrij & R. Bull (eds), *Psychology and Law: Truthfulness, Accuracy and Credibility*. New York: McGraw-Hill

Memon, A., Wark, L., Koehnken, G., & Bull, R. (1997) Context effects and event memory: how powerful are the effects? In D. Payne & F. Conrad (eds), *Intersections in Basic and Applied Memory Research*. New York: Lawrence Erlbaum Associates

Merritt, K.A., Ornstein, P.A. & Spiker, B. (1994) Children's memory for a salient medical procedure: Implications for testimony. *Pediatrics*, 94, 17–23

Merry, S. (1981) Defensible space undefended: social factors in crime control through environmental design. *Urban Affairs Quarterly*, 16, 397–422

Messerschmidt, J. (1993) *Masculinities and Crime*. Lanham, MD: Rowman & Littlefield

Messner, S.F. (1988) Research on cultural and socioeconomic factors in criminal violence. *Psychiatric Clinics of North America*, 11, 511–525

Milavsky, J.R., Kessler, R.C., Stipp, H. & Rubens, W.S. (1982) *Television Aggression: a Panel Study*. New York: Academic Press

Milgram, S. (1963) Behavioural study of obedience. *Journal of Abnormal and Social Psychology*, 67, 371–378

Mirrlees-Black, C. & Allen, J. (1998) Concern about Crime: Findings from the 1998 British Crime Survey. *Home Office Statistical Bulletin Issue 83/98*. London: Home Office

Mirrlees-Black, C., Budd, T., Partridge, S. & Mayhew, P. (1998) The 1998 British Crime Survey. *Home Office Statistical Bulletin Issue 21/98*. London: Home Office

Moir, A. & Jessel, D. (1997) *A Mind to Crime: The Controversial Link between Mind and Criminal Behaviour*. London: Signet

Morison, P. & Gardner, H. (1978) Dragons and dinosaurs: The child's capacity to differentiate fantasy from reality. *Child Development*, 49, 642–648

Moscovici, S. (1976) *Social Influence and Social Change*. London: Academic Press

Moscovici, S. (1980) Towards a theory of conversion behaviour. In L. Berkowitz (ed.), *Advances in Experimental Social Psychology*, vol. 13, pp. 208–39. New York: Academic Press

Moscovici, S. (1985) Social influence and conformity. In G. Linzey & E. Aronson (eds), *Handbook of social psychology*, 3rd edition. New York: Random House

Moyes, T. Tennent, T.G. & Bedford, A.P. (1985) Long-term follow-up study of a ward-based behaviour modification programme for adolescents with acting-out and conduct problems. *British Journal of Psychiatry*, 147, 300–305

Muirhead, J. (1997) Assessment of anger and negative affect as they relate to the prediction of criminal violence in a federal inmate population: A retrospective study. Unpublished doctoral dissertation. Carleton University, Ottawa, Canada

Mulder, M. & Vrij, A. (1996) Explaining conversation rules to children: an intervention study to facilitate children's accurate responses. *Child Abuse and Neglect*, 7, 623–631

Murphy, P., Williams, J. & Dunning, E. (1990) *Football on Trial: Spectator Violence and Developments in the Football World*. London: Routledge

Myers, D.G. & Kaplin, M.F. (1976) Group-induced polarization in simulated juries. *Personality and Social Psychology Bulletin*, 2, 63–66

Neisser, U. & Harsch, N. (1992) Phantom flashbulbs: false recollections of hearing the news about Challenger. In E. Winograd & U. Neisser (eds), *Affect and Accuracy in Recall: Studies of 'Flashbulb' Memories*, pp. 9–31. Cambridge: Cambridge University Press

Neitzel, M.T. (1979) *Crime and its Modification: A Social Learning Perspective*. Oxford: Pergamon

Nemeth, C. (1977) Interactions between jurors as a function of majority vs. unanimity decision rules. *Journal of Applied Social Psychology*, 7, 38–56

Newburn, T. & Stanko, E. (eds) (1994) *Just Boys Doing Business?* London: Routledge

Newman, O. (1972) *Defensible Space*. New York: Macmillan

Newson, E. (1994) Video violence and the protection of children. *Psychology Review*, 1(2), 2–6

Newton, A. (1980) The effects of imprisonment. *Criminal Justice Abstracts*, 12, 134–151

Offord, D.R. (1982) Family backgrounds of male and female delinquents. In J. Gunn & D.P. Farrington (eds), *Abnormal Offenders, Delinquency, and the Criminal Justice System*. Chichester: Wiley

Oleson, J.C. (1996) Psychological profiling: does it actually work? *Forensic Update*, 46, July, 11–14

Orne, M.T. (1979) The use and misuse of hypnosis in court. *International Journal of Clinical and Experimental Hypnosis*, 27, 311–341

Ouston, J. (1984) Delinquency, family background and educational attainment. *British Journal of Criminology*, 24, 2–26

Paik, H. & Comstock, G. (1994) The effects of television violence on antisocial behaviour: a meta-analysis. *Communication Research*, 21 (4), 516–546

Paivio, A. (1971) *Imagery and Verbal Processes*. New York: Holt, Rinehart and Winston

Parke, R., Berkowitz, L., Leyens, J., West, S. & Sebastian, R. (1977) Some effects of violent and non-violent movies on the behaviour of juvenile delinquents. In

Berkowitz (ed.), *Advances in experimental psychology*, vol. 10. New York: Academic Press

Passingham, R.E. (1972) Crime and personality: A review of Eysenck's theory. In V.D. Nebylitsin and J.A. Gray (eds), *Biological Bases of Individual Behaviour*. New York: Academic Press

Pearson, G. (1987) *The New Heroin Users*. Oxford: Blackwell

Pennington, N. & Hastie, R. (1986) Evidence evaluation in complex decision making. *Journal of Personality and Social Psychology*, 51, 242–258

Pennington, N. & Hastie, R. (1993) The Story Model for jury decision making. In Hastie, R. (ed.), *Inside the Juror: the psychology of juror decision making*. Cambridge: Cambridge University Press

Perris, E.E., Myers, N.A. & Clifton, R.K. (1990) Long term memory for a single infancy experience. *Child Development*, 61, 1796–1807

Peterson, M.A., Braiker, H.B. & Polich, S.M. (1981) *Who commits crimes?* Cambridge, MA: Olegeschlager, Gunn & Hain

Pezdek, K. & Roe, C. (1995) The effect of memory trace strength on suggestibility: *Journal of Experimental Child Psychology*, 60, 116–123

Pfeifer, D. & Ogloff, J. (1991) Ambiguity and guilt determination: a modern racism perspective. *Journal of Applied Social Psychology*, 23, 767–790

Phillips, D.P. (1983) The impact of mass media on homicide. *American Sociological Review*, 48, 560–568

Phillips, D.P. (1986) Natural experiments on the effects of media violence on fatal aggression: Strengths and weaknesses of a new approach. In L. Berkowitz (ed.), *Advances in experimental social psychology*, vol. 19, pp. 207–250. New York: Academic Press

Piaget, J. (1926) *The language and thought of the child*. London: Routledge & Kegan Paul

Piaget, J. (1932) *The Moral Development of the Child*. Harmonsworth: Penguin

Pickel, K.L. (1998) Unusualness and threat as possible causes of "weapon focus". *Memory*, 6, 277–295

Pickel, K.L. (1999) The Influence of Context on the "Weapon Focus" Effect. *Law and Human Behaviour*, 23(3), 299–311

Piliavin, I. & Briar, S. (1964) Police encounters with juveniles. *American Journal of Sociology*, 70, 206–214

Pinizzotto, A. J. & Finkel, N. J. (1990) Criminal personality profiling: an outcome and process study. *Law and Human Behaviour*, 14(3), 215–233

Pinizzotto, A.J. (1984) Forensic psychology: criminal personality profiling. *Journal of Police Science and Administration*, 12, 32–40

Pollard, C. (1998) Zero Tolerance: Short-term fix, Long-term Liability? In N. Dennis (ed.), *Zero Tolerance. Policing a Free Society*. IEA Health and Welfare Unit. Lancing: Hartington Fine Arts Ltd

Pollard, P. (1992) Judgements about victims and attackers in depicted rapes: A review. *British Journal of Social Psychology*, 31, 307–326

Poole, D. & White, L. (1991) Effects of question repetition on the eyewitness testimony of children and adults. *Developmental Psychology*, 27, 975–986

Poole, D. & White, L. (1993) Two years later: effect of question repetition on the eyewitness testimony of children and adults. *Developmental Psychology*, 29, 844–853

Poole, D. & White, L. (1995) Tell me again and again: stability and change in the repeated testimonies of children and adults. In M. Zaragoza, J. Graham, G. Hall, R. Hirschman and Y. Ben-Porah (eds), *Memory and Testament in the Child Witness*. Thousand Oaks, CA: Sage

Pratap, A. (1990) "Romance and a little rape". *Time*, 13 August, p. 69

Provenso, E.F. (1991) *Video Kids – Making sense of Nintendo*. Harvard: Harvard University Press

Quigley, B.M., Johnson, A.B. & Byrne, D. (1995, June) Mock jury sentencing decisions: A meta-analysis of the attractiveness–leniency effect. Paper presented at the meeting of the American Psychological Society. New York

Repetto, T. (1976) Crime prevention through environmental policy: a critique. *American Behavioural Scientist*, 20, 275–288

Rice, M.E., Quinsey, V.L. & Houghton, R. (1990) Predicting treatment outcome and recidivism among patients in a maximum security token economy. *Behavioral Sciences and the Law*, 8, 313–326

Roebuck, R. & Wilding, J. (1993) Effects of vowel variety and sample length on identification of a speaker in a line-up. *Applied Cognitive Psychology*, 7, 475–481

Ross, L.D. (1977) The intuitive psychologist and his shortcomings: distortions in the attribution process. In L. Berkowitz (ed.), *Advances in Experimental Social Psychology*, vol. 10, pp. 173–220. New York: Academic Press

Ross, R.R. & Mackay, H.B. (1976) A study of institutional treatment programs. *International Journal of Offender Therapy and Comparative Criminology*, 20, 165–173

Roy, D.F. (1991) Improving recall by eyewitnesses through the cognitive interview. *The Psychologist*, 4(9), 398–400

Rudy, L. & Goodman, G.S. (1991) Effects of participants on children's reports: Implications for children's testimony. *Developmental Psychology*, 27, 527–538

Russell, D.E.H. (1983) The incidence and prevalence of intra-familial and extra-familial sexual abuse of female children. *Child Abuse and Neglect*, 7, 133–146

Russell, D.E.H. (1984) *Sexual Exploitation*. Beverley Hills: Sage

Rutter, M. (1971) Parent–child separation: Psychological effects on the children. *American Journal of Psychiatry*, 139, 21–33

Saks, M.J. (1974) Ignorance of science is no excuse. *Trial*, 10, 18–20

Saks, M.J. (1977) *Jury verdicts: The role of group size and social decision rule*. Lexington, MA: Lexington Books

Saladin, M., Saper, Z. & Breen, L. (1988) Perceived attractiveness and attributions of criminality: what is beautiful is not criminal. *Canadian Journal of Criminology*, 30, 251–259

Sanders, G.L. (1984) The effects of context cues on eyewitness identification responses. *Journal of Applied Social Psychology*, 14, 386–397

Sheldon, W.H. & Stevens, S.S. (1942) *The Varieties of Temperament*. New York: Harper

Sheldon, W.H., Hartl, E.M. & McDermott, E. (1949) *Varieties of Delinquent Youth: An Introduction to Constitutional Psychiatry*. New York: Harper

Smith, B.D., Davidson, R.A., Smith, D.L., Goldstein, H. & Perlstein, W. (1989) Sensation-seeking and arousal: Effects of strong stimulation on electrodermal and memory task performance. *Personality and Individual Differences*, 10, 671–679

Smith, E.R. & Mackie, D.M. (1995) *Social Psychology*. New York: Worth Publishers, Inc

Smith, M.C. (1983) Hypnotic memory enhancement of witnesses: Does it work? *Psychological Bulletin*, 94, 87–94

Spence, S.H. & Marziller, J.S. (1981) Social skills training with adolescent male offenders: 2. Short-term, long-term and generalisation effects. *Behaviour Research and Therapy*, 19, 349–368

Spencer, J. & Flin, R. (1993) *The Evidence of Children: The Law and the Psychology*. London: Blackstone

Sprorer, S.L., Penrod, S.D., Read, D. & Cutler, B.L. (1995) Choosing, confidence and accuracy: a meta-analysis of the confidency–accuracy relation in eyewitness identification studies. *Psychological Bulletin*, 118, 315–327

Stack, S. (1984) Income inequality and property crime. *Criminology*, 22, 229–257

Stalnaker, J.M. & Riddle, E.E. (1932) The effect of hypnosis on long-delayed recall. *Journal of General Psychology*, 6, 429–440

Stasser, G. & Stewart, D. (1992) Discovery of hidden profiles by decision-making groups: Solving a problem versus making a judgement. *Journal of Personality and Social Psychology*, 63, 426–434

Stewart, J.E. (1980) Defendant's attractiveness as a factor in the outcome of criminal trials: An observational study. *Journal of Applied Psychology*, 10, 348–361

Stewart, J.E. (1985) Appearance and punishment: The attraction–leniency effect in the courtroom. *Journal of Social Psychology*, 125, 373–378

Strodtbeck, F.L. & Hook, L. (1961) The social dimensions of a twelve-man jury. *Sociometry*, 24, 397–415

Sutherland, E.H. (1951) Critique of Sheldon's varieties of delinquent youth. *American Sociological Review*, 16, 10–13

Sutherland, E.H. & Cressey, D.R. (1974) *Principles of Criminology*, 9th edition. New York: Lippincott

Synder, H. & Sickmund, M. (1995). *Juvenile Offenders and Victims: A national Report*. Washington DC: Office of Juvenile Justice and Delinquency Prevention

Taylor, R.B. & Brooks, D.K. (1980) Temporary territories: Responses to intrusions in a public setting. *Population and Environment*, 3, 135–145

Toch, H. & Adams, K. (1989) *The Disturbed Violent Offender*. New Haven: Yale University Press

Towl, G.J. & Crighton. D.A. (1996) *The handbook of psychology for forensic practitioners*. London: Routledge

Towl, G.J. (1993) Anger control groupwork in practice. *Issues in Criminological and Legal Psychology*, 20, 75–77

Towl, G.J. (1995) Anger management groupwork. *Issues in Criminological and Legal Psychology*, 23, 31–35

Tucker, A., Merton, P. & Luszcz, M. (1990) The effect of repeated interviews on young children's eyewitness memory. *Australian and New Zealand Journal of Criminology*, 23, 117–123

Tulving, E. & Thomson, D.M. (1973) Encoding specificity and retrieval processes in episodic memory. *Psychological Review*, 80, 353–370

Underwager, R. & Wakefield, H. (1990) *The real world of child interrogations*. Springfield, Illinois: Charles C. Thomas

Vingoe, F.J. (1991) The truth and nothing but the truth about forensic hypnosis. *The Psychologist*, 14(9), 395–397

Vrij, A. (1998) Psychological Factors in Eyewitness Testimony. In A. Memon, A. Vrij & R. Bull (eds), *Psychology and Law: Truthfulness, Accuracy and Credibility*. McGraw-Hill

Walker, N. & Farrington, D.P. (1981) Reconviction rates of adult males after different sentences. *British Journal of Criminology*, 21, 357–360

Walster, E. (1966) Assignment of responsibility for important events. *Journal of Personality and Social Psychology*, 3, 73–79

Wells, G.L. (1978) Applied eyewitness-testimony research; system variables and estimator variables. *Journal of Personality and Social Psychology*, 36, 1546–1557

Wells, G.L. (1993) What do we know about eyewitness identification? *American Psychologist*, 48, 553–571

Wells, G.L. & Bradfield, A.L. (1998) "Good, you identified the suspect": Feedback to eyewitness distorts their reports of the witnessing experience. *Journal of Applied Psychology*, 83(3), 360–376

Wells, G.L., Wright, E.F. & Bradfield, A.L. (1999) Witness to Crime: social and cognitive factors governing the validity of people's reports. In R. Roesch, S.D. Hart and J.R.P. Ogloff (eds), *Psychology and Law: The State of the Discipline*. New York: Kluwer Academic/Plenum Publishers

Wells, J. (1995) *Crime and Unemployment*. London: Employment Policy Institute

West, D. (1982) *Delinquency: Its Roots, Careers and Prospects*. London: Heinemann

Wheeler, H. (1985) Pornography and rape: A feminist perspective. In A.W. Burgess (ed.), *Rape and Sexual Assault*. New York: Garland

Wiegman, O. & van Schie, E.G.M. (1998) Video game playing and its relation with aggressive and prosocial behaviour. *British Journal of Social Psychology*, 37, 367–378

Wilding, J., Cook, S. & Davis, J. (2000) Sound familiar? *The Psychologist*, 13(11), 558–562

Wilson, J.Q. & Kelling, G.L. (1982) 'Broken Windows'. *Atlantic Monthly*, March, 29–38

Wilson, S. (1980) Vandalism and "defensible space" on London housing estates. In R. Clarke & P. Mayhew (eds), *Designing out crime*. London: HMSO

Wood, W., Wong, F.Y. & Chachere, J.G. (1991) Effects of media violence on viewers' aggression in unconstrained social interaction. *Psychological Bulletin*, 109, 371–383

Wootton, B. (1959) *Social Science and Social Pathology*. London: Allen & Unwin

Wrightsman, L.S., Nietzel, M.T. & Fortune, W.H. (1994) *Psychology and the Legal System*, 3rd edition. California: Brooks/Cole

www.cabinet-office.gov.uk/womens-unit/fear

www.zerotolerance.org.uk/splash.htm

Yarmey, A.D., Yarmey, M.J. & Yarmey, A.L. (1996) Accuracy of eyewitness identification in showups and lineups. *Law and Human Behaviour*, 20, 459–477

Yuille, J.C. & Cutshall, J.L. (1986) A case study of eyewitness memory of a crime. *Journal of Applied Psychology*, 71, 291–301

Yuille, J. (1993) We must study forensic eyewitnesses to know about them. *American Psychologist*, 48, 572–573

Zamble, E. & Porporino, F.J. (1988) *Coping, Behavior, and Adaptation in Prison Inmates*. Berlin: Springer-Verlag

Zamble, E. & Quinsey, V.L. (1997) *The criminal recidivism process*. Cambridge: Cambridge University Press

Zeisel, H. (1971) And then there were none. The diminution of the federal jury. *University of Chicago Law Review*, 38, 710–724

Zillman, D. & Bryant, J. (1984) Effects of massive exposure to pornography. In N. Malamuth & E. Donnerstein (eds), *Pornography and Sexual Aggression*. Orlando: Academic Press

Zillmann, D. (1993) Mental control of angry aggression. In D. Wegner & J. Pennebaker (eds), *Handbook of mental control*, vol. 5, pp. 370–392. Englewood Cliffs, NJ: Prentice Hall

Zuckerman, M. (1969) Variables affecting deprivation results. In J.P. Zubek (ed.), *Sensory Deprivation: Fifteen Years of Research*. New York: Appleton-Century-Crofts

Zuckerman, M., Kuhlman, M. & Caurac, K. (1988) What lies beyond E and N? Factor analysis of scales believed to measure basic dimensions of personality. *Journal of Personality and Social Psychology*, 54, 96–107

Index

Page numbers given in **bold** indicate the page on which a term has been defined.